KANAZAWA
The Other Side of Japan

by RUTH STEVENS

Kanazawa : The Other Side of Japan
© 1979 by Ruth P. Stevens, 108 E.38th St., #1107, New York, N.Y.
10016 USA
Edited by Kaneko Kenji, Oasis Magazine.
Published by Kanazawa Tourist Association,
located at Kanazawa Chamber of Commerce,
9-13 Oyama-cho, Kanazawa,
tel. (0762)63-1151
Printed by Nakagawa Taisho Printing Co., Kanazawa, Japan

First edition, 1979
First printing, revised edition, 1984

Preface

In years past, Japan has been on the receiving end of international communication, a country dedicated to investigating foreign technology and ideas and adapting them to fit Japanese society. Recently, however, many Japanese people have begun to recognize that international exchange is a two-way street. The Japanese must also work to increase foreign understanding of themselves.

Professor Donald Keene has suggested that Japan often settles for too selective a self-introduction. Perhaps thinking that foreign interest is only superficial or that foreigners' ability to comprehend the intricacies of Japanese thought and culture is limited, the Japanese themselves have kept the best parts, some of their most valuable treasures, hidden. Kanazawa is one of these gems. This city has everything--a long history, elegant architecture, lively nightlife, and an emphasis on crafts, arts, tea ceremony and noh theater--a broad sampling of the things most foreign visitors find fascinating about Japan, all in a medium-sized, manageable town.

Japanese have always known about Kanazawa, if only as the city of Kenrokuen, one of Japan's three greatest gardens. Most people also know it as a well-preserved old castle town, the second largest city on the Japan Seacoast, and notorious for its severe winters.

This is the 'back' of Japan, and few foreigners have included it in their itineraries. Five years ago, when I first came to live here, it was such a treat to see a fellow foreigner on the street that we few foreign residents would telephone each other with eager reports of a new face glimpsed in passing.

Now such encounters are more frequent. Kanazawa is enjoying the benefits of the general travel 'boom' and, more specifically, the increasing interest shown in out-of-the-way Japan by tourists who have already 'done' the major spots like Tōkyō, Kyōto and Nara. And we who know Kanazawa well feel the need for a simple means to share the pleasures of our adopted city with other English speakers.

The result is this book, a practical and, I hope, useful guide to visiting Kanazawa. The first half is a general introduction with helpful information and suggestions for how best to enjoy what the city has to offer. In the second section, the city is divided geographically into areas. Kanazawa is not yet geared for international tourism--this is one of the city's greatest charms. But foreign visitors will be able to find English speakers here and there, many of whom are noted in this book. Although most spots described here can be appreciated without Japanese language ability, some, like crafts workshops, would benefit from a translator.

We have made editorial decisions somewhat arbitrarily. Romanization of Japanese words follows the modified Hepburn system more or less consistently. Those not appearing in the *Concise Oxford Dictionary,* Sixth Edition, have been italicized. Japanese names are written with the family name first, with the exception of people who have foreign given names. Readers will no doubt find some of the information in this book dated at the outset. Prices rise, stores move, new bus routes are introduced--it's impossible to keep up with the city's growth and change. But I do humbly take responsibility and apologize in advance for any errors. Suggestions and comments from readers will be most welcome.

I began this project over a year ago with one general purpose in mind--to introduce my favorite city to other English speakers. At the same time, I hoped to do something in the way of expressing my gratitude to Kanazawa for the five delightful years I've spent here. Far from repaying my debts, however, I've found myself even further obligated to the hundreds of people who gave their time and support to this project. A brief word in acknowledgement appears at the end of the book.

Welcome to Kanazawa. I hope this book helps you enjoy our city, either from your armchair or on a real visit. If you see a blond woman on a giant green bicycle, that's me. Please wave me down and let me know how you're enjoying your visit.

Preface to the Revised Edition

As the original preface predicted, much has changed about Kanazawa in the five years since we first published *Kanazawa: The Other Side of Japan.* Certainly, the physical changes have been legion; this we expected. But less predictable were what I might call the spiritual changes in the city.

There is a palpable new air about Kanazawa in recent years. People are proud of their historical role as a major center of culture and education. But they are also actively building toward the future. There is talk of the "New Kanazawa" and what its image should be; and talk of internationalism, of industrial development, of technological innovation.

Some of us outsiders, captured by the charm of Old Japan and cognizant of the potential dangers of development, may hesitate to applaud such change. But I am happy to report that in Kanazawa the modern talk contains a strong sense of tradition. Rather than abandon the old, people plan to build upon it. Kanazawa was once Japan's largest and wealthiest fiefdom, they say. It was at the forefront of education, of Western learning, and of culture. We should encourage the natural vitality of this city to emerge again.

To this end, much activity has been planned and executed - so much that on a recent visit I found some parts of the town hardly recognizable. A new international convention center has arisen behind the New Grand Hotel, for example. The Kōrinbō area is being renovated to reassume its place as a commercial center of the city.

However Kanazawa may have changed, the essence that prompted this guidebook's preparation remains. For this reason, and for others less noble but more practical, we have kept alterations for this revised edition to a minimum. We have done our best to make other additions and subtractions, but we beg your indulgence for the inevitable oversights.

Again, the Society to Introduce Kanazawa to the World welcomes you. Though I have since returned to the U.S., I too, with a slight twinge of envy, wish you a pleasant visit to Kanazawa.

New York
August 1984

Ruth P. Stevens

① Ishikawa Gate of the former Kanazawa Castle, now a national university.

② A Kenrokuen pine with *yuki-tsuri* protection against heavy snow.

③ The Maeda lords' guest parlor in Seisonkaku Villa.

④ April cherry-viewing by the castle's solid rock wall.

⑤ June iris seen from Hanami Bashi in Kenrokuen.

Annual Events and Festivals

①. Secluded garden of the Terashima samurai family.
②. A Kaga tea ceremony room.
③. Feudal firemen show off their Kaga Tobi acrobatics.
④. Lord Maeda Toshiie in the Hyakumangoku Festival parade.
⑤. Kaga Hōshō noh theater.

①. Souvenir cakes, crackers and barley candy.
②. Making Okiagari dolls.
③. Elegant Kaga dinner includes *jibu* stew, sweet shrimp sashimi and baked sea bream.
④. Hand-painted kimono of bright Kaga Yūzen design.
⑤. Local crafts: pottery, lacquerware, dolls, silks and woodwork.

④

⑤

We Care.

At Japan Air Lines we care. We care about everything. So whether it's a coffee cup that needs refilling or a child that needs attention, we'll be there. We'll be there giving you something even more than good service. Good feelings.

For reservations, call your travel agent or JAL direct...

It's always a pleasure.

JAPAN AIR LINES

Contents

FOREWORD

I am delighted to introduce to you this guidebook to Kanazawa City in English. Kanazawa is a storehouse of nature and history, still preserving the atmosphere of an old castle town. It is famous throughout Japan as a city of education and culture. The people of Kanazawa place great importance on arts and traditional crafts. Kanazawa has long been a popular tourist city in Japan; certainly foreign visitors will also find it interesting.

I am grateful to Ms. Ruth Stevens for her efforts in investigating and writing this book. Her book will surely be effective in introducing our prefecture to more and more foreign visitors. We Japanese have welcomed many foreign visitors, especially to industrialized and heavily populated Ōsaka and Tōkyō, but the areas on the Japan Sea coast are not yet well known. I believe that a good route to discovering the best parts of Japan lies in knowing Kanazawa. This is a city which incorporates such Japanese traditions as noh, tea ceremony and Japanese dancing into everyday life. Here, traditional crafts such as Kaga Yūzen, Kutani pottery, Kaga *maki-e* and Wajima lacquerware are not only produced but in constant use by the people.

It would be hard to understand the real beauty and spirit of Japan without visiting such a regional city as Kanazawa. For these reasons, I believe this book will serve as an excellent bridge to international understanding.

Yōichi Nakanishi, Governor

Let me offer my congratulations on the occasion of the publication of 'Kanazawa: The Other Side of Japan' by Ruth Stevens. I am impressed by the efforts she has made, and I am further pleased at the enormous support shown by the people of Kanazawa and that the book is being published locally.

Beginning with Buffalo, N.Y., Kanazawa has established sister-city relations with cities in five different countries. Through these relationships and various exchange programs, we have deepened international understanding and communication. Thanks to these projects, foreign visitors have been kind enough to say, 'Kanazawa is a truly Japanese city. It is rare to find the beauty of a traditional Japanese castle town preserved so well.'

Kanazawa is, however, somewhat off the path well-trodden by foreign tourists, so we haven't had the opportunity to entertain many visitors from abroad. We are delighted that with this book, hitherto untapped tourist resources as well as Japanese traditions and character will become available to the rest of the world.

Ms. Stevens' subtitle is extremely provocative. Compared with the industrialized, crowded, but nevertheless well-known cities of the Pacific Coast, this other side of Japan, the back side, preserves the most Japanese qualities of Japan. We are proud that Ms. Stevens has recognized this.

Since coming to Kanazawa in 1974, Ms. Stevens has worked variously as a teacher at our Municipal Technical High School, a newspaper columnist and an instructor at Kanazawa Economics College. At the same time, she has invested many hours in investigating the city in great detail and writing this book. Everyone has noticed her tall figure riding around town on her bicycle. Rather than a mere English translation of a Japanese guidebook, this is written through the eyes of a foreigner, reflecting the seriousness and thoughtful consideration of Ms. Stevens herself. As a result, it should serve as a convenient and stimulating guide.

I am looking forward to not only an increase in the number of foreign visitors to Kanazawa, but also increased understanding of our city by foreign readers and deepened friendship between Japanese and the people of other countries. Let me again express my gratitude to Ms. Stevens for her efforts.

Noboru Egawa, Mayor

序　文

　このたび英文による金沢の案内書が出版されることを心からおよろこびいたします。

　金沢は、自然と歴史の宝庫といわれる石川県の中心として、古い城下町の面影を今も残しており、一方、教育文化都市としても日本有数の街であります。市民は美術工芸や伝統芸能や学術文化を大切にしており、日本では大変人気のある観光都市のひとつで、外国の皆さんにも興味あるところだと思います。ルース・スティブンス嬢がここに住み、多くの努力を払って調査・執筆されたことに敬意を表するとともに、より多くの方々に金沢を知っていただくのに大変役立つ本を書かれたことを感謝します。

　外国から日本に来られる方々は少なくありませんが、日本海に面した当地は、必ずしも良く知られておらず、従って金沢も外国の方には東京や大阪ほどポピュラーではありません。しかし本当の日本の良さや美しさを知るには、この街を知るのが早道だと私は信じています。日本の経済発展やスモッグの東京は良く知られているかも知れませんが、能やお茶や踊りが生活に生かされ、美しい庭園や伝統の洗練を受けた生活工芸──例えば加賀友禅や九谷焼や加賀蒔絵や輪島塗などが作られ使われ続けている──本物の日本の美や心は、（日本の）地方都市、なかでも金沢のような街に来なければ理解できないでしょう。その意味で、この本はすばらしい国際理解の橋になると信じています。

石川県知事　中　西　陽　一

　このたび本市在住のアメリカ人ルース・スティブンス嬢の手になる英文ガイドブック「金沢案内──もう一面の日本」が出版されることになり、著者のご苦労に敬意を表するとともに、心からのお祝いを申し上げる次第です。また私にとって、この出版が市民の方々の協力により地元金沢でなされたことも、喜びを一層大きくするものです。

　金沢市は米国バッファロー市始め海外5都市と姉妹関係にあり、また国際生活体験や世界青少年交流協会等を通じても国際親善と交流を深めてきました。これら交流による来訪者は勿論、その他一般観光客など本市を訪れる外人客から、私達はいつも「金沢は、本当に日本らしい、日本的な伝統を今も残す全国でも数少ない美しい古都である」とのお賞めの言葉を頂戴してまいりました。

　しかし現実には、金沢は、いわゆる表日本の東京、箱根、から伊勢、京都、奈良、さらには瀬戸内といった来日外人観光客に踏み慣らされたメインルートから外れているため、来沢する一般の外人観光客の数はそう大きなものではありませんでした。

　今回の出版により、金沢の国際的には隠れた観光資源が紹介、宣伝されるのみならず、本市の持つ日本的な伝統、個性といったものが広く世界に紹介されるならば、私達にとっても望外の幸せであります。

　スティブンスさんがこの本につけたサブタイトル「もう一面の日本」は極めて示唆に富んだ言葉です。もし、これが表日本の画一化された都市や踏み慣らされた観光ルート、そして人口の密集する工業地帯等に対比する意味でのもう一面の日本、裏日本の金沢であるとするならば、金沢こそは個性豊かな最も日本らしいものを保存している町ということになります。私達は、このことに強い誇りを感ずるものです。

　スティブンスさんは1974年の来沢以来、金沢市立工業高校教諭、英文毎日コラムニスト、金沢経済大学講師として活躍されるかたわら、長い時間をかけて市内をくまなく歩いて綿密な調査、取材をし、それをもとに本書を書き上げられました。長身の彼女が自転車で町を走る姿はよく見かけられたものです。従って、本書は、従来の日本の観光案内書を単に英訳したに過ぎない通り一辺のものと違い、外国人の眼を通して見た英文の書き下ろしであり、何よりも、彼女自身が自分の足で行った調査に基づくオリジナルであるところに魅力があります。

　その上、彼女の真面目な人柄、やさしい思いやりが全篇に反映されていて、外人向けの金沢案内書としては、正に打ってつけの非常に便利で親切なガイドブックになっています。

　私は、この本が、単に金沢への外人観光客の誘致に役立つだけでなく、もっと広い意味で、外国人読者が金沢に関する正しい理解を深められることによって金沢市と外国間の正しい相互理解が深まり、さらに国際間の親善と友情の促進に寄与することと大いに期待しております。

　　1979年7月

金沢市長　江　川　　　昇

Saigawa

As though to soothe one's heart, this river flows:
My life runs smooth beside its flowing flank.

Springlike in spring, in summer summersome,
Such flowers bloom along the riverbank
That, as I sit among them, things I'd known
Only from books and therefore barely knew –
Feelings of tenderness, of love bestowed —
Bloom to become, of my own knowledge, true.

And still this marvellous river flows away,
Its endless balm by light winds ruffled blue.

(1913) by Murō Saisei

Hyakumangoku Festival. (June 14th)

Historical Outline

One day about 1200 years ago, as Imohori Tōgorō strolled home from a long afternoon of digging potatoes at his nearby mountain plot, he was greeted by an astonishing sight. Crowded into the narrow dirt road by his simple hut were long lines of warriors, porters, horsemen and maidservants, and in their center, he saw an elaborate lacquered palanquin. Its lattice door slid open, and out stepped a lovely young lady, who addressed the bewildered Tōgorō. She explained that she was Wako of Hase and that the goddess of mercy, Kannon, had appeared before her father in a dream with the advice that she find the peasant Tōgorō in the Kaga district and become his wife.

Tōgorō managed to overcome his shock, and admitting that he had been visited by a similar vision, gladly accepted Wako into his household. But stipulating that as a farmer's wife, she would no longer be needing the services of her retainers, he sent them back to her family in Yamato.

The Tōgorō couple lived happily for years, except that the new bride was perhaps somewhat homesick at times. At one point, her father, fearing for his beloved daughter's welfare, sent along a bundle of gold so she could enjoy at least some of the luxuries of her maiden days. But Tōgorō, a simple peasant unaware of its value, innocently fed the gold to the ducks. When his wife cried out in protest, Tōgorō answered that gold is really nothing special. To prove it, he shouldered a sack of potatoes and led her off to Oyama, the nearby town.

Coming to the local well, Tōgorō began scrubbing his potatoes as usual in the clear water. Suddenly gold began to appear, floating up brightly through the depths, as it often did in local rivers and streams. They gathered up the gold, distributed it among their neighbors and commissioned a statue to the Kannon goddess who had brought them together.

The couple lived happily, if simply, ever after, and their story became a legend in the Kaga district. The well itself can be found in Kenrokuen Park, and the legend provides Kanazawa with its name, meaning Marsh of Gold.

The Tōgorō story has as many variations and interpretations as it has tellers, but it does provide some clues to early life in this district. Kaga (Ishikawa Prefecture consists of the two former provinces of Kaga and Noto) was basically an agrarian society, although there was some trade with northern provinces. Peasants were ruled by richer peasants who sometimes became so powerful as to be labeled lords, setting up short-lived dynasties, only to become corrupt and decayed, finally giving way to a rival clan.

One of these, the Togashi family, managed to maintain control over Kaga for several centuries. Designated *shugo,* or governor, by the Kamakura Bakufu government in the late 1100's, they built a fortress at Takao, not far from Tōgorō's home, and ruled more or less benevolently, relying for survival on taxes from rice, border traffic and their own vast holdings. But as the period of the Warring States (Sengoku Jidai, 1467–1567) approached, life became more difficult for the Togashi. Rival lords battled one another all over Japan. The farmers, who were providing the economic base and the cannon fodder, eventually protested, sparking widespread agrarian rebellion.

In the Hokuriku district (now Fukui, Ishikawa and Toyama prefectures), the flames of uprising were fanned by Rennyo (1415 –1499), the radical Buddhist saint from Kyōto's Honganji temple, who preached the promise of life with the merciful Amida Buddha after death. The simplistic doctrine appealed to the farmers. They eagerly joined the militant Ikkō-shū, the 'single-minded religion' which developed from the Jōdo (Pure Land) Sect. The reign of the last Togashi lord, Masachika, ruler of a divided family and a seething populace, finally came to an end in 1488, when the farmer-fanatics conquered the Takao stronghold. The Buddhists became the rulers at a fortress-temple, Kanazawa Gobō (also known as Oyama Gobō, at the site of the present Kanazawa University), and political power was diffused among various priests and small-scale samurai.

The Ikkō Sect maintained control over Kaga for about 100 years, long enough to leave a lasting impression on local culture. Kaga was known as the 'peasants' country,' where taxes were low and the common people were allowed to live in peace. The teachings of the True Jōdo Sect (Shin-shū) continued to spread among the expanding population. Political harmony was maintained by Rennyo's brilliant skill at organizing the villages horizontally into cells around local temples, connected with Kanazawa Gobō and thus with Honganji itself.

But in the country surrounding the peaceful 'peasants' kingdom,' the Sengoku era was still in full swing. Lords from Niigata to the northeast and Fukui to the southwest had their greedy eyes on Kaga. Several decades of battles, maneuvers and political intrigue ensued, resulting eventually in nation-wide domination by Oda Nobunaga of Owari (Nagoya). In 1580, Nobunaga placed General Sakuma Morimasa in charge of Kaga, where he destroyed the Kanazawa Gobō temple and built a small castle in its place. With the arrival three years later of Nobunaga's powerful retainer, Maeda Toshiie, Kaga settled down for the three centuries of stability and prosperity which supported the flowering of Kanazawa City.

The Edo Period

Maeda Toshiie was also a native of Owari, born in Arako Village (now part of Nagoya) in 1538. He was only the fourth son of the village headman, but his skill with the spear and his obvious military talents caught the eye of Nobunaga, who raised Toshiie to

Lord Maeda Toshiie.
(K.Nakayama
Prefectural Art Museum)

Interior of Kanazawa Castle in
its prime, complete with bonsai
collection and teahouse. (City
Cultural Properties Office)

head of the Maeda family. Not only a skilled warrior, Maeda was
also an astute politician. He strengthened his position as Nobunaga's retainer with success on the battlefield and then went on to
survive the hazardous series of power transfers, from Nobunaga to
Toyotomi Hideyoshi and finally to Tokugawa Ieyasu. Maeda's
eventual reward was the wealthiest fief in Japan--the Kaga district
which produced a million *koku,* or five million bushels of rice,
annually. (Wealth was measured in rice, the main staple and
general medium of exchange.)

In the precarious Edo period, any daimyō found himself in a
delicate position. The Maedas, as foreigners to Kaga, had to strug-
gle with the remnants of the militant local Buddhists as well as the
constant tension which existed between the four social classes of
the district, the samurai, farmers, artisans and merchants. As lords
of Japan's most productive and potentially threatening fief, the
Maedas also had to deal with suspicions of treachery on the part of
the Tokugawa shōgunate.

Lord Toshiie skillfully established a position of balance and
taught his descendants well. The second generation Maeda,
Toshinaga, showed some signs of ambitions beyond Kaga, but he
wisely resisted the temptation to challenge the increasingly strong
Tokugawas. Instead, Toshinaga continued Toshiie's policies of
stabilizing the Maeda power by remodeling the city around the
castle and setting up a local hierarchy, with the Maedas at the top.

Beginning with the third lord, Toshitsune, the spirit of
Kanazawa as a wealthy castle town (*jōkamachi*) began to develop.
The abundant tax revenue was no longer needed for military
purposes, so the lords invested in culture. They called master
craftsmen from Edo and Kyōto and set up schools and workshops.
Noh theater and tea ceremony were special Maeda interests. At
one time there were two noh stages within the castle walls. Tea
houses and accompanying gardens were built all over the city. As
the lords' enthusiasm developed, their retainers also took up
lessons. Eventually, these past-times, normally limited to the lei-

sured aristocracy, filtered down to the common people, the base
on which their continued popularity rests today.

The 300 years of peace and affluence of the Edo period turned
Kanazawa into Japan's fourth largest city--a thriving metropolis of
120,000, producing lacquer and silks and enjoying the cultural
refinements made possible by Maeda patronage.

Meiji Era Kanazawa

The Meiji Restoration in Japan was a peculiarly peaceful revolu-
tion, transforming nearly every aspect of society with only traces
of the agony which usually accompanies such far-reaching change.
Kanazawa stands as a case in point. By the mid-1800's, the city
was already economically weakened--a series of famines, years of
mismanagement, and the increasing strength of the merchant class
undermined the base of the feudal system. So, when off in Edo
feudalism was officially abolished and the country was opened to
foreign trade, the local system gave up with hardly a whimper.
There was some resistance--the new Ishikawa prefectural government was moved to nearby Mikawa town for a year (1872—73)
until the disgruntled samurai cooled down--but most people
adjusted peaceably to the new age.

At the time, few citizens could imagine the effects the changes
were to have on Kanazawa's future. The samurai were in the most
painful position. Unskilled and jobless, many of them emigrated to
other regions for a new start. After centuries of isolation and
impractical cultural pursuits, the remaining population (reduced to
about 94,000) was hardly any better prepared to participate in
Japan's industrialization. Instead, the people concentrated on
adapting their local skills and products to modern demands.
Cottage industries in textiles, lacquer and pottery were expanded
and developed. Feudal schools were transformed into modern
institutions of higher learning.

The lack of heavy industry has been a blessing for Kanazawa in
many ways. The city escaped being bombed during World War II,
and since then the people have striven to preserve the best of the
old ways while accommodating the city to the modern world.
Kanazawa citizens maintain a deep sense of pride in their cultural
traditions, and visitors will find reflections of this feeling everywhere in the city.

Practical Information

HOW TO GET HERE

The quiet charm of Kanazawa has been preserved partly because it is still slightly off the beaten tourist track, and six to seven hours by train from Tōkyō. But in no way is the city inaccessible. For a quick trip, the most convenient transportation is by All Nippon Airways. Four round-trip flights a day, between Haneda and Komatsu airports, are met by a 45-minute city bus from Kanazawa Station. The most picturesque train route, passing through the Karuizawa and Nagano mountains, takes seven hours. On this line between Kanazawa and Ueno, there are five direct trains, each way, a day. More expensive, but faster at 5½ hours, is taking the Bullet Train, Hikari, from Tōkyō Station to Maibara or Nagoya, and changing to a limited express (*tokkyū*). From Kansai district Kanazawa is within day-trip range: 3½ hours from Ōsaka, 3 hours from Kyōto and 3 hours from Nagoya.

As part of a leisurely tour of Japan, Kanazawa can be combined with several other spots. Try the Hokuriku route between Tōkyō and Kyōto, stopping in Matsumoto, Takayama, Noto Peninsula and Kanazawa, and then moving down to Kyōto via Eiheiji temple and Tōjimbō seacoast in Fukui prefecture. Other interesting stops might be Yatsuo, a paper-making center, Takaoka which is famous for bronzework bells and statuary, the mountain villages and hot springs of Gokayama, the secluded moss temple of Heisenji near Katsuyama or the Echizen pottery village at Takefu. A 'wide-ken' round-trip ticket, including train between Tōkyō and Ōsaka via Hokuriku and bus around Noto peninsula, is available at major JTB offices.

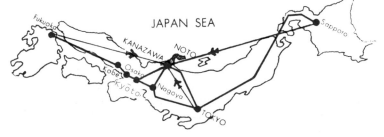

WHEN TO COME

One proverb which always crops up in conversations about Kanazawa is, *Bentō o wasuretemo, kasa o wasureruna,* or 'Even if you forget your lunchbox, never forget your umbrella.' Hokuriku district is known for long and severe winters. The daily snowfall, although picturesque in Kenrokuen Park, is rarely brightened by sunshine. The snow is wet and heavy, so an umbrella is a must from November to March. Again in mid-June, the *tsuyu* rainy season makes us heed the proverb, until mid-July, when the weather turns hot and sticky. Clear, comfortable weather can be relied upon in spring and fall, when the city's tile roofs sparkle and we can forget both umbrella and lunchbox, and spend the noon hour strolling by Saigawa river or soaking up the sun in Central Park.

BEFORE YOU COME

Seasoned travelers often like to do some investigating before setting off on a trip. Readings and places connected with Kanazawa are listed below for them. Those who prefer to avoid prejudice can leave the list for later comparison with their own impressions.

Background Reading

Although many would argue that the 'real,' traditional, Japan is found more easily here than in the big cities of the Pacific coast, Kanazawa has never received much foreign attention. The late Edo-period illegal trade through nearby seaports was a short-lived, if exciting, phenomenon. Since the opening of Japan at the end of the last century, foreigners, particularly writers, have concentrated on Kantō and Kansai. Nevertheless, a smattering of material in English on Hokuriku is available.

The earliest account is found in *A Diplomat in Japan,* by Sir Ernest M. Satow (Philadelphia, Lippincott, 1921). In 1867, Satow traveled with Sir Harry Parkes throughout Niigata and Hokuriku, in search of west coast ports suitable for foreign trade. Included in his memoirs is a delightful description of his run-in with the Japanese negotiating style on an overnight stay in Kanazawa.

Another fascinating early record is a commentary on a visit to

Hokuriku in 1889 by Percival Lowell, the Boston astronomer, discoverer of Pluto, and independently wealthy Japanophile. Lowell arrived in Japan in 1883, seven years before the better-known Lafcadio Hearn. His *Noto: An Unexplored Corner of Japan,* was published in 1891 by Houghton Mifflin and became an influential introduction of Japan to western readers. But these days the book is out of print, and copies are well nigh unobtainable. There is one each in the Library of Congress and the Diet Library. Kanazawa's only copy is in the possession of Mr. Miyazaki Masaaki, who has translated it into Japanese.

Other noted travelers have recorded their impressions of Kanazawa and Hokuriku (for example, C. Yee, *The Silent Traveler in Japan,* Tuttle, 1974, and Fosco Maraini, *The Island of the Fisherwomen,* Harcourt, Brace and World, 1962), and articles appear from time to time in periodicals, scholarly journals and anthologies on 'unexplored' Japan. More recently, Prof. Morton Huber has published a sympathethic account of the villages submerged by the new dam on the Tedori River. The slim volume illustrated with his own sketches and watercolors is now sold out, but available in numerous Ishikawa prefectural schools and libraries. Ask for *Villages of Tedori River Gorge: The Final Curtain Descends.*

The bulk of commentary on Kanazawa has been written in Japanese, including, curiously enough, the memoirs of some of the early, and very influential, foreign missionaries. But here and there Japanese pieces turn up in translation. The great haiku poet, Bashō, stayed here long enough to leave some memorable poetic impressions. His travel diary has been translated by Prof. Yuasa Nobuyuki, in a widely available Penguin Classic, *The Narrow Road to the Deep North,* 1966.

A novel based on a tragic tale of bureaucratic corruption during a 19th century Kaga famine was translated by a local English teacher for use as a school reader. Visitors to the Seven Jizō Temple in Higashiyama which memorializes the unfortunate peasants involved in a similar incident, or to the Tenpo People's Monument behind the station, will be particularly interested in reading *People of the Tenpo Era,* by Katsuo Kinya. The Prefectural Social Education International Cultural Center library has a copy, or you can order it directly from the publisher, Motoyoshi Sangyo Inc., 232–3 Kita Yasue-chō, Kanazawa 920, for ¥300.

The well-known essayist and critic, Yoshida Kenichi, includes his trip to Kanazawa in his book, *Japan is a Circle* (Kodansha, 1975). His insights, especially his loving description of that winter libation, *kotsuzake,* hold appeal for both Japanese and foreigners.

Kanazawa's own contributions to Japanese literature have not been small, and some works of several of the most famous native authors are available in English. Only a few of the stories are about Kanazawa itself, but references to these gentlemen (and one lady, Kaga no Chiyo) pop up everywhere around the city, so some familiarity with them in advance may be worthwhile.

Short Stories & Poetry

> *Modern Japanese Stories* (ed. I. Morris, Tuttle, 1962) has stories by Murō Saisei, Tokuda Shūsei and Inoue Yasushi.
>
> *The Izu Dancer and Other Stories* (Tuttle, 1974) has a piece by Inoue Yasushi.
>
> *Modern Japanese Literature* (ed. D. Keene, Tuttle, 1957) carries one story by Izumi Kyōka.
>
> *The Counterfeiter* (Tuttle, 1965) is a collection of Inoue Yasushi's stories.
>
> *Japanese Folktales of Kaga and Noto* (Hokkoku Publishing, 1981). Stories collected and translated by Yamazaki Kazuhiro with Ruth P. Stevens.
>
> Saisei's poems can be found in *An Anthology of Modern Japanese Poetry* (ed. and tr. I. Kono and R. Fukuda, Kenkyūsha, 1957) and *Anthology of Modern Japanese Poetry* (tr. and comp. M. Shiffert and U. Sawa, Tuttle, 1972).

Novels (all by Inoue Yasushi, who attended Shikō, the Fourth Higher School which prece ded Kanazawa University)

> *Flood* (Tōkyō, Hara Publishing, 1964)
>
> *The Hunting Gun* (Tuttle, 1961)
>
> *Journey Beyond Samarkand* (Kodansha, 1971)
>
> *Lou-lan* (Tōkyō, Hara Publishing, 1964)
>
> *The Roof Tile of Tempyō* (U. Tōkyō Press, 1975)
>
> *Tun-huang* (Kodansha, 1978)

Kanazawa in Japan

During the feudal period , the Kanazawa ruled by the Maedas was the third largest city in Japan, and the clan's influence was felt nationally. Visitors touring Kyōto's Katsura Imperial Villa, or strolling around Daitokuji temple, for example, will be reminded that a Maeda lord presented this incense burner, or a Maeda daughter brought that screen as part of her dowry. And several of the buildings preserved in Meiji Village, outside of Nagoya, are from Kanazawa, notably a barbaric prison and a lecture hall from Shikō, the Fourth Higher School.

Particularly in Tōkyō, evidence of the Maeda's glory remains strong. Until they donated the property to the country, the Maeda's family villa stood at the present site of Tōkyō University's Hongō campus. Akamon, the red gate which still symbolizes the school, was the mansion's entryway. Their western-style, Meiji period mansion, in Komaba, now houses the Tōkyō Museum of Modern Literature (東京都近代文学館, 目黒区駒場43—55, tel. 466—5150), a 15-minute walk from Shibuya Station. Another fine Kaga-related museum the Hatakeyama Collection, (畠山記念館, 港区白金台 2 —10— 2 , tel. 447—5787) preserves the tea ceremony treasures of the Hatakeyama family, the early lords of Noto. The museum, surrounded by beautiful grounds and tea houses, is next to the well-known Hannya-en country restaurant, a five-minute walk from Takanawadai subway station.

Although the best way to enjoy Kaga cooking is to visit Kanazawa, those who can't make it (or can't live without it) can try one of the several Kaga restaurants in Tōkyō. One, an Akasaka branch of the extensive Asada Group, is very expensive and patronized chiefly by politicians and expense-account businessmen (浅 田 tel. 585—6606). More reasonably priced is Totoraku (とと楽) in the basement of Roppongi's Ibis Hotel (tel. 479—0606). Other possiblities include Ōshima (大志満) in the basement of the Hotel Pacific near Shinagawa Station, (tel. 446—9903), and Tōgen (桃 源) near Meidi-ya Supermarket in Roppongi (tel. 405—5751).

Ishikawa Prefecture runs a Tōkyō office stocked with pamphlets, maps and useful information, on the third floor of Kokusai Kankō Kaikan, at the Yaesu Exit side of Tōkyō Station (tel. 231—

4030). Kanazawa City's Tōkyō Office is on the fifth floor of the Zenkokutoshikaikan Bldg., 2-4-2 Hirakawa-cho, Chiyoda-ku, tel. 262-5519. The nearest subway stop is Akasakamitsuke.

WHERE TO STAY

Hotels

English is generally not understood at the medium-priced business-style hotels. For help with reservations, ask one of the several English-speaking employees at JTB's main office in Musashi.

Adventurous couples shouldn't forget the notorious love hotels found in every neighborhood. They can be identified by a profusion of garish neon saying *hoteru* (ホテル). After nine or so, a room for overnight can cost as little as ¥3,000.

New Grand Hotel ニューグランド・ホテル(高岡町) Takaoka Machi tel. 33—1311

The New Grand is Kanazawa's best, English is spoken, and the service is excellent. Single rooms, from ¥7,000 without meals, are narrow by western standards--a semi-double is recommended. Western food on the 12th floor, and the Chinese buffet lunch on the 3rd floor is a bargain. Sunset from the cosy cocktail lounge, Dichter, on the 12th floor, shouldn't be missed. Neither should breakfast on the 12th floor on a clear morning--both the view and the French toast are praiseworthy. A branch of the famous local inn, Kincharyō, in the basement offers Kaga cooking. Parking in the building. Credit cards, of course.

Sky Hotel スカイホテル（武蔵町15－1） tel. 33—2233

A cut above the usual 'business hotel,' with a great view. Lobby on the 10th floor. Single, ¥7,000; double, ¥11,000; twin, ¥13,000; In the center of Musashi.

Kanazawa Miyako Hotel 金沢都ホテル（駅前） tel. 31—2202

Directly across the station. Refurbished in 1983. Japanese and French restaurants on the 7th floor. Single, ¥7,000; semi-double, ¥11,000; twin, double, ¥12,000.

Holiday Inn tel. 23—1111

Big rooms with American-size beds. To the left of the station exit. Ground floor coffee shop has free refills. The 12th floor restaurant/lounge has an extensive appetizer list. Single, ¥7,500;

double, ¥13,000; twin, ¥14,000.

Hotel New Kanazawa   tel. 23−2255
Conveniently across from the station, to the right. Single,
¥5,500; double, ¥10,000; twin, ¥10,000.

International Hotel Kanazawa   tel. 96−0111
Plush hotel in Takao. Restaurants, convention hall, tea ceremony house and swimming pool.

Hakuunrō Hotel (See Yuwaku Hot Spring, p. 35)

New Grand Inn ニューグランド・イン   Kenroku Moto Machi tel. 22−1211
Business style, but retaining the fine service of the New Grand
Hotel. Single, ¥5,300; double, ¥7,900; twin, ¥10,500. Near
Kenrokuen Park.

Kanazawa Station Hotel   金沢ステーションホテル（此花町8－8）   tel. 23−2600
Business and 'special' rooms, across from the station, to the left.
Single, ¥5,500; double, ¥9,900; twin, ¥9,500.

Daiichi Hotel   第一ホテル（広坂1－2）   tel. 22−2011
Business style, with small rooms, but a great location on
Hirosaka-dōri. Single, ¥4,000; double or twin, ¥7,200.

Kanazawa Prince Hotel 金沢プリンスホテル（片町2−23−7）   tel. 23−2131
Right in Katamachi, perfect for night owls. Deluxe rooms also
available. Single, ¥5,500; double, ¥11,000; twin, ¥9,000.

Koseinenkin Kaikan 厚生年金会館（石引4−17−1）4-17-1 Ishibiki tel. 22−0011
Good location for tourism, at the top of Kenrokuen Park.
Single, ¥4,840; double, ¥7,920.

Pension Kanazawa 金沢ペンション（長町3−8−4）3-8-4 Nagamachi tel. 61−3489
In Nagamachi, near the samurai house area, with garden coffee
shop. Cheap for five people--a dorm-like room for ¥16,000.
Single, ¥3,600; twin, ¥7,500. Separate baths.

Ladies Hotel レディースホテル（橋場町10−38）   10-38 Hashiba-chō tel. 22−1531
Women only; beside Asano River. Japanese and western rooms,
all ¥4,000 per person.

Hotel Oka   岡旅館（堀川町5－2）   5-2 Horikawa-chō tel. 63−5351
Japanese and western rooms, near station. With two meals,
¥10,000, and ¥5,400 without.

Chaya Restel 茶屋レステル（本町2−17−12）2-17-12 Honchō tel. 61−6215
Cheapest western-style place near the station. Single, ¥3,000,

Quiet ryokan entrance.
(Oasis)

double, with bath, ¥7,000.

Ryokan (Inns) -- First Class

Asadaya　浅田屋（十間町 3）　　　23 Jukken Machi tel. 31−2228
　　Very new and elegant (not a spot of plastic in the place), with prices to match. Overnight, including dinner and breakfast, is around ¥30,000 per person. A cheaper chance to experience such luxury is the excellent *bentō* lunch (reservations necessary) for about ¥4,500.

Tsubajin　つば甚（寺町 5 − 1 − 8 ）　　5-1-8 Teramachi tel. 41−2181
　　Better known as a connoisseur's restaurant (lunch about ¥7,000, dinner, ¥10,000 up), Tsubajin also serves overnight guests. As is the case with yachts, if you have to ask the price at an elegant *ryokan*, you can't afford it--overnight, with two meals, runs about ¥30,000.

Kincharyō　金茶寮（寺町 1 ）　　　　1 Teramachi tel. 43−2121
　　One of the most charming *ryokan*, with six tiny separate houses spreading down the hill overlooking Saigawa, Kincharyō is also one of the most expensive. Luncheon, ¥10,000; dinner, ¥13,000; overnight, ¥40,000. But if you fancy sleeping where Reischauer and various prime ministers and princes did, the money will be well spent. Their Kaga cooking is also available in a branch shop in the New Grand Hotel basement.

Nishitsu にし津（大手町 9 − 5 ） 9-5 Ōtemachi tel. 61−6168

Nishitsu caters to an exclusive clientele, mainly elite Tōkyō businessmen, so it isn't very well known in Kanazawa. But the mistress likes it that way. A former geisha of legendary beauty and refinement, she chooses her customers carefully. An introduction from a reliable source is almost always necessary. But for the chance to experience the depths of true Japanese courtesy and taste, it's worth the extra trouble. Overnight is fixed at ¥20,000.

Kinjōrō 金城楼（橋場町） Hashiba-chō tel. 21−8188

This elegant, 100-year old inn is equally famous for its delicious meals. An inexpensive sample is available at lunchtime when *bentō* run between ¥1,500 and ¥3,000 (reservations necessary). Overnight, with two meals, is about ¥30,000. All rooms have a garden view and private bath.

Yama No O 山乃尾（東山 1 - 31- 25） 1-31-25 Higashiyama tel. 52−5171

Behind the Higashi pleasure district and formerly used mainly for assignations with geisha, Yama No O is now open to the public, but still very elegant. You can enjoy viewing the superb garden from one of the small, private rest houses scattered around its edges. What they call a 'simple luncheon' is ¥8,000 up, and an overnight runs from ¥25,000, including two meals.

Miyabo みやぼ（下柿木畠） Shimo Kakinokibatake tel. 31−4228

Formerly the tea house of Mr. Inagaki, Kanazawa's first mayor after the feudal age ended, Miyabo is surrounded by one of the oldest private gardens in the city. Depending on the room, an overnight is between ¥8,000 and ¥15,000, including dinner and breakfast. Garden fans who don't want to spend so much can catch a glimpse from the third floor rear window of the neighboring building.

Ryokan (Inns)--Moderate

Unlike the elegant *ryokan,* where meals are automatically included, at cheaper inns the price is often negotiable, depending on food included, length of stay and desirability of the room.

Yamatoku 山徳（広坂 1 − 2 −14） 1-2-14 Hirosaka tel. 31−4171

Good sightseeing location, near the city hall, in a homey, 3-story wooden structure. ¥3,500 without meals. Relaxed, family style atmosphere.

Murataya 村田屋（片町 1 － 5 － 2 ）　　1-5-2 Katamachi tel. 63—0455
Right off main Tatemachi shopping street. Japanese style rooms with shared bath and toilets. ¥6,600 with two meals, ¥3,800 without.

Nakamura 中村（広坂 1 － 6 － 6 ）　　1-6-6 Hirosaka tel. 31—1806
Quiet, family place on the edge of downtown. ¥3,500, including breakfast.

Itaya いたや（本町 2 －17－ 3 ）　　2-17-3 Honchō tel. 63—5451
Near station. ¥5,000 with two meals, ¥4,000 without.

Kinkōsō 金港荘（此花町 2 －39）　　2-39 Konohana-chō tel. 65—5725
Near station. Overnight, ¥2,900. No meals.

Shibaya しばや（本町 2 －19－ 7 ）　　2-19-7 Honchō tel. 22—3270
Near station. ¥2,800 without meals, ¥3,300 with breakfast.

Bonronan （梵論庵 ）　　2-87-1 Izumi Honmachi tel. 44—5670
Near the Kanazawa High School playing field. ¥2,500 with 2 meals. Maximum 8 people.

Minshuku (Family Inns)

There are Japanese style *minshuku* everywhere, so only those with some special advantage have been included here. It's best to ask at the City Information Booth outside the station to help with reservations.

Kōganji 高岸寺（寺町 5 － 2 －25）　　　　tel. 41—2280
An old temple in Teramachi with a nice view of Saigawa and the city. ¥4,000 with two meals. ¥1,000-down is necessary to make a reservation.

Ikegame いけ亀（野町 2 － 1 － 6 ）　　2-1-6 Nomachi tel. 41—0306
Large 80-year old former Japanese restaurant beside Shinmeigu and Saigawa Ōhashi bridge. Convenient to downtown. ¥3,200 with two meals.

Yōgetsu 陽 月（東山 1 －13－22）　　1-13-22 Higashiyama tel. 52—0497
Former geisha house in the Higashi district. Lovely interior. ¥3,500 with two meals.

Hirosaka Pension 広坂ペンション（広坂 1 － 2 －32）　　tel. 22—2837
Best location, between Kenrokuen Park and downtown on Hirosaka-dōri. Above a bakery. No meals, beds only. ¥3,000 for a short bunk bed.

Pension Raspberry ペンション・ラズベリー（瓢箪町25−27）

25-27 Hyōtan-machi tel. 23−0757

Western style (i.e., beds), run by Mr. and Mrs. Saida, who have traveled all over Europe. ¥3,500, including breakfast. Short walk from Musashi, toward Kobashi.

Youth Hostels

With a year's stay in Japan, one photo and ¥1,100, a foreigner can get a Japanese YH card, at the JYH Office in the Social Education Center's Bunkan. International YH cards are only available in Ōsaka and Tōkyō.

Izuminodai YH 泉野台YH（泉が丘−1−31） 1-1-31 Izumigaoka tel. 41−2802

Although crowded in summers, it's open to non-YH members, and a good bargain, except that you have to be in by 9:00 p.m. ¥2,500 including dinner and breakfast, ¥1,500 without meals (¥1,000 for members). Take bus #30 and get off at Izumino Sanchōme. Or the walk from downtown, past Ninjadera, is worth the time. The road is lined with temples interspersed with artisans--lacquer, basketry, tatami.

Matsuiya 松井屋（片町１−９−３） 1-9-3 Katamachi tel. 21−0275

Conveniently located downtown, but almost always full (perhaps you could squeeze in during winter or the June rainy season), and only open to YH members. Most visitors reserve by post card or phone. ¥2,700 with dinner and breakfast or ¥1,700 without.

Kanazawa YH 金沢ＹＨ（末広町37） 37 Suehiro-chō tel. 52−3414

The location at Utatsuyama is beautiful, but quite a hike when the buses (#5) stop. Last bus from the station leaves at 8:30. Curfew, of course, at 9:00. ¥1,900 for nonmembers without meals.

Hot Springs

Hot spring overnights are an institution in Japan. Could there be a better excuse than 'medicinal purposes' for a night away from home? Groups from offices, clubs and schools organize annual outings, usually to the big hotels of Kaga Onsen, down the coast near Kaga City.

For road-weary travelers, the rowdy spas may not be appropriate. There are several quiet possibilities close to Kanazawa, suitable for a relaxing bath and overnight after a day of city sightseeing. Most places include dinner and breakfast in the price. If you wish to stay in town through the evening, arrange to skip dinner when you make your reservation.

Taki No Sō 滝の荘（末町）   Suemachi tel. 29—0003

A charming old inn some ways up Saigawa river , and nestled in a hollow beside a waterfall, Taki No Sō specializes in river fish and mountain vegetables, with a hot spring bath and low prices. Luncheon or dinner begins at ¥4,000, overnight from ¥7,000. Only 20 minutes from town by cab. Nearby is the entrance to Tatsumi Yōsui, the underground waterway which runs through Kanazawa.

Ishiya   石屋（深谷温泉）   Fukatani Machi tel. 58—2133

A large old inn with modern improvements providing all the comforts. The enormous garden is graced with a private noh stage, the banquet rooms are beautifully decorated, and the corridors are lined with cases displaying crafts and knick-knacks. But the bath is best of all--coffee-colored water which smooths the skin. Prices begin at ¥7,000. Ishiya is one of several inns at Fukatani Onsen, 20 minutes by cab, up behind Morimoto.

Yuwaku Hot Spring   湯涌温泉

Most hot spring spas nowadays have gone completely commercial, with garish signs, bars and strip shows. But Yuwaku maintains the atmosphere of an old-fashioned, sleepy mountain village. It's close enough for an overnight from Kanazawa, especially when combined with a look at neighboring Edo Mura. There are several small hotels and inns, ranging from the modest Atarashiya (about ¥8,000 a night, tel. 35—1011) to the first-class Hakuunrō Hotel. Overlooking man-made Lake Gyokusen, Hakuunrō has no fewer than four baths (perfumed, fountain-decorated, bubbling spring, coed), western and Japanese rooms and a country mixed-grill dinner cooked and served on a plow. The Americans who took it over during the Occupation built a swimming pool, now open only a few weeks in summer, Hakuunrō's facade is incongruously half Chinese and half Spanish, but the interior is Japanese.

The prices are also Japanese--overnight and two meals for ¥25,000. Ms. Katō speaks English. (白雲楼 (湯涌温泉)   tel. 35—1111).

ENGLISH INFORMATION SOURCES

–The Society to Introduce Kanazawa to the World is a non-profit organization that was formed in 1977. Beside publishing this guidebook, the Society also teaches Japanese to resident foreigners and sponsors a 3-week intensive summer seminar annually. International Business Seminars also aid Japanese with their English for overseas transactions. The Society will arrange for goodwill volunteer guides. (See opposite.) Located on the 4th floor of the Social Education Center (Shakyō Center). Tel. 31—3291, ext. 205. Mon.–Fri., 10:00–4:30.

–The International Culture Center has a library with many English books and current magazines. Space for reading and studying. In front of the above Society's office. Tel. 31—3291, ext. 244 or 245. Mon.–Sat., 10:30–6:30.

–Kanazawa City Tourism Section is on the 3rd floor of the new City Hall Building. They have pamphlets and information on everything. Tel. 20—2194. Mon.–Fri., 9:00–5:30, Sat. 9:00–10:00.

--JTB's main office in Musashi is the best for general travel information on Japan, but they can also answer questions, investigate details or make local reservations. Several of the employees speak some English. Tel. 64—2266. Open Mon.–Fri., 10:00–6:00, and Sat. 10:00–1:00.

--The New Grand and Sky hotels have English-speaking front desk clerks.

--For some English that doesn't talk back, try the small English book sections at Utsunomiya, Hokkoku Shorin and Maruzen bookstores.

HELPFUL INFORMATION

General Travel Information

JTB (日本交通公社) is the best bet. English spoken. Main office in Musashi, branches in Daiwa (first floor) and the station.

10:00–6:00, Mon.–Fri.; 10:00–1:00, Sat.: Main office, tel. 64–2266.

Hokuriku Kōkū Service, for air reservations and tickets only. English can be used intermittently, depending on their staff schedules. 9:00–6:30, Mon.–Fri.; 9:00–5:00 Sat.; 10:30–5:00, Sun. and holidays. tel. 63–7117. 1-2-24 Kōrinbō.

Train tickets are sold in three places: the station, the JTB main office in Musashi, and Nihon Ryokō, at the Katamachi intersection, 9:30–5:30, Mon.–Fri.; 9:30–12:30, Sat.

Other travel bureaus:

Nihon Ryokō, 1-6-13 Katamachi, tel. 62–0411.

Kinki Nihon Tourist, 1-1-34 Katamachi, tel. 32–0561.

Tōkyū Kankō 1-11-14 Owari-chō, tel. 22–0109. Mr. Ueda speaks English.

New Orient Express, 3-43 Ikedamachi, tel. 63–3441.

Nisso Tourist Bureau, 1-7-14 Katamachi, tel. 63–9494.

Tōbu Travel, 15–24 Shōwamachi, tel. 31–0190.

English Guide

Kanazawa SGG goodwill volunteer guides are part of the national system established by the Japan National Tourist Organization. Call the Society to Introduce Kanazawa to the World office (31–3291, ext. 205) for a guide in English, Chinese, German, or French. Home visits can also be arranged. Mrs. Yoshiko Hayakawa is a licensed, English-speaking guide with much experience and knowledge about the city. Call her at 63–0762.

Currency Exchange

The fastest, most convenient service is available at the Sanwa Bank (三和銀行) in Musashi or the Hokuriku Bank (北陸銀行) in Minami-chō (second floor).

Immigration

The local Immigration Office (Nyūkoku Kanri Jimusho), a branch of the Nagoya office, is located at Kanazawa Port. Only three buses a day head for the port directly (#74), so try taking one of the frequent ones for Kanaiwa Town (#60 or #61), and get a taxi from there. 8:30–5:00 Mon.–Fri.; 8:30–12:30, Sat. Tel. 68–2488. Call first--sometimes they're closed. The office is on the second floor of the building to the left.

City Information Booth is just
outside the station. (H.Ikeuchi)

Cheap instant photos can be had from the machine by the side entrance to the Blue Ribbons Building on Tatemachi shopping street. Four for ¥300.

International Telephone and Telegram

The Kanazawa Telegraph Office, 2-9-1 Hikoso, is open 24 hours, for cables and phone calls, tel. 20-4541.

International Mail

Overseas packages are accepted at two city post offices: Minami Post Office, 6-17-1 Izumino (8:00− 8:00; Sun. until 5:00), and Chūō Post Office, 1-1 Sanja (open 24 hours). English-speaking Mr. Nozaki Mitsuyoshi works at the Chūō Post Office, tel. 33− 2490.

International Florist

Hanamasa Florist, 2-1-10 Kōrinbō, is a member of FTD. They have an English pamphlet from which to choose.

Movies

An English list of current movies is posted in the International Culture Center.

First Run,	Kanazawa Gekijō	tel. 61-0837
Japanese		1-7-23 Katamachi
First Run,	Tōei	tel. 31-5853
Foreign (in original language)		2-9-1 Katamachi
	Plaza	tel. 31-3043
		2-9-2 Katamachi
	Grand	tel. 21-3011
		2-9-3 Katamachi

	Cinema 1 and 2	tel. 33-3700
		2-7-19 Katamachi
	Palace	tel. 31-5853
		2-9-1 Katamachi
	Teatoru	tel. 64-1140 2-1-13 Hikoso
	Roxy	tel. 61-3691 Basement of Kanazawa Bldg. (across from station)
Second run	Star	tel. 31-0222 3-5-24 Ishibiki
Second run	Roppongi	tel. 0762-75-6161 Mattō City, near the Bypass; car necessary.
Second run or porn	Ekimae	tel. 31-1838 6-10 Kasaichi
	Bunka Gekijō	tel. 61-1372 Basement of Kanazawa Bldg. (across from station)
Porn	Nikkatsu	tel. 31-4061 2-9-2 Katamachi

All Night Places

Twenty-four-hour places have come into vogue lately, so die-hard insomniacs can stop muttering about rolled-up sidewalks and hick towns. Other than the garish Mr. Donuts, most all night places serve light food, drinks and coffee. Try Yellow USA near the station, Goendama on Saigawa Ōdōri (Saiwai-chō), or Uchū-ken, in downtown Katamachi.

Playguide

Concert tickets are sold at the Playguides on the first floors of Daiwa and Meitetsu Marukoshi departments stores. Cheap movie tickets are sold in advance at many shops, like tobacco places and record stores, as well as on the first floor of Meitetsu. About ¥200 cheaper than at the door, they are also available on the same day as the movie is playing.

Emergency Phone Numbers (In Japanese)

Fire: 119
Police: 110　　　　　　　Weather: 177
Ambulance: 119　　　　Time: 117

Churches

Catholic, Hirosaka-dōri, daily mass at 7:00 a.m.; Sun., also at 8:30, 9:30. and 6:00 p.m.; Wed. also at 6:00 p.m.

United Church of Christ, Kōrinbō (Kanazawa Kyōkai), services on Sun., 10:15 a.m. and 7:00 p.m. and Wed., 7:30 p.m.

Friendship Associations

Japan-Soviet Society, 1-7-14 Katamachi, tel. 63—9494.

Japan-France Society, Plaza Miki, 6-22 Oyama-chō, tel. 32—3257. (Ms. Ikeda)

Japan-America Society, International Cultural Center, 3-2-15 Honda-machi, tel. 31—3291.

Japan-Brazil Society, 3-10-6 Honda-machi, tel. 32—3330. (Dr. Iino)

Coin Laundries

Kit Coin Laundry, behind the New Grand Hotel, 8:00—10:30 daily. Kodatsuno, near New Tanuki and Joe House, 7:00—10:00 daily.

Shoe Repair

Mr. Minute: Daiwa, sixth floor. While-you-wait service. Also keys made.

SPORTS, HEALTH AND BEAUTY

Doctors

The following doctors speak good English, with the exception of the acupuncture and oriental medicine specialists, who can, however, read and write it fluently. For emergency or extreme cases, it may be best to go directly to the University Hospital (Daigaku Byōin) in Kodatsuno. (tel. 62—8151)

Surgery: Dr. Mai Masayoshi, Cancer Research Institute (Ganken Byōin), 4-85 Yoneizumi, tel. 41—8245. Home: 22—7636.

Ob-gyn: Dr. Matsumoto Hirofumi, Red Cross Hospital (Nisseki Byōin), 2 Minma, tel. 42—8131. Home: 44—6333.

Internal Medicine, Pediatrics: Dr. Kadoya Motoko, 1-11-7 Honda-machi, tel. 22—6880.

Opthalmology: Dr. Fujimura Kazumasa, 2-5-36 Arimatsu, tel. 44—5768. Dr. Tanabe Jōji, tel. 62—8151, ext. 3527.

Dentistry: Dr. Iino Takeshi, 3-10-6 Honda-machi, tel. 32—1301.

Acupuncture: Dr. Nakamura Kanesuke, 2-14-36 Higashiyama, tel. 52—2005.

Oriental Medicine: Dr. Taru Atsufumi, 5-12 Wakakusa-machi, tel. 41—4771.

Exercise Centers

Nagae Training Center: Open 10:00—9:30, daily, for free exercise (no trainer). ¥500 for visitors. 2-4-5 Izumino. Tel. 41—5007. Even those with no interest in exercise would benefit from meeting Ms. Terry Nagae, the unique, English-speaking owner.

Koseinenkin Kaikan: Good equipment and training courses in the early afternoons. 10:00—12:00 for women only, 1:00—8:00 for both sexes. ¥330 for two hours.

Yoga

Trainer Ms. Sanmi speaks some English and holds classes at Kosaka Kōminkan, Fri. 7:00—9:00. ¥3,000 membership fee plus monthly tuition. Her home phone number is 42—2715.

Bathhouses

Kusatsu Onsen, 5-5-5 Teramachi, is the best public bath in Kanazawa. A new building, it's not much on traditional atmosphere, but the equipment, convenience and cleanliness are unparalleled. The second floor has a regular *sentō*-style neighborhood public bath. The third floor (take the elevator) is divided into private 'family baths' of different flavors—milk, lemon, Chinese medicinal and regular. A great experience in any season. Open daily, 2:00 p.m.—2:00 a.m., except the 11th and 12th of every month.

Sauna and Massage

Men-only sauna-massage places (of varying respectability) are found everywhere. The following are the only places in Kanazawa serving both men and women. Oriental-style massage parlors, often including acupuncture and moxabustion treatment, are found in nearly every neighborhood.

Daiwa Sauna, 2-3-15 Katamachi, open daily.

Men: Sauna, ¥1,200, massage, ¥2,500, 24 hours; for an extra ¥800, you can sack out on a couch overnight.

Women: Sauna, ¥1,000; massage, ¥2,500. Noon—2:00 a.m. Slightly sleazy at night.

Beauty Salons

The following three places are used to having foreign customers.

Tableau, basement of Blue Ribbons Bldg. on Tatemachi-dōri; 10:00—8:00; Sun., 9:00— 6:00.

Kizawa, basement of Hokkoku Bank Bldg., Katamachi Intersection, 10:00—8:00; Sun. 8:30—6:00.

Gion, 1-12-18 Katamachi, 10:00—5:30.

Hasegawa, behind Sky Plaza, 9:30—7:00, also closed 2nd Sun.

(Kanazawa barbers and beauty shops are closed on Mondays.)

Hiking

The nearest good hiking spot is Iōzan, the area famous for medicinal herbs and grasses (but not for amateur pharmacists-- many are poisonous). Take the 8:15 a.m., #14 bus from the station to the Iōzan Sports Center, and then you're on your own. There are several trails and one excellent orienteering course. If you make a reservation well in advance (forget school holidays), you can stay overnight at the Sports Center for the unbelievable price of ¥2,200, which includes three meals. Tel. 29—1591. For more serious hikers, the nearest challenges are Mt. Tateyama in Toyama, and Mt. Hakusan, both limited to summer assault.

Bicycling

A peaceful, 8-kilometer bike path runs between Katamachi (near Saigawa Shrine) and the sea, along sparkling Saigawa river. Path ends at a park with artificial lakes for boating. A bird sanctuary and swimming pool make it a great place for picnicking. It connects with trails extending clear out into Noto Peninsula. On the other direction, although the roads are narrow and somewhat dangerous, the way out to Edo Mura makes a pleasant ride. Actually, the return trip, an easy downhill coast, is more pleasant.

Swimming

The heated, indoor City Pool, near Arimatsu, is open 1:00 p.m. to 7:00 p.m., year-round, except Tuesday. Sunday is from 11:00— 4:00 p.m. Two hours for adults cost ¥250. The outdoor pool at the same center opens when someone decides it's warm enough. The Prefectural Kenmin Pool, down by the seaside, is a beautiful-looking complex, but not recommended for actual swimming. It's open only from mid-July through August, just when the kiddies are out of school, and it's always packed.

Although it's frowned upon locally, seaside bathing is nice at Kanaiwa. Take a #60 or #61 bus to Kanaiwa and keep walking, 5 minutes from the bus station. Most people flock to Uchinada Beach, a 1-kilometer walk from the end of the electric train line, which is supplied with lifeguards, litter and loudspeakers. Direct buses leave from Kanazawa station during the season (mid-July through August, only).

Golf

The best course around here is at Katayamazu Hot Springs, about 1½ hours away by #42 bus (be sure to take the bus via Awazu, not Katayamazu; get off at Golfjōmae). The nearest course is at Kanazawa Golf Club, this side of Yuwaku Hot Springs. Take a #12 bus, and get off at Nakamura. Call the club from there (tel. 29–1515), and they'll pick you up. Equipment is available for rent.

Field Athletics

This is Japanese for 'obstacle course.' A creative and challenging one, set up at the far side of Kenmin Park at Utatsuyama, is open to energetic souls from April to November.

Tennis

People with rackets can just go down to the Kenrokuen Courts by Hirosaka-dōri and start swinging. Otherwise, Jumbo Bowl Tennis Club has a visitors system. When their members aren't using all the courts (count out Sat., Sun. and holidays). Visitors may (unofficially) borrow shoes and a racket, and play 2 hours for ¥300. Best bet is early morning. Check for free courts by phone, tel. 44–7121 ('*Aite imasuka?*'). 6:30 a.m.–9:30 p.m. daily. Many buses pass Jumbo Bowl. Ask at the station bus information desk for the fastest way. Get off at Nishi Izumi. Iōzen Sports Center offers courts only. Tatsunokuchi Kōen outside Tsurugi has courts and lessons and rents rackets.

Skiing

The following ski slopes are accessible by public transportation for day trips from Kanazawa. They all rent equipment (up to 27-centimeter shoe size). Bus times vary with the season, so you have to check schedules again in advance. The only constant is that there are only a few in each direction, so if you miss one, your day can be ruined.

Shishiku Kōgen: 45 minutes away. Bus #47 from the station. Get off at Ichinomiya and walk 20 minutes.

Dainichi: 1½ hours away. Bus #47 from Kenrokuenshita to the slopes.

Ichirino: 1½ hours away. Bus #47 from the station, or the electric train from Nomachi, to Hakusanshita. Change to the bus for Ichirino slopes.

Shiramine: 2 hours away. Bus #47 from the station to the slopes.

Overnight reservations can be made with JTB. They also organize many overnight and day trips, near and far, with inexpensive, all-inclusive fares.

THINGS TO DO

There's more to visiting a foreign country than exploring temples and trying the local food. Visitors with time on their hands or a desire to go beyond sightseeing may wish to try something from the following list.

Tea Ceremony: Ms. Matsuda Sōyo teaches tea in her lovely home (8 Kiyokawa-chō) on Tues., 10:30—4:00 and Sat., 1:00—5:00, and she welcomes foreigners. In fact, for several years she has been sponsoring a tea-in-English class--Japanese tea students and a foreign English teacher meet one evening a week to exchange instruction. Visitors may make arrangements for a tea lesson through the Society to Introduce Kanazawa to the World (tel. 31—3291, ext. 205) or Mrs. Sonoko Matsuda, her sister-in-law, in the evenings (tel. 43—6655).

Flower Arrangement: Mrs. Okada Emiko speaks excellent English and teaches Ohara School arrangement in her home (1-1 Nagadohei) on Wed. and Thurs. or by appointment. (tel. 61—5063 or through SGG). The fee varies with the price of the flowers that day.

Aoki Cooking School: Language isn't necessary for learning some local cooking. Try the general Japanese cooking class on Tues. afternoon at 1:30, for two hours (about ¥2,000). After the class you can eat what you've made, so it becomes an inexpensive lunch after a morning at the samurai houses and Yūzen factory in Nagamachi. Although residents must sign up for a term, Mrs. Aoki is willing to give tourists a one-shot deal. Apply in advance if possi-

Tea ceremonies are popular and frequent. (Hokkoku Press)

ble, but the morning of the same day is fine for individuals or a small group. Another possibility is the *kaiseki* (tea ceremony food) class on the third Mon. of the month, ¥6,000 for 3 hours, beginning at 1:30. 1-1 Nagamachi.

Culture Centers: Both the Hokkoku and Chūnichi local newspapers run a *bunka sentaa*, offering a wide range of courses (traditional arts, crafts, sports, languages, cooking, etc.) at low prices. At Chūnichi (2-7-15 Kōrinbō, 8 F, tel. 33−1977), you can pay by the month for weekly classes. Hokkoku (3-2-1 Hondamachi, tel. 22−0101) requires a membership fee plus three months' tuition. Japanese ability is not necessary for understanding and enjoyment of most arts and crafts lessons. Laporto Culture School, a branch of the Hokkoku Bunka Center, has programs geared to the young (Tel. 20−8800).

Kimono School: Visitors are welcome to watch classes in donning kimono at the Bunka Fukusō Gakuin, run by Mr. and Mrs. Murakami. Beginners' classes every Thurs., 1:00−3:00, advanced on Mon., 1:00−3:00 and 6:00−8:00. Although women may enter the classroom, men must wait downstairs until the students have struggled into the basic underclothes. It's best to call (tel. 42−2330) or drop by in advance to let them know you're coming. 1−5 Kiyokawa-chō.

Martial Arts: The new Ishikawa Prefectural Budōkan in Naruwa (8-3 Kosaka-machi Nishi) holds classes every Mon, Wed. and Fri. evenings from 4:00−6:00 (children) and 6:00−7:00 (adults) in judō, *kendō* and *kyūdō* (archery). Observers are welcome, and if you call in advance (51–5721), the fellows in the office will arrange for a guide.

Central Fish Market: This circus swings into business at 3:30 a.m., when the fishermen auction their catch to the wholesalers. The noisy spectacle is worth the agony of getting up in the middle of the night, except in mid-winter, when the balance is tipped by the cold. The action continues until 6:00 or so, when the vegetables go on sale. Reward yourself with a bowl of noodles at one of the market's restaurants. Wear rubber boots, if possible. Cab is the only possible transportation at that hour. Say 'Chūo Ichiba' to the driver. In operation daily except Sun.

Planetarium: It's open at the Children's Center (Jidōkaikan) in Hōshima-machi, from 3:30 to 4:10 daily except Mon.

Courthouse: Witness trials involving gangland murder, bureaucratic corruption or environmental pollution. With the exception of very controversial issues, most cases involve quickly settled, petty disputes, so the visitors gallery is usually empty. Apply at the reception desk at either side of the building (*'Bōchō sasete itadakemasenka?'*) anytime from 10:00–12:30 and 1:00–4:30. Mon.-Fri.

City Assembly: Observe city politics in action at the plenary sessions held four times a year. The speeches, on topics previously settled in committee, contain no surprises and little excitement, but, unlike the trapped assembly members, visitors may slip out any time. Call the Tourism Section (tel. 20–2194) for exact dates. Drop by the assembly's 4th floor office a few minutes in advance to pick up a pass (*'Bōchō sasete itadakemasenka?'*). Enter the visitors gallery from the 7th floor. No smoking, photos or catcalls.

Noh Theater: Noh or some other traditional performing art is held almost every Sat. and Sun., usually for free, at the Noh Theater above Kenrokuen Park. Professional noh is regularly scheduled on the first Sun. of the month, about ¥1,000.

Home Visit: The City Office sponsors a system whereby foreigners may visit Japanese homes. Call English-speaking Mr. Kunisawa of the General Affairs Section (tel.20–2075). Also contact the Society to Introduce Kanazawa to the World (tel. 31–3291, ext. 205).

Tea Ceremony: Memorial for tea master Sen Sōshitsu at Gesshinji in Higashiyama, on the 23rd of every month. Memorial for silk dyer Miyazaki Yūzensai at Ryūkokuji in Higashiyama, on the 17th of every month. Memorial for their *fudō* deity, at the lotus-surrounded Hasudera in Jingūji, on the 27th of every month.

Shintō Rites: Oyama Shrine holds rites on the 27th, the day of Lord Maeda Toshiie's death, and on the first, to begin the month properly. Both at 10:00 a.m. Gokoku Shrine holds memorial services for the war dead daily at 11:00 a.m.

Early Risers Club: The Hayaoki-kai gathers daily at Kanazawa Shrine in Kenrokuen, for sunrise, tea and talk. Anyone welcome. The hour depends on the season, ranging from 4:00 in summer to 7:00 or so in winter.

The prefectural theater's strong wooden beams set off the power of noh. (Oasis)

NHK FM Request Hour: You can be a member of the studio audience on this 3:10, Saturday afternoon show, if you show up at the NHK information desk between 3:05 and 6:00.

MRO Pal Do Sunday: Everyone is welcome to participate in MRO's Sunday afternoon radio show, when it's held at the 'satellite studio' on the 5th floor of the Pal Do building, across from Daiwa, between 1:20 and 2:15.

Horseraces: Lose your shirt at the racetrack in Hatta town, on Sat., Sun. and Mon., from April though December. Nine races a day, between noon and 4:00 p.m., are met by special buses, leaving every 15 minutes from the Central Hotel, across from the station. The first bus is at 10:30.

Exhibitions: A constant stream of exhibitions--historical, cultural and commercial--are held at the department stores and various galleries around town.

Going Around the City

GETTING AROUND

Kanazawa is small enough to be well suited to walking tours--
it only takes an hour to walk from the station clear across town to
Daijōji temple. And much of Kanazawa's charm is to be found in
the old back streets, the original main roads of the castle town.
Winding by old shops and houses, they maintain the atmosphere of
the Edo period. Buses travel almost exclusively on the broad
avenues built in this century, over the filled-in moats or where a
fire leveled a neighborhood.

If the winding back streets constitute one of Kanazawa's attractions, they are also a tourist's nightmare. Streets are rarely laid out
at 90° angles, so even a keen sense of direction will be befuddled.
In fact, some speculate that this is the reason for the confusing
jumble--invading troops would have a hard time making their way
through this maze to the castle. In any case, unless you wish
deliberately to wander around aimlessly, say in the Higashiyama
temple district, it's helpful to rely on a map.

Rent-a-cycle

A bicyclist, one who doesn't mind getting off to push up the
steep hills, can get around best in Kanazawa. One-way streets, no-
parking signs, expensive parking lots--all can be ignored. The one
thing that demands attention is the weather. Much of June and
November, and all of the first three months of the year, Kanazawa
citizens are chained to their umbrellas. Only the old men coming
down from the mountains, wrapped in warm straw matting and
waterproof hats, will venture out on a bicycle or motor scooter.

The rent-a-cycle office at the station is out to the left, beside
the bus platforms. Tel. 21−0947. (See Map on p.106.) The seats
can't be raised any higher than to suit a person of 5'8" or so. Open
8:00−5:30. It costs ¥1,000 a day. To keep the bike overnight,
convincing details about where you are staying and how long, etc.,
will be necessary. Ask for their bike route map.

Hire Car

For those in a hurry, especially a group of 3 or 4, a hire taxi
is most convenient. The rates usually run around ¥4,000 − an
hour. Try English-speaking Mr. Matsubara Yoshio, who worked
for many years at the U.S. Naval Base in Yokosuka. He now works

for Naruwa Taxi Co., tel. 52—2141. His home phone is 37—4539. Most other drivers are accustomed to half or full day tours of the most famous spots, so if you can't get Mr. Matsubara, make your own list, hire a cab through JTB and leave the logistics up to the driver. The biggest taxi company is Ishikawa Kōtsū, tel. 31—4131, but they refuse early morning calls, so for a crack-of-dawn train departure, try Fuji Kōtsū, tel. 52—6121 or Kintetsu Taxi, tel. 21—3265.

Bus

For outlying districts and cross-town jaunts, the city bus system (Hokutetsu) is the best bet. There are two circle lines, buses #1 and #2, which offer a good, if fleeting, view of the city in a short time. Fares are still cheap, and the signs are numbered as well as color-coded by general direction. The drawbacks of bus riding are the crowds at rush hour (8:00—9:00 and 5:00—6:00), and the early hour of the last bus--most routes peter out around 8:30 or 9:00 p.m. The other problem is that the number system can be confusing. Several long-distance buses with different destinations may have the same number. A notable example is #41, the airport bus. There are five different #41 buses, and only one goes to Komatsu Airport. Be sure to check with the driver as you get on.

A bus map appears on page 94. For bus information at the station, ask at the tiny Hokutetsu information window on the outside platform. State the destination, and someone will steer you to the right stop.

There are two types of bus. The majority are 'one-man,' with a ticket machine. On inner-city buses, the fare is fixed at ¥140. But on buses going outside the ¥140 limit, you take a ticket as you enter the middle door. The number on your ticket and the corresponding fare are written above the front window. As you get off, put the exact fare and the ticket in the box. There is a machine for changing coins, but drivers are not always able to change a bill. The second kind of bus has a conductor standing at the center door, which serves as entrance and exit. He will tell you when the fare is over ¥140.

The national bus company (Kokutetsu), operates mainly suburban buses, convenient for trips to outlying areas and neighboring prefectures. Ask about times and destinations at their information booth, situated between the city bus terminal and the railroad station.

Electric Train

There are two rickety, picturesque trolleys (*densha*) running from Kanazawa Station to Uchinada, and from Nomachi Station, via Tsurugi, to Hakusanshita.

Rent-a-car

Not recommended for city sightseeing, but great for getting around the prefecture. All sorts of cars are available, beginning at ¥4,800 for six hours, at two companies in front of the station.

Bus Tours

All in Japanese, with flags and the works. Hurried, but convenient. Buses leave from and return to Kanazawa Station. Make reservations through JTB or at the Hokutetsu offices in Kingeki Bldg., in Katamachi (tel. 62–8216), and at the left as you leave the station (tel. 62–8211).

Kenrokuen Course: 8:40 or 1:20, April–October; 8:40 or 1:00, Nov.–March; Oyama Shrine, Utatsuyama, Seisonkaku, Ace Kanazawa, Nagamachi Samurai Houses, Kenrokuen Park. ¥1,620. About four hours.

Jōkamachi Course: 8:30, for four hours. Modern Literature Museum, Honda Museum, Edo Mura, Ninjadera, Ace Kanazawa. ¥2,580.

Hyakumangoku Course: 8:30, for 8 hours. Modern Literature Museum, Honda Museum, Edo Mura, Ninjadera, Ace Kanazawa, Oyama Shrine, Utatsuyama, Seisonkaku, Nagamachi Samurai Houses, Kenrokuen Park. ¥4,670.

WHAT TO NOTICE

City Layout: Upon arriving in Kanazawa, head directly for a high vantage point, like the top of the Sky or New Grand hotels. Then look down over the city. A 360° sweep reveals that Kanazawa is built on a narrow plain between the Alps foothills and the Japan Sea. Notice the three finger-like ridges, divided by the Asano and Saigawa rivers. Keeping an eye on these three hills, Utatsuyama, Kodatsuno and Teramachi, will help you maintain some sense of direction when walking around town. Kanazawa Castle and

Kenrokuen are built on the tapering end of the middle ridge, and the town circles around them.

Greenery: Kanazawa is sometimes called *mori no miyako,* or the Wooded Capital. The Maeda lords, always conscious of military preparedness, ordered fruit trees planted everywhere for emergency food supplies. The city became uniquely lush, with apricots, figs and peaches in every garden, and the natural sweets became an important part of the people's diet. Now that sugar is readily available, families are choosing to build more traditional Japanese gardens. The pines and cedars have taken over again.

Japanese have a deep-seated respect for trees. The most impressive evidence of this feeling is the deliberate protection of trees blocking a widened road. In most countries they would be cut down without a second thought to make way for the traffic, but in several spots around Kanazawa, the road has been built around them. Find examples across the street from the International Culture Center and near Asadaya Inn in Jukkenmachi.

Architecture: Kanazawa's architectural style is completely dictated by the weather. Houses are built to withstand the long winter, but open enough to provide some relief from summer's humidity. These considerations have given rise to several features unique to the Hokuriku area. Many houses along the back streets retain some or all of them.

Traditional Kaga house on a quiet back street.

The city is best known for its shiny tile roofs which, when viewed from above, seem to flow like the waves on the nearby Japan Sea. Their sparkling glaze is found only in Snow Country. Reflecting the precious winter sun, they help melt the snow whose weight threatens the strength of the house's supporting pillars. About one-third of the way up the roof runs a wooden or tile rim to keep the fast-melting snow from sliding down on passersby. Nevertheless, every winter seems to have its tragic newspaper account of buried children or a crushed snow shoveler.

It's only relatively recently, however, that tiles came into wide use. Most buildings were covered with thick boards weighted down with rows of stones. Although the wood might rot quickly, it's said that the people counted on the rocks for a handy weapon in an emergency. From a high place it's still possible to see such roofs here and there around town.

The other characteristics are visible from the front of the house. Just under the main roof is a smaller one, called *koyane,* which is often edged above with figured tiles. These make a pretty decoration on an otherwise dull facade, but their main purpose is practical. When the snow melts and begins a slow slide down the main roof, it curls under the beams and rests against the mud wall. A row of tiles in this spot protects the house from seepage.

Just above these tiles, many houses have barred or permanently shut windows, indicating a storeroom. In the Edo period the townspeople were forbidden to look upon a procession of the lord and his retainers. Windowless storerooms in the front of the house guaranteed that this rule would be observed. Careful scrutiny, however, reveals that some families were able to evade a rule or two, like the ban on 3-storied houses. Some are designed with three stories at the back of the house, but with an innocent two-story front.

Hanging below the *koyane,* Kanazawa houses often have a narrow board running the length of the front windows. This, too, is for snow protection. And the level of the board is raised slightly at the doorway, breaking the severe line with a graceful curve. The door itself is often one massive square of wood, kept shut during the winter, in which a smaller, person-sized entrance has been cut out for everyday use.

There's one distinctive feature of Kanazawa houses that may be as much a product of the people's character as of the weather. This is the *sodegaeshi*, a trapezoidal sleeve at both sides of the house between the main roof and the *koyane*. Ostensibly to cut the severity of the strong winds blowing in through the chinks, some argue that Kanazawa people are equally interested in creating as much privacy between their homes as is possible in the town's cramped quarters. Dark bamboo slatted curtains, called *mushiko*, which hang outside the house, may also fall into this psychological category. City folk can watch passers-by through the curtains from inside their houses without being seen themselves.

Kanazawa Dialect: With the widespread influence of radio, television and national magazines, 'standard' Japanese (i.e., that spoken in Tōkyō) is understood all over Japan. But regional accents and dialects remain the favorite mode of communication in most areas. The easy intimacy of shared roots can be established early in a conversation between strangers, and, likewise, outsiders are immediately recognizable.

Kanazawa Dialect, characterized by a rolling tone at the pauses and certain feminine-sounding verb endings, is easily distinguishable in local shops (especially Ōmichō), restaurants and on the street. For those who understand some Japanese, a brief list of typical Kanazawa expressions appears below. Local people are delighted (and amused) to hear them used by foreigners.

Kanazawa	*Standard Japanese*	*English*
Ah, honnan!	Ah, sō desu ka!	Is that so!
Anyatō	Arigatō	Thank you
Nān (with rising tone)	Dō itashimashite	Don't mention it
Chokkoshi	Sukoshi	A little
Tabemasshi (feminine)	Otabe nasai	Please eat
Honnagaya	Hai, sō desu	Yes, that's right
Nenne	Akachan; kodomo	Baby; child
Dara! (Be careful using this one)	Baka!; Chigau!	You fool!; Oh, no!

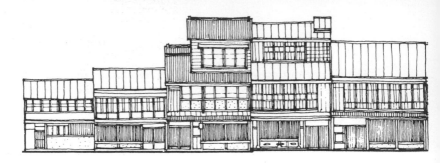

Old and New: The city has had its share of fires, but like Kyōto, Kanazawa escaped being bombed during World War II. This is partly because of its lack of military importance (industrial Toyama and Fukui were destroyed), and partly due, it is to be hoped, to American respect for the cultural heritage of Japan. There may be spiritual scars left on Kanazawa, but physically, the city has been able to preserve many of the characteristics of a provincial castle town: narrow streets, old shops and samurai houses surrounded by earthen walls.

On the other hand, this asset can also be considered a defect. One of the most challenging local controversies is under what conditions to preserve old neighborhoods. The modern residents of the Higashi geisha district, for example, protested vehemently when moves were made to designate it a protected area. They were afraid that as home improvements were forbidden, property values would decrease. And they disliked the idea of going to such lengths to preserve the slightly embarrassing former red light district. At this point, despite the difficulties, old and new coexist peacefully, if under only a temporary truce.

Sprinklers: Down the center of Kanazawa main streets runs a line of metal caps. When the snow falls, the underground water is switched on, and the low spray washes away the slush. A clever system for a city where it's rarely cold enough to freeze, but it does cause some inconvenience to the fashion-conscious--blocked-up water at the curbs makes rubber boots imperative for much of the winter. And no matter how clear the main streets may be, the narrow ones are left snowbound until spring.

Waterways: The ubiquitous stone, and more recently concrete, waterways (*yōsui*) running through town had several early purposes: they irrigated fields, provided fire protection and swept away waste. Some are covered over with wooden platforms and decorated with

potted plants, creating a welcome front yard for cramped city dwellers. The water can be controlled by sluice gates at the main rivers. When they are closed, the junk accumulated in the bottom can be an eyesore, but usually the cool, clear water is delightful.

'Where Are You Going?' Traditionally, rumor and gossip have been one of the chief recreational activities of small-town Japan. The high interest shown by Kanazawa people in everyone around them is no exception. A casual greeting often heard here is *'Doko ikunya?'* or 'Where are you going?' Fortunately, it's not necessary to answer clearly--a simple *'Chotto...'* ('Just...') will suffice. But foreigners are subject to a different kind of scrutiny in Kanazawa. Still rare here, foreigners are either stared at curiously, or bombarded with English nonsense or squeals of *'Gaijin! Gaijin!'* There are, however, overwhelming compensations. Whereas a Japanese person entering this small town might be struck by the reserve of the local residents, for a foreigner, Kanazawa people will go out of their way to be friendly and helpful.

Umebachi: The Maeda's family crest, a stylized plum blossom of five circular petals, can be seen everywhere--on temples, on sake cups and in kimono designs. One elegant nightclub in Katamachi was thoughtless enough to install carpeting with an *umebachi* design, and the hostesses confess that many fastidious customers are uncomfortable treading on it.

Buddhism: It's been 400 years since Kanazawa was controlled by militant monks and a religiously inspired peasant government, but the influence of Buddhism remains strong. Notice the abundance of temples and Buddhist supply stores. Religion is a profitable business here. Nearly every home has a family altar enshrining the ancestors which needs to be stocked with bells, embroidered cloths and incense. Statues of *jizō*, the guardian god of children, are found everywhere in Japan, but in Kanazawa they seem to get special attention. Devoted old grandmothers will pause on their way past a *jizō* figure to leave a candle, a red bib or a piece of fruit. These same old ladies are the ones who will mutter an unconscious prayer to the Amida Buddha when a son gets into college or a daughter-in-law enters the delivery room. The holy words taught by St. Rennyo and other Shinshū sect priests are actually *'Namu Amida Butsu,'* but in Kanazawa dialect they come out sounding like a tongue twister: *'Namandabu.'* According to the simplest version of Shinshū's teachings, mere utterance of the words is enough to insure salvation. The phrase still springs to people's lips at times of uncertainty or relief.

Yuki-tsuri: From early November, umbrella-like bamboo and straw rope contraptions go up in every garden in the city. Not a bush or lantern escapes a girdle or cover of some sort. Without them, flimsy branches and stones would easily crack under the weight of Kanazawa's wet snow. Calling a company of specialists every winter can be expensive, so some families make their own *yuki-tsuri* of plastic or clothesline. On a gnarled pine, the *yuki-tsuri* can be majestic, but when bushes are fitted with their strait-jackets, they look downright pathetic. One longs for March when the snows are gone and the branches are liberated at last.

Medicinal Herbs: Toyama Prefecture has long been famous for its medicine, and many of the herbs and grasses came from the Hakusan foothills near Kanazawa. Herbs were gathered according to Chinese learning and local folklore. The processed product was then sold through a unique door-to-door system. Each family would keep a chest containing a variety of medicines to use as the need arose. Once a year, the salesman would visit to collect money for what was used and restock the chest. Toyama medicines are still used by many Kanazawa families. And there are traditional medicine shops in every neighborhood of town.

Gardens: For a well-preserved city known as 'Little Kyōto' and boasting one of the Big Three Gardens of Japan, Kanazawa has a curious dearth of public gardens. This is due in part to the severity of the winters--upkeep is more expensive and troublesome than usual. The influence of the Jōdo Shinshū sect of Buddhism may be another reason. Zen, which has created some of Japan's most breathtaking gardens, is overshadowed in Ishikawa by the

Yukitsuri tree supports go up in Kenrokuen. (Oasis)

pragmatic, 'Peasants' Buddhism,' Jōdo Shinshū. Zen developed later, under the Maedas, and in those days there were some magnificent temple gardens in the city. But few temples today enjoy the popular enthusiasm and financial resources necessary to support such luxuries.

Town Names: In the Edo period, Kanazawa neighborhoods had colorful, informative names. Some referred to the people who lived there, like the towns for blacksmiths and metal workers. Others were named for their physical characteristics, like Cherry Tree Town, Old Temple Town or Single Pine. After the war, the number of names was cut down to create larger districts. These were marked off into *chome,* or numbered sections. Whether this supposedly progressive reorganization was actually for the convenience of the post office, as stated, or due to inexplicable bureaucratic churlishness is not clear. In many areas, residents and taxi drivers stubbornly cling to the old names. It's easier and more personal to remember Persimmon Field or 13-house Town than to distinguish between Katamachi 1-*chome* and 2-*chome*.

Night Views: Kanazawa is not included in the Big Three of spectacular Japanese night views (they are Kōbe, Hakodate and Nagasaki), but there are some beautiful spots here for an evening stroll. Lovers have already discovered the attractions of Utatsu-yama, where there are several secluded look-out points with a clear view of twinkling lights in the town and suburbs. On the horizon, the misty beams of fishing boats glisten, but their meaning is slightly discomforting: squid and shrimp are attracted to light, so the fishermen just turn on the generators and scoop up the catch.

Gutters: Along every street in town runs a gutter covered by removable metal sheets or cement blocks. The gutters' main function seems to be snow removal. During the winter, notice the housewives out stuffing them full of accumulated snow (snow shoveling is women's work in Japan). Drivers have to be cautious on Kanazawa's narrow streets, but the gutters complicate their problems. Don't be surprised if you see several men heaving a back wheel out of an uncovered ditch.

Welfare Services: The sidewalk at every crossing is patterned in yellow raised dots, to identify the spot for blind people. When the green pedestrian light goes on, a recorded melody announces that it's safe to cross. With a *'peopeo'* for a narrow street and *'kako-kako'* for a larger road, the sounds effectively catch the attention of children and handicapped people.

Traditional Arts: Thanks to the Maeda family's patronage, Kanazawa is permeated with traditional Japanese culture. Everyone seems to be taking lessons in something, and there are always recitals, exhibitions and performances, both professional and amateur, being held at the city's auditoriums. Noh theater and tea ceremony are perhaps the most influential. Although noh is difficult to understand and hardly an idle pastime, Kanazawa people feel special affection for the Hōshō School, which is based here. When walking around the quiet back streets, you'll often hear through an open window the deep rumbles of an *utai* chanting lesson.

Kanazawa's most popular school of tea is Ura Senke, introduced here in the mid-1600's by an early Ura master. Along with Kyōto, Kanazawa is one of the few cities in Japan producing all the equipment necessary for tea ceremony, from silk wiping cloths to iron kettles. The only thing that Kanazawa lacks is the tea itself. But utensil shops are everywhere, each garden seems to have a tea house, and a tea ceremony is held on any pretext--an anniversary, an exhibition, or just for itself.

Kanazawa also has its 'own' tea school, Sōwa-ryū, founded by tea master Kanamori Sōwa. (Sōwa-ryū is also found to a lesser extent in Takayama.) There is one flower arrangement school unique to Kanazawa, Kaga Koryū, which concentrates on *seika*, traditional styles using locally grown flowers and branches.

Sake: Every region of Japan has its own sake. Travelers enjoy sampling the local brews, which often aren't available elsewhere. The three biggest Kanazawa companies are Manzairaku, Nichiei and Fukumasamune, all *amakuchi*, meaning on the sweet side. For a drier, *karakuchi* sake, try Noto's Sōgen or Fukumasamune's Kuro-obi. Sake is served everywhere, but it goes best with Japanese dishes. Each shop has its house brand, so to try all of them, you have to latch onto the Japanese custom of *hashigo* (ladder) barhopping--heading off for another shop almost as soon as you've entered the first.

Internationality: As a city facing out across the Japan Sea,

Kanazawa takes a natural interest in things foreign. Since the seafaring days of Zeniya Gohei, indeed since priests like Kōbō Daishi returned from China through Noto Peninsula to introduce Buddhism into Japan, or, as some speculate, since humans first entered Japan via Noto, international communication has been important here. Since the war, Japan has been actively pursuing international friendship. Sister-city relationships have been established in five countries. Notice the symbol of Kanazawa's tie with Buffalo, New York, in the bronze buffalo pawing the ground in front of Kankō Kaikan in Hondamachi.

Universities: Among their other cultural activities, the Maedas set about making Kanazawa an academic center. They collected books, both Japanese and foreign, on a wide range of subjects—medicine, art, literature—and Kanazawa people proudly proclaimed the city *tenka no shofu* --a library of Japan. Today Kanazawa has a national university, several private colleges and a municipal arts college, all within the city limits. Not only do Kanazawa young people have good oportunities for higher education, but many students from other areas of Japan come here to school and settle down after graduation. The old city enjoys a constant rejuvenating stream. For tourists, this means a plethora of cheap restaurants and drinking spots as well as the appealing vitality students bring to a town.

Industry: Although a thriving city of 416,000, Kanazawa has generally lagged behind neighboring Toyama and Fukui in terms of industrial development. Several reasons may be advanced for this situation. Most obvious are Ishikawa's scarce energy resources and comparative distance from the markets. More speculatively, it is often said that Kanazawa's people are too caught up in formalities to do business competitively. Substantive business affairs are only discussed after many polite cups of tea and exchanges of pleasantries. And although Kanazawa dialect establishes trust and intimacy, its vagueness can hamper working relationships. Another possible reason is the city's long-standing interest in the arts and education. People's energies go into their noh chanting lessons, and budget allocations are diverted to schools and theaters.

However, Kanazawa does play a major role in the industries of Hokuriku, which are particularly strong in textiles and machinery production. Recently, too, industrial development has accelerated in Kanazawa, and the city is increasingly recognized as a hospitable environment for business and industry.

Fashion: You still see kimono frequently on Kanazawa streets, and not only on holidays--many people prefer kimono for everyday wear. They enjoy the luxury of fine clothes, despite the unpredictable weather. According to the proverb, people won't go out without clean white *tabi*, even on a rainy day: *Ame ga futtemo shiroi tabi da.* And the air and the streets are so clean here that there's no risk in wearing expensive kimono often. In Tōkyō, the silk would become grubby after only a day outdoors.

In terms of local dialect and cooking, Kanazawa may be closer to Kansai, but fashion follows Tōkyō· The stylish young people strutting up and down Tatemachi-dōri are indistinguishable from their fellow fad-followers in Harajuku. The same trend goes for Japanese clothing. A new bride from Kyōto often feels after arriving here that her carefully prepared kimono are out of date and unwearable. And conversely, a Kōbe-born bride returning home for a visit may deliberately pack something a little less than up-to-the-minute so as not to be too conspicuous. In other areas Kanazawa may be accused of being backward and conservative, but fashion is a colorful and stimulating exception.

Belgian visitors tie fortunes to the trees of Kanazawa Shrine. (H.Nakatani)

SHOPPING

Japanese tourists, obligated to buy local souvenirs for the folks back home, head straight for the 'Famous Products' of Kanazawa, like Kutani pottery and Yūzen silk goods. These are reviewed below, with suggestions for shopping and visiting workshops. Foreigners, who may be interested in a broader range of Japanese products, should also consult the Shopping sections of each area.

Don't neglect the junk stores, where persistence is rewarded with beautiful bargains. There are several clusters of them around: in Musashi, behind Ōmichō and at the end of the Yoko Yasue-chō Arcade; in Shin Tatemachi street; around Hirokōji intersection and out toward Nomachi.

Kaga Yūzen

Yūzen silk is painted by a complicated and time-consuming process, in bold, clear designs which are popular for kimono. It is also distinguishable by the fine white lines surrounding each petal

Painstaking and delicate hand-painting on Kaga Yūzen silk. (Oasis)

or leaf where paste was applied to keep the colors from running together. The Yūzen process is limited to Kyōto and Kanazawa, having been introduced in both cities by the 17th century dyer, Miyazaki Yūzensai.

A picture which invariably appears in tourist brochures for Kanazawa is of the Saigawa or Asano rivers when the rubber-booted dyers are washing out the paste in one of the last steps of

A long, slow job---tracing Kaga Yūzen paintings with paste. (Oasis)

the process. It's hard these days to catch a glimpse of the colorful spectacle, and when we do, it's more often than not deliberately staged for the guidebook's camera. Nevertheless, every once in awhile, a stroller crossing the Saigawa Ōhashi bridge finds himself in luck.

A complete explanation of the process and the chance to watch the hand-painters are available at Saihitsuan in Nagamachi. Those who wish to see the large-scale cooperative factories should visit Yūzen Danchi near Kanaiwa. Miyazaki Yūzensai's grave is at Ryūkokuji in Higashiyama, and a memorial tea ceremony is held there by the dyers' association on the 17th of every month.

A good place for buying silk is Erihana in Tatemachi. Handpainted kimono may be beyond the tourist's budget, but wallets, neckties and purses make good souvenirs. A more folksy shop is Kiguraya in Owari-chō, which specializes in silk purses and handbags.

Clear river water washes the paste out of Yūzen silk. (H.Ikeuchi)

Kutani Pottery

The development of Ishikawa's best known product is still sur-rounded in mystery. Historians and potters agree that in the mid-1600's kilns were established near Yamanaka Hot Springs under the patronage of a Maeda branch family. According to legend, a samurai named Gotō was sent to Kyūshu to learn pottery tech-niques and returned to teach others here. This ware, called Ko-kutani, was imitative of Chinese pottery, with deep, distinctive, over-glazed colors. For reasons still unclear, these kilns were later destroyed. Excavations in the early 1970's resulted in further confusion, since only a few of the unearthed shards resembled known Ko-kutani. Previously collected, well-preserved Ko-kutani, in fact, resembled Imari ware from Kyūshu, leading critics to ques-tion the authenticity of prefectural pride in Kutani.

Regardless of Ko-kutani's origins, it remains a strikingly beauti-ful ware and all the more precious because of its rarity. The best permanent exhibition is in the Prefectural Art Museum beside Kenrokuen Park. Modern Kutani in production since the Meiji period tends to gaudiness, but some understated pieces appealing to western taste are available, particularly from individual artists.

There are Kutani shops all over Kanazawa, with concentrations near Kenrokuen and the station. Recommended is Moroeya across from Daiwa, which offers a broad range of styles and prices and will pack for shipping.

A convenient introduction to the Kutani process can be found at the tourist-oriented centers, like Ace Kanazawa where potters will demonstrate and explain their work, or the Kankō Bussankan.

It's not easy to investigate Kutani deeply. Most of the pottery is produced in factories for the mass market, and very few places perform the whole process in the usual sense of the word, 'kiln.' Of the individual potters scattered around the city, Mr. Mannen Saburō speaks English and would welcome foreign visitors to his studio at 1-11-1 Teramachi. Call first (42−2088), to fix a time.

For those who wish to view the factory process, the best thing to do is call up Mr. Nishida at the Kutani Bussan Company in Terai town (07615−7−2121) and ask him to act as guide. He speaks some English and will arrange for visits to the various workshops. To get to his sales outlet, take the Terai-bound bus (#41) and get

off at Ao, just after crossing Tedori River.

Lacquerware

Like almost every cultural tradition in Kaga, lacquerware blossomed under the wealthy Maeda clan. The famous lacquer painter Igarashi Dōho was invited here by Lord Toshitsune to teach his skills to the craftsmen retained by the castle. Dōho's speciality was *maki-e,* the raised lacquer painting often found today on tea caddies, calligraphy equipment boxes and Buddhist altars. *Maki-e* means 'sprinkle painting.' Before the last of many coats dries, gold or silver powder and leaf is placed on top. It is then lacquered and polished again in a complex and delicate series of steps.

Most of the preparatory work for Kaga *maki-e,* the woodcutting and basic lacquering, is done outside of Kanazawa, in the countryside. These processes are now concentrated in Wajima and Yamanaka, and they have become famous in their own right. Wajima lacquerware is known for its durability and its lustrous black and dark red hues. It is truly beautiful, but recently the prices have shot up so quickly, that many people are choosing the more reasonable Yamanaka lacquerware. Since anything other than the finest lacquer will warp and crack with a change in humidity, it is not always a suitable gift for friends in foreign countries.

The basic lacquerware processes are demonstrated frequently. Most accessible is Kankō Bussankan's craft center. But delicate *maki-e* is done in small, unprepossessing workshops around town, and it is difficult to visit them without an introduction. *Maki-e* is widely exhibited and sold. There are lacquerware shops everywhere in Kanazawa, but Nosaku on Hirosaka-dōri and Ishida on the main street in Katamachi seem to have particularly good selections.

Gold and Silver Leaf

Kanazawa is the only major center of metallic leaf art left in Japan. Although machines are in wide use now, until recently the soft metal was pounded by hand. Two workers would place a blob between sheets of special oil paper and hammer in turn to a beat, while the gold or silver became thinner and thinner.

This process is sometimes displayed at the Kankō Bussankan, and the oil paper-making technique is explained at Danpūen near Edo Mura. But Mr. Yasue's gold leaf museum near the station is most convenient and thorough.

Gold and silver leaf souvenirs consist mainly of cheap plastic dishes and trays, or extremely expensive folding screens and lacquerware. There is little middle ground. But the work is so beautiful that an ambitious shopper may consider it a challenge to find the perfect piece. One interesting and reliable gift is a small box of gold leaf fragments, suitable for sprinkling over gourmet dishes or decorating cups of warm sake.

Ōhi Pottery

The first Ōhi Chōzaemon, a *rakuyaki* potter in Kyōto, came to Kanazawa in the 17th century with tea master Sen Sōshitsu. In Ōhi Machi, on the edge of town, he found a suitable clay and began using *ame-gusuri,* a glaze the color of brown sugar. The results pleased the tea master, and Chōzaemon's descendants have been producing the distinctive light brown ware ever since.

During the Edo period, the Maeda lords, who sponsored and encouraged the arts, also kept them strictly controlled. Chōzaemon and his descendants were the only artisans allowed to make Ōhi-yaki, and they were permitted to make only that. Their line has continued to flourish. The ninth Chōzaemon still works at his Hashiba home, assisted by his son Toshirō, who will become the tenth Chōzaemon at his father's retirement.

Since the Meiji Restoration loosened the legal controls on the arts, several other Kanazawa families have begun producing Ōhi-yaki. These artists, such as Chōami across and down the street from Chōzaemon, and Chōraku opposite the New Grand Hotel, are only grudgingly tolerated by the Chōzaemon line. But it's up to the buyer to decide on the comparative value of the Chōzaemon name versus the more reasonably priced pieces of the newcomers.

Ōhi-yaki itself is light, warm and lovely to touch.

Unfortunately, none of the artists encourages casual workshop visits. Buyers and browsers are of course welcome to the show-rooms out front, where they can soak up some of the atmosphere. The nearest most visitors get to Ōhi-yaki production is the mould-your-own tea bowl opportunity offered at Chōraku's shop. Ōhi-yaki is sometimes used at the public tea ceremonies held on the 23rd of every month at Gesshinji, where the first Chōzaemon's grave lies.

Paulownia Craft

Paulownia (*kiri*) became popular as a carving material because it is soft, and the deep grain is easily exposed. Instead of using varnish, craftsmen roast the hollowed vase or *hibachi* over a coke fire until it takes on a quiet brown luster. This is improved with age and handling--*kiri* is not a souvenir to put away on a shelf.

Kanazawa's unique contribution to *kiri* craft is the application of raised lacquer designs. Most often flowers or birds, they make an effective contrast, without overpowering the natural wood. And the small size of the lacquered area keeps the price down, in comparison with regular lacquerware.

Uesaka's shop down the street from Kenrokuen has the widest selection of *kiri* products. Kankō Bussankan offers a limited view of the process. Home factories, as usual, are busy and don't encourage visitors.

Buddhist Altars

Although the ornate family altars native to this region hardly make a suitable souvenir, shoppers may enjoy poking around the Buddhist supply stores centered around Yoko Yasue-chō and Nomachi. The goods on display also include embroidered cloths, bells, candles, incense and other paraphernalia in a glittering, fragrant atmosphere.

As a 'Buddhist Metropolis' which turned to the arts, Kanazawa was uniquely suited to Buddhist altar production. With his vast organizational talent, St. Rennyo created the demand in every pious home and Shinshū temple. The craftsmen later invited to Kanazawa by the Maeda lords provided the necessary talent.

Since many separate skills go into one altar, it's difficult for a visitor to watch the whole process in one place. Each step—carpentry, lacquer, *maki-e,* woodcarving and metalwork—is performed at a separate workshop. Furthermore, since a fine altar takes six months to make, usually according to a special order, what you will be able to see changes from day to day. But the craftspeople are proud of their work, and with proper introduction, happy to show it off. Visit old Mr. Sawada at his Yasue-chō sales shop, and he'll show you the small workshops in the back.

Cakes and Snacks

Beautifully wrapped, often symbolizing a famous place, season or historical anecdote, and always gladly received, local cakes make a great souvenir. Cakes from the tea-loving Kaga region, particularly from Morihachi and Moroeya, are nationally famous. But smaller shops, too, have creative designs and interesting tastes. Heavy cakes (*omogashi*), made with sweet bean jam or *mochi* pounded rice, harden and go stale in a few days. The dry cakes (*higashi*), cast in delicate shapes from hand-carved wooden molds, will keep for months.

Making Rakugan cakes at Moroeya. (Moroeya)

Representative Kaga cakes are on sale at the Station Department Store, Kankō Bussankan, the first floor of Daiwa and the basement of Meitetsu Marukoshi (they have the widest selection, including samples from Toyama and Fukui), as well as at the individual shops. Visitors to the shops themselves, who request to see the cake-making process in action, may be permitted entry to the factory (try saying, *'Kōba o misete itadakemasenka?'*). Some cake-making is on display at Kankō Bussankan's third floor crafts section.

The little wooden boxes of sticky brown fish and nuts on sale at every souvenir stand are *tsukudani,* a concoction made by long, slow boiling in a mixture of soy sauce and *ame,* natural barley sugar. Since both the *gori* fish and *kurumi* walnuts used in this popular hors-d'oeuvre are increasingly hard to find, *tsukudani* is becoming something of a delicacy. The *gori tsukudani* has a strong flavor which goes well with warm sake, and the slightly tart walnuts make a wonderful light dessert with coffee, brandy or ice cream.

Toys

It's not surprising that in a country with severe winters there should be a tradition of crafting children's toys. Kaga folk toys, developed in those long winter evenings, were improved upon during the Edo period in response to general prosperity and the sponsorship of the Maeda lords.

The most famous of these is Hachiman Okiagari, a papier maché, roly-poly baby, swaddled in a red kimono. The figure is based on the legend that the baby Emperor Ōjin (201–310) was wrapped in red, and that such a doll will bring health and happiness to children. Local people use the Okiagari as a congratulatory gift at childbirth or New Year's, or as a get-well-soon present.

Although not a toy as such, miniature Kaga lion head carvings are found displayed in most Hokuriku homes. During festivals, or whenever there's a good excuse, neighborhood people perform the lion dance in the street. Several men are covered with a large, colorful cloth to form the body, and one man operates the wooden head, carved like that of *shishi,* the mythical Chinese lion. To the tune of a bamboo flute and the beat of the drums, a young boy makes a ritual attack with a long stave, in a rather ferocious but graceful dance. Compared with other prefectures, the Kaga lion dance is good training in martial arts--the boy gets a good workout, and the lion always 'dies' in the end.

It's said that Lord Maeda Toshiie was charmed by the lion dances which welcomed him at his triumphal entry into Kanazawa Castle in 1583. He later ordered that the art be expanded and propagated throughout his domain. While boys practiced busily at the neighborhood shrine grounds, lion head carving flourished. The heads are made from lightweight paulownia wood. Many are

Kaga dolls performing the Shishimai lion dance. (Nakashima Menya)

on display at the Chōmin Bunkakan in Musashi, and miniatures are sold at every souvenir stand. To watch them being carved, visit Mr. Chida in Tsurugi or the Kankō Bussankan.

Later Maeda lords invited doll craftsmen here from Kyōto. The fine collection of *hina* dolls on display in Seisonkaku for the March dolls festival are an example of their work. The only style remaining from this tradition is Kaga Ningyō, a molded and polished earthen doll usually dressed as a Kagatobi fireman in his Dezome-shiki regalia.

Less well known, but very appealing, are the small mechanical dolls, a rice-eating mouse (Kome-kui Nezumi) and a rice cake-pounding bunny (Mochi-tsuki Usagi). Both were developed as an alternate source of income during the lean years of the Tenpo Famine in the 1880's. The mouse became nationally known when he appeared on a New Year's stamp in the year of the rat several years ago.

Kaga dolls are available everywhere, especially at Nakashima Menya in Musashi. Visitors may watch doll making at the Naka-shima Menya factory in Nanatsuka.

TOUR SUGGESTIONS

Walking Tours

The City Tourism Section has organized three walking-tour courses, covering the Central district, Higashiyama and Teramachi. They are printed in Japanese, but the illustrated maps are easy to follow. Directional and explanatory signs have been erected at major spots along the way. The maps are available at the station, the major hotels and department stores, and the City Hall Tourism Section. The estimated time is around 4 hours for each course.

Half-day Tours

Each of these three- or four-hour routes begins at Kenrokuen Park (start early to avoid the crowds) and heads off in a different direction. Any could be extended to a full day by filling in from the area sections in the second part of this book. For quick shopping and a look at local crafts production, try the Kankō Bussankan beside Kenrokuen.

1. Ishikawa Gate, Kenrokuen, Prefectural History Museum, Saihitsuan Yūzen Silk Center, Nagamachi Samurai Houses
2. Kenrokuen, Ishikawa Gate, Oyama Shrine, Terashima Family House, Higashiyama
3. Ishikawa Gate, Kenrokuen, Prefectural Art Museum, Honda Museum, Edo Mura
4. Ishikawa Gate, Kenrokuen, Nakamura Memorial Museum, Daijōji, Teramachi

Full Day Tour

Moving clockwise according to the map, make a rough circle, adding or subtracting as you like.

Kenrokuen–(walk)–Nakamura Memorial Museum–(cab)–
Daijōji–(bus)–Ninjadera–(bus)–Prefectural History Museum–
(walk the rest of the way)–Saihitsuan Yūzen Silk Center–Oyama
Shrine–Ōmichō–Terashima Family House–Higashiyama

More Than One Day

After (or instead of) doing all the 'musts', try some of these lesser known but equally worthwhile places:

Yasue Gold Leaf Museum
Shōenji temple

Ōmichō market
People's Culture Center
Yonekawa Samurai House
Shima Geisha House
Gyokusen-en Garden
Noh Theater
City Folk Museum
Kaga Crafts Museum
Daijōji temple
Kita Family House
Danpūen

Three restaurants deserving special recommendation are Koto-buki-ya in Musashi, Terakiya in Teramachi and Zenigame near Yuwaku Hot Spring.

Rainy Day Tour

Sad to say, rainy day contingency plans are a must for Kanazawa. Strolling around the castle or wandering from temple to temple loses much of its appeal when the feet are wet and the umbrella heavy. There are some satisfactory substitutes: museums, department stores (especially the toy department), or movies. Arcades like Yoko Yasue-chō and Ōmicho may be cold, but at least they're dry. Try the crafts center at Kankō Bussankan, or take a circle line bus ride on #1 or #2. The answer for rain in combination with tired feet or a craving for English may be the International Culture Center's English library, or a Japanese novel in translation in the Modern Literature Museum's reading room.

Crafts and Traditional Products Tours

A convenient introduction to local crafts production can be found on Kankō Bussankan's third floor. Those with a deeper interest in these Kanazawa 'famous products' may investigate their respective workshops (See 'Shopping'). A crafts-oriented tour might also include the City Folk Museum, Danpūen and the City Arts College (Bidai).

For those with the time to visit various other traditional workshops, here follows a list of accessible places. Studios which double as sales outlets can be approached freely. An interpreter would make the experience even more worthwhile. For workshops in private homes, make an appointment in advance by telephone. Unless the craftsperson speaks English, a translator will be necessary. Contact Kanazawa SGG, tel. 31–3291, ext. 205. (See 'English Guide'.) Keep in mind that in Japan, where proper and rules of etiquette are treated seriously, an unannounced visit may be considered an intrusion by a busy professional. Some artists in town, notably the makers of tea kettles and Japanese swords, refuse casual visitors. (Of course, serious customers are another matter entirely.) The craftspeople on this list are either running retail shops or have otherwise agreed to show visitors their work.

Shops

lanterns, umbrellas--Igarashi
calligraphy brushes--Matsuda
tabi socks--Miyanaga
bamboo--Hashimoto
fishing lures--Meboso
hanko chops--Hosoji
mizuhiki paper decorations--Tsuda
wigs--Shimazaki
bonsai--Hosokawa
sake--Manzairaku
silk bags--Kiguraya
washi Japanese paper--Saitō
shamisen--Fukushima
tōfu bean curd--Morohashi
geta clogs--Yamada
tatami--There is a tatami shop in every neighborhood, each humming with activity, bright and open with plate glass windows and a friendly, relaxed atmosphere. Particularly recommended for those in the area beyond Rokuto Plaza in Teramachi is Hayashi Tatami, 1-19-34 Yayoi.

Private Homes

—metalwork--Mr. Kazawa Yoshiaki and his father, Yoshiteru, do just about anything connected with metal. They'd be bored sticking only to their main source of livelihood, making silver rims for tea bowls and lacquer incense boxes, so they have branched out into all kinds of creative inlay work, Damascene, filigree and *hanko* chops, mixing the alloys and drawing the wire in their own shop. They're happy to explain the processes and show off their master-pieces—exquisite boxes, jewelry and utensils, which make the rounds of crafts exhibitions. Tea teachers would be delighted to get their hands on some of the things, but the Kazawas won't sell.

Kaga Damascene sake pot. (Y.Kazawa)

It's hard to part with a piece after putting in two years of sustained effort. Tel. 61−3919. 8-3 Hyōtanmachi, near Nishi Betsuin.

—woodcarving--Mr. Ishizaki Shūhō is willing to show visitors his camphor-wood carving, mainly intricate *ranma* transoms and fanciful statuary. He works on only a few things at a time, and most of his apprentices have become independent and moved away, so the studio isn't as busy as it once was. But Ishizaki Sensei is still actively working on his own designs and customers' orders. Call 43−9666 to fix a time, and take along an interpreter so as not to miss his thoughtful comments on his craft and its requirements. 303 Sanhaimu, 1-4-13 Teramachi.

—noh masks--Mr. Mukai Shōun carves noh figures, lion heads and his speciality, noh masks, in a bright workroom in his home. He is very friendly and will happily explain about his work (he refuses to 'antique' his masks, saying they should wear naturally with age)

and show off his certificates and prizes. The noh masks aren't for
the casual collector--they begin at ¥300,000. 2-4-28 Nagamachi.
Tel. 61–0079.

—fingernail weaving--Ms. Sakamoto Yukiko studied fingernail
weaving techniques at Nishijin in Kyōto. She does the painstaking
work at her little house in a bamboo wood, mainly weaving silk obi
for Kyōto customers. She is also studying painting, in hopes of
later combining some Kanazawa-influenced designs with the Kyōto
skills. Visitors are welcome. Tel. 44–1751. The house is up at the
edge of the mountains, so take a cab (or call her again when you
get close). Drop by the Yamashina fossil beds while you're in the
area. 47-30 Tsu Yamashina.

—papermaking--There are still three or four Japanese paper (*washi*)
makers left in Futamata town, out at the base of Iōzan. Among
them is Saitō Hiroshi, who has been experimenting with various
techniques for 20 years. He uses the bark of the *kōzo* plant (paper
mulberry) to make a tough but soft paper called Kaga Kōzo. According to the season, the process moves from cultivating, gather-
ing, washing and boiling, to pounding, grinding and finally sifting
it through a bamboo screen into thin sheets. Visitors are welcome
to watch whatever process is going on at the time. Mr. Saitō also
has a library on *washi,* much of it in English, which includes several
of his samples and detailed discussions of regional papermaking.
Call him at 36–1062, and take the Kokutetsu bus to Futamata.
The Saitōs live across from the post office. While you are there,
drop into Honsenji, the once-majestic temple which served as
Rennyo's headquarters. It's Nine Mountains-Eight Oceans Garden
is now in disrepair, but you can see a monument containing bone
relics of Rennyo. Notice too the tall stone which illustrates his
height. The present head priest is his descendant, of the 21st
generation.

—embroidery--The Kobayashi family preserves Kaga *shishū* em-
broidery techniques passed down since the Edo period. Ten or so
full-time workers stitch beautiful designs on kimono, obi and
Buddhist altar cloths, using silk or metallic threads. Visitors are
welcome at their home factory at 130 Tōriki 1 chome (take bus #50
and get off at Shin Kanda) between 9:00 and 5:00, except Sunday.
Tel. 91–5150.

Four Seasons

Kaga Cooking

Second only to Kenrokuen Park, Kanazawa is most famous for *Kaga no aji,* the taste of local cooking. The nearby Japan Sea provides most of the ingredients, like tiny sweet shrimps and winter crabs, but vegetables and game from the Japan Alps foothills and freshwater fish from the city's two rivers are also widely appreciated.

Like most Kanazawa traditions, Kaga cooking is closely tied to the Maeda clan. Cooks for the castle lived in Daidokoro Machi (or Kitchen Town, the present Kikugawa-chō), and were expected to come up with fresh delicacies to please the lords and their attend-

Jibu

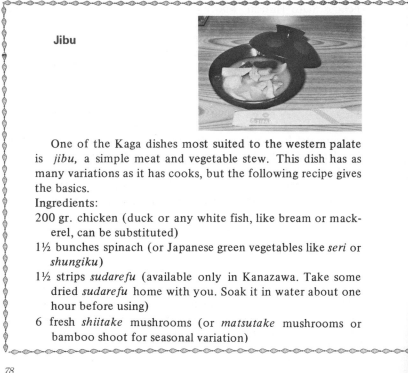

One of the Kaga dishes most suited to the western palate is *jibu,* a simple meat and vegetable stew. This dish has as many variations as it has cooks, but the following recipe gives the basics.

Ingredients:

200 gr. chicken (duck or any white fish, like bream or mackerel, can be substituted)

1½ bunches spinach (or Japanese green vegetables like *seri* or *shungiku*)

1½ strips *sudarefu* (available only in Kanazawa. Take some dried *sudarefu* home with you. Soak it in water about one hour before using)

6 fresh *shiitake* mushrooms (or *matsutake* mushrooms or bamboo shoot for seasonal variation)

ants. The results are famous throughout Japan. Tourists flock here year-round, their mouths watering for a taste of *jibu,* or *gori,* or *kabura-zushi.* But the appeal of these dishes depends on the visitor's enthusiasm for Japanese food in general, and no small amount of time devoted to getting accustomed to new tastes.

Foreigners can decide for themselves how far to go in sampling Kaga cooking. Good luck--and don't forget there's a good assortment of European restaurants to fall back on.

This list includes not only Kaga specialities, but whatever is particularly good in Kanazawa according to the season. All Japanese restaurants, especially *kappō* style counter places, are conscious of seasonal changes and vary their menus frequently.

2 c. *dashi* stock
4 T. *shōyu* soy sauce   flour
2 T. sugar   *wasabi* (green horseradish)

Cooking directions:

1. Bone and cut chicken or other meat into bite-size pieces. (Some cooks then marinate the meat in a mixture of 6 parts sake and 4 parts *shōyu* for 5 minutes to deepen the flavor.) Dust the meat with flour.
2. Boil the spinach. Cut the bunches of leaves into 3—4 cm. lengths. Run *sudarefu* through some hot water. Cut into 3—4 cm. lengths.
3. Prepare *dashi.* Add sugar and *shōyu,* tasting as you go. Add *sudarefu* and mushrooms. Boil over medium heat, 7—8 minutes. Remove *sudarefu* and mushrooms from *dashi.* Dip spinach into dashi, just to pick up its flavor. Remove immediately.
4. Add floured meat to *dashi.* Cook over low heat 4—5 minutes. Dashi will thicken. Remove meat. Arrange meat and vegetables in 6 individual dishes (covered lacquer bowls are preferred in Kanazawa). Top with thickened sauce and *wasabi.* Serves 6.

Spring

Local Specialities

—**kuma no sashimi:** tiny slices of raw bearmeat, eaten like fish sashimi, with *wasabi* horseradish and soy sauce. A novelty dish with few fans, it's found at mountain hot spring spas like Chūgū and at Tsurugi's Wataya and Kokin in Katamachi.

—**gori:** Although perhaps Kanazawa's best known delicacy, this tiny gray river fish, distinguished by a fat head and two outsized fins, is rather expensive and less than wildly popular. It is most often found boiled down with soy sauce as a sake accompaniment (*tsukudani*). Some restaurants serve *gori* in *miso* soup or deep fried with salt. And one specialty restaurant, Goriya, makes every imaginable dish from *gori*.

—**oshizushi:** Pressed rice and fish, often found at festivals. (See Fall)

—**takenoko:** Bamboo shoot isn't unique to Kanazawa, but in late May it's fun to visit Bessho, the small village outside of town which devotes itself to serving a wide variety of bamboo shoot dishes, from sashimi to tempura. (See Calendar)

Other Good Things

Mountain vegetables, like *warabi* ferns and *fukinoto,* which push their heads up through the melting snow; *takuan* pickles; fish like *iwashi no dango* (sardine balls), in soup or *oden; tai* (sea bream); natural oysters (*tennen gaki*); *isasa,* a tiny Tedori River fish available for only two or three weeks and served alive with vinegar and soy sauce or in soup (*odorigui,* or 'dancing' soup).

Summer

Local Specialities

—**dojō no kabayaki:** Loach, a thin river fish, grilled with soy and sake sauce. This dish is said to have originated with the Nagasaki Christians who were exiled to Utatsuyama in the late Edo period. One of their few sources of income was catching *dojō* in the Asano River, grilling it and selling it in town.

—**kinugoshi tōfu:** Soft and slippery bean curd, so refined it could have been strained through silk. In many neighborhoods, it's still peddled every day by old men with wooden handcarts.Refreshing in summer served with soy sauce, ginger and chopped scallions. Around the foot of Mt. Hakusan can be found an unusual, hard bean curd, *Hakusan katadōfu,* which has had most of the water pressed out, and is often deep fried or used in tempura. It was developed because watery, soft *tōfu* is too difficult to transport in mountainous regions. *Katadōfu* can be tied up with string and carried anywhere.

—himuro manjū: heavy, sweet bean cakes, eaten in Kanazawa on July first in connection with the Maeda family's ice house. (See Calendar and Kenrokuen)

Other Good Things
Seasonal fish: freshwater *iwana* and *ayu* from Saigawa river, and *awabi* (abalone) and *baigai* (a snail-like shellfish) from the sea around Noto Peninsula.

Fall

Local Specialities

—Hakusan nameko: tiny, wild mushrooms covered with a natural jelly, often found in soups or with grated *daikon* radish on top of *soba* noodles.

—Kaga renkon: lotus root grown locally since the Edo period when cultivation was introduced here by the retainers of Lord Maeda from Owari, near Nagoya. Served vinegared, or blended with ground sesame paste, or in tempura.

—oshizushi: eaten at spring and fall festivals . Vinegared rice and fish are pressed into a square wooden tub and left to pickle slightly overnight. Producing neat, tasty squares is no mean trick, and such ability is the mark of a good Kaga housewife. Sold in grocery stores and at Shibazushi shops.

Other Good Things
Matsutake dobin mushi (a delicate, clear mushroom soup); *akinasu,* autumn eggplants; *jinenjo,* a mountain yam; *tachiuo shioyaki,* grilled, salted sea fish; *kuri gohan,* rice cooked with chestnuts.

Winter
Local Specialities
—crabs: either *zuwaigani,* the hairless male crab, or *kōbakogani,* tiny female crabs with delicious eggs still attached. Usually served cold, with vinegar, or in *nabe* hot pots.

—amaebi: small, sweet shrimps eaten raw, with vinegared rice as sushi, or by themselves as sashimi. Their delicate taste is satisfactory compensation for the miserable winter weather.

—jibu: This stew of duck and various vegetables, like spinach, Chinese mushrooms and wheat gluten, is always a part of Kaga dinners, available year-round, but most delicious in winter. Because the sauce is thickened with flour, unusual in Japanese cuisine, there is speculation that *jibu* has its origins in Portugal and may have been introduced to Kanazawa by Takayama Ukon, the Christian daimyō protected by Maeda Toshiie. The wheat gluten used in *jibu* is *sudarefu,* a type unique to Kanazawa, rolled thin in a bamboo screen.

—kabura-zushi: a sandwich of sliced turnips and *buri* (yellowtail), pickled in malted rice and salt. Its unique taste takes some getting used to.

—kobujime: white fish wrapped in *konbu* seaweed and preserved for a few days until the flavors blend.

—tsugumi: ouzel, a wild bird found in the nearby mountains. It was popular grilled over charcoal and eaten in *yakitori* or whole (bones, head and all), until 1947, when it was designated an endangered species and the dish was banned. Some unscrupulous restaurants get around this law by importing ouzels from China and Spain.

—fukuume: red and white cakes, made of a waffle cup shaped like the Maeda family plumflower crest and stuffed with sweet bean jam. They are sold only during the New Year's season. Similar waffle cakes, called *futtoku,* are filled with tiny doll-shaped candies or fortunes.

Other Good Things
Daikonzushi, long white radishes pickled in malted rice with herring; *madara shioyaki,* grilled cod; *tara no kotsuke,* cod sashimi dipped in cod eggs; *konowata,* the insides of sea cucumber--it sounds awful, but actually goes nicely with sake.

CALENDAR

Festivals, ceremonies and other seasonal events are going on constantly in Kanazawa. Participation in some local activities livens up a routine sightseeing schedule, and gives a visitor a sense of belonging. If nothing on this list coincides with your stay, consult the section on 'Things to Do' for some ideas.

JANUARY

1   Hatsumōde. The first visit to a shrine begins at midnight of the 31st and continues for days, depending on people's schedules. The big shrines, Oyama, Keta Taisha in Hakui and Shirayama in Tsurugi, are most popular, but any neighborhood shrine is lively with kimono-clad visitors. New Year's is mainly a family holiday. People stay at home or call on relatives, where they eat, drink and play special New Year's games. One such game, found only in Kanazawa, is Hata Genpei, a kind of Capture the Flag played on the tatami. It originated in the Edo period, based on the battling Heike and Genji families, and became popular here because some of the fleeing Heike took refuge in Noto.

1−3   Kenrokuen open for free.

6 or 8   Dezomeshiki. 'Kaga Tobi' demonstrations of the Kaga firemen's famous traditional skills, at Saigawa near Sakurabashi bridge. Spurting hoses and ladder-top acrobatics are very

Rythmic Kaga Manzai story-telling at Setsubun season. (M.Imamura)

Hata Genpei New Year's game. (Jidō Kaikan)

exciting. The firemen, wearing only loincloths and *happi* coats, keep themselves warm with plenty of sake.

15   Sagichō. People bring samples of their first calligraphy and used New Year's decorations to their local shrines, where they are burned. Particularly lively at Ishiura Shrine and Shinmeigū. Eating some of the *mochi* rice cakes grilled on this day insures health in the coming year.

15   Adults Day brings all 20-year-olds to local community centers for congratulatory speeches and coming-of-age ceremonies. The streets are colorful with kimono.

23–26 Kanshugyō (Deep Winter Ascetic Practices). Priests from Daijōji temple tramp all over, wearing straw sandals (no *tabi*) and carrying an iron staff and a bell, chanting sutras and receiving charitable gifts from the townspeople. Anyone is welcome to join, or watch, or contribute. After *zazen* meditation at 4:30 a.m., they leave the temple around 9:00 and walk until noon, circling through Teramachi, Kōrinbō and Nagamachi.

25   Tanshinsai service at Oyama Shrine celebrates Lord Maeda Toshiie's birthday. 10:00 a.m.

FEBRUARY

4   Setsubun. On the last day of winter, people purify their homes by scattering dried beans, and calling for good luck to enter and devils to leave. Rites are also held at shrines around town, like Oyama and Ishiura (the latter holds its ceremonies the day before Setsubun). But the best is Kobashi Sugawara Shrine, which has a performance of Kaga Manzai on the evening of Setsubun. This is a comic dance

performed at New Year's, usually at private homes, to pray for the peace and prosperity of the household. Accompanied by sake, drums and laughter, five old gentlemen dance and tell a story unique to Kaga. Although designated a National Folk Treasure, the art is fast dying out.

8   Harikuyō (Needle Mass). Held at Bunka Fukusō Gakuin sewing school, for tired and broken needles. Visitors welcome to the 10:00 a.m. ceremony.

10−16 Dekumawashi. Ōguchi Village is preserving the lively puppet theater which was developed on those long winter nights in the mountains below Hakusan. The shows run from 8:30 p.m. for a week, at the new Community Center. Call Mr. Zenzai in advance, to arrange for an overnight stay with a village family. Tel. 076196−7120. The bus for Shiramine (#47) leaves Kanazawa Station at 5:00 p.m. Get off at Higashi Futakuchi. Definitely worth the trip. Read up about the puppets and the villages in Mr. Huber's book (See 'Before You Come'). Dekumawashi is also performed in Fukaze Shin Machi, an area beyond Nonoichi settled by displaced villagers from the Tedori River Valley. But performances are erratic, and there are no buses to the town. If you miss the Ōguchi Village shows, call Mr. Minami Fujio, the town head (tel. 07619−3−1791), to find out Fukaze Shin Machi's schedule .

11   Kenkoku Kinenbi. National Founding Day observed at Oyama Shrine, 10:00 a.m.

17   Kinensai. The traditional blessing of the year's rice is now extended to cover all foods and products. Oyama Shrine, at 10:00 a.m.

late   Wild daffodils peeking up through the snow at Wakasa Bay in Fukui make a popular destination for Sunday drivers.

late   Graduation Art Exhibition at Bidai. Student work in fine arts, crafts and industrial design, well displayed.

28   Chinkasai. Annual prayers to the Sun Goddess, to protect the nation from fires. Oyama Shrine, at 10:00 a.m.

MARCH

all month Elegant doll set is on display at Seisonkaku in Kenroku-
en, to celebrate Dolls Festival (*hina matsuri*) on March 3.

1—3 Musa no Gyōki. Held at Kōsaiji in Ōgimachi. An unusual
wintertime airing of temple treasures, including many
salvaged from Oyama Gobō. Legend has it that this day is
invariably overcast, so take your umbrella.

15 Nehan-e. The ceremony in memory of the death of
Gautama Buddha. Although held on Feb. 15 at most
temples, Raikyōji in Higashiyama has an interesting service
in March. All day the temple passes out rice dumplings,
which devotees may take away to roast and eat at home.

20 or so Vernal Equinox Day. Most temples are open and welcoming visitors. People customarily visit family graves at
Nodayama and Utatsuyama, and eat *ohagi* bean cakes.
Shōenji's gruesome Buddhist hell paintings are on display for
free. Another exotic event is the annual display of an outlandish, mummy-like head at Zengyōji temple in Tenjin-
machi. The owners admit their ignorance of the origins and
authenticity of the hairy, 3-faced figure, which combines a
man, a woman and the mythical *kappa* water sprite.

late Saiseiki. Memorial service held for Kanazawa's most famous literary talent, on the anniversary of his death (it's
usually scheduled for a Sunday thereabouts). A bus from
the Modern Literature Museum carries devotees to Murō
Saisei's grave, where they read poetry and present flowers.
A memorial lecture is also held. Check with the Museum
for the date and details.

end Professors and students of Kanazawa University Medical
School hold a memorial service at the Utatsuyama graves of
all those who donated their bodies to the school.

APRIL

8 Hana Matsuri celebrates the birth of Gautama Buddha. A
small Buddha statue is set on a white elephant and worshippers dowse it with sweet tea. The ceremony is held at a
different temple every year. Call the Higashi Betsuin office,
tel. 61—6432, for the location.

15 Yasue Hachiman Shrine's festival day--it always rains.

mid-late Cherry Blossom Season. Kenrokuen is open for free through the evening, and the grass below Ishikawa Gate is mobbed with merry-makers. Every year a few drunks hurt themselves trying to scale the castle walls. Cherry viewing is quieter at Utatsuyama, the Saigawa riverbank and Ōtebori.

19–20 Spring Festival at Gokoku Shrine, when the shrine maidens dance.

25 Rennyoki. Anniversary of the death of Rennyo, the influential priest who inspired the Buddhist 'peasant kingdom' in Kaga in the 16th century. Families gather at Rennyodō temples at Daijōjiyama and Utatsuyama.

29 Ningyōkuyō (Doll Mass) at Kishimōjin in Higashiyama. After years of loving care, it doesn't seem right to throw worn out or broken dolls away. Instead they are respectfully burned at this temple. Flower shows and tea ceremonies are also held. It's a good opportunity to examine the colorful insides of Kishimōjin.

29 Tenchōsai, at all shrines, celebrates the Emperor's birthday. Oyama Shrine ceremonies begin at 10:00 a.m.

MAY

all month *Takenoko* (bamboo shoot) is dug up fresh and served in all sorts of delicious styles at Bessho village out beyond Nodayama. Make a reservation for set dinners, ¥2,000, served by the Miyakawa family, 11:00–8:00 daily. Tel. 42–0360. From April 20 to May 20 only. Take a #20 or #21 bus and get off at Besshomachi, or go by cab.

early Taue. Demonstrations of traditional rice planting are held at Edo Mura. The day changes annually, so call 35–1111 for the exact date. Mr. Kuroda speaks English.

3–5 Kutani Teacup Festival in Terai town offers some good bargains. Special buses from Kanazawa station take about 1 hour.

5 Carp kites fly over houses as families with sons celebrate the Boys Festival. The shrine at Ataka Barrier, where Yoshitsune escaped arrest, holds its annual festival.

5 Shōbuyu. People put fragrant iris (*shōbu*) in their bathwater on this day. A good day to try a public bathhouse.

5–15   The wisteria begins to bloom all over town. It's especially beautiful at Kenrokuen, Oyama Shrine and Honda Woods.

12   The iris (*kakitsubata*) begins to bloom at Kenrokuen. Go early in the morning to hear them 'pop' as they open. *Kakitsubata* last through June.

15   Shinji Noh. It's curious that in a city so influenced by noh theater, there is only one regular outdoor noh performance, at rustic Ōno Minato Shrine in Kanaiwa. For the last 370 years, an annual show has been held for the gods--notice that the stage faces the shrine to give the gods a good view-- to thank them for the Tokugawa's victory at Sekigahara.

15   Shinmeigū in Hirokōji celebrates its spring festival with *aburi-mochi,* grilled rice cakes.

17   Yūzen silk dyers gather at Ryūkokuji in Higashiyama to honor the developer of the Yūzen process, with memorial services, a tea ceremony and geisha dances.

21   The hemorrhoid-curing Buddha is on display at Sanbōji in Higashiyama.

22–3   Mikawa's colorful spring festival is marked by floats paraded around by the young men of the town. The 22nd, either daytime or evening, is the better day. The best route to this old fishing town is by train.

JUNE

1   *Ayu* (sweetfish) season begins. The elusive river fish challenges anglers at upper Saigawa and Asano rivers.

early   National High School Sumō Tournament is held on a Sunday at the open air stadium on Utatsuyama. Shouldn't be missed.

early   Azaleas begin to come out all around the city. Kenrokuen, with both iris and azaleas, is lovlier than ever.

early   Open-air beer gardens at various buildings begin business as the evenings warm up. Just crane your neck for the rooftop strings of lights, or try the Fukui Bank (strip show), Hokkoku Bank (*karaoke* singing), Daiichi Seimei (Hawaiiana), or the New Grand Hotel (quiet, on the 3rd floor).

12   Plum Rain Season begins. Ends in mid-July, when the humidity of summer sets in.

13–15 Hyakumangoku Festival. The city's largest. Visit Oyama

Shrine for tea ceremony, flower exhibitions and demonstrations of martial arts; Central Park for folk dancing in the evening; Kankō Kaikan for a geisha dance show. Highlights are the all-day tea ceremony at Kenrokuen (indoors at Seisonkaku and various park tea houses, as well as outdoors at the Plum Garden), and the parade, in traditional costume, along the main streets around the castle. Kenrokuen opens for free on the 13th and 14th. Detailed festival schedules are available from the City Hall Tourism Section.

30   Ōbarai at Oyama Shrine. Semi-annual general purification rites, to cleanse people's hearts and bodies. 4:00 p.m.

JULY

1   In celebration of the Maedas' annual gift to the Tokugawas of ice preserved in underground storehouses, Kanazawa people eat sweet *manjū* bean cakes. In the days when sweets were scarce, a cake was thought to insure the family's health through the coming summer's heat.

1   Visitors to the Hitotsukyū ceremony at Kōgenji in Kotatsuno will be safe from illness and accident for a whole year.

7   *Tanabata* (Weaver Star Festival). Little girls decorate bamboo branches with wishes written on colored paper, and hang them in front of their houses. The authentic disposal of the branches, by sending them floating down the rivers, has been banned for environmental reasons, so the festival does little more than liven up the streets. A Tanabata Party is held at the Children's Center (Jidō Kaikan) in Hōshima-machi.

9–10   Kakikōza. The lecture series on various topics at Higashi Betsuin attracts hundreds of people. 7:00–9:00 p.m.

10 or so Shisetsu-ki. The founder of Kanazawa's main school of noh is buried at Zenshōji in Higashiyama. Hōshō School's headmaster, students, teachers and admirers gather for a memorial service at Shisetsu's grave.

mid   Swimming season begins. See 'Helpful Information.'

mid   The early *obon*, Festival of the Dead, is observed at some shrines and temples. Shrines celebrate with *bon odori* dancing, and temples burn lanterns in the cool of the evening.

15–16 *Kiriko* lanterns lit at Gokoku Shrine, in memory of the war

Kiriko lanterns brighten family graves
at Obon season. (M.Imamura)

dead.

16   Mantōkai. Relatives place *kiriko* paper lanterns in front
of graves at Daijōji, and in the early evening, the priests visit
each one, chanting sutras as they go.

mid   Sacred lotus flowers bloom at Hasudera, through August.
Tea is served to the public on the 27th of every month.

20 or so   The ancient *mushi-okuri* ritual to rid the villages of
mosquitoes is still performed at some rural spots near Mattō.
Farm boys beat big drums and march with torches through
the rice fields. The custom began in the late 15th century,
when Togashi Masachika, the local lord, was conquered by
the Ikkō Ikki peasants' rebellion. Togashi cursed the
people, saying that bugs would torment them forever. The
frightened farmers decided to take some action to protect
themselves. The increasing use of DDT and other pesticides
has made the ritual almost obsolete.

24–25   Ōno town's summer festival. Three brightly costumed villagers, representing the Mountain Demons, visit each house
—it takes two full days—to exorcise demons with flutes and
drums. Take bus #61 from Musashi.

31   Toyokuni Shrine on Utatsuyama holds its evening *obon*
summer dance and *sennichi mairi.* A visit to the shrine on
this day is worth 1,000 days of visits.

AUGUST

1   Haiku poetry party held at Senkōji temple in honor of
Chiyo, the great poetess who is buried there.

1–3   Ōno Minato Shrine Festival, in Kanaiwa town, famous for
carved wooden floats. The shrine's god is said to spend
these two nights in the sea, visiting.

early   Mushiboshi (Airing of Temple Treasures). Most temples
put out their scrolls, embroidered cloths and old sutras to
prevent mildew and bugs, and give people a chance to ad-

mire the treasures. Recommended are Nishi Betsuin and Chikakuji, both near the station. Chikakuji brings out a bloodstained *furoshiki* cloth which was used to wrap a sliced-off head in an Edo-period vendetta. A samurai son avenged his father's death by placing the murderer's head on his father's grave at this temple.

early   Saigawa Festival. City-sponsored summer festival, with games, dancing, fireworks and other traditional and modern entertainments. Details available at the City Hall Tourism Section.

9—10   Kakikōza. At Higashi Betsuin. See July 9—10.

mid   *Bon odori* at local shrines and temples. The Festival of the Dead is usually held in mid-August in rural districts, so around Ishikawa, late *obon* is livelier than the citified *obon* of July. Traffic snarls the town, as the crowds come back from Tōkyō and Ōsaka to visit family graves. Many restaurants and shops take short vacations, but there's some relaxing summer event practically every night, to make up for the hectic days. And *obon* traditionally signifies the end of the worst summer heat, when the rice ears fatten, and harvesting will begin soon. Several temples celebrate '46, 000 Days' on which one visit is worth that many days of prayer.

mid   Yūzen Tōrō Nagashi. Silk painters give thanks to the river by sending exquisite, hand-painted paper lanterns floating down the Asano at dusk, to the plaintive notes from *komuso* (mendicant priest) *shakuhachi* players, with baskets covering their heads. The best view is from between Tenjinbashi and the Ōhashi bridges.

mid   Corn Fair Festival at Kannon-in temple in Higashiyama. See the Tōgorōs' Kannon statue, pray at the 33 stations representing Koya-san temple's holy spots, and take home the silkiest ear of corn you can find (*mōke*, 'more hair,' is a homonym for 'profit').

mid   Futamata town's Iyasaka Odori, celebrating a local victory in the Heike-Genji battles, is an Intangible Cultural Treasure.

mid   Doctors involved in medical research at Kanazawa University Hospital hold a memorial service at Tentokuin for the souls of the rabbits, mice and dogs used in their experiments.

15   Prayer for Peace at Gokoku Shrine. On the anniversary of the Emperor's radio address ending World War II, government officials and dignitaries join the people in prayer at the prefectural shrine dedicated to the war dead.

15   Sakata Odori. *Obon* dancing in Hatta village, near the racetrack, is one of the few preserving colorful costumes and live music (no records).

15, 16 Jongara Odori. The most famous local *obon* dance, held at the Nonoichi Primary School grounds. Well organized by enthusiastic citizens, it celebrates the days when people from all levels of society would dance together during the benevolent, Heian-era rule of Lord Togashi. Although they are complicated, you can soon catch onto the repetitive steps and join the hundreds of dancers in the circle.

20   Daibutsu Festival at Renshoji. In memory of the dead from the terrible fire of 1736, people gather with bright lanterns before the Great Buddha.

end   Sankosan (moon-viewing). At around 2:00 a.m., a thin crescent moon rises over Utatsuyama. Those watching from Suwa Shrine on the Teramachi ridge, can see three moonbeams extending from the moon to the earth. Participants greet the moon with Shinto ceremonies.

SEPTEMBER

early Public tea ceremony honoring the famous Momoyama painter, Tawaraya Sotatsu, held at Hoenji on a Sunday.

mid   Meigetsu (Full Moon). People buy moon-viewing bean cakes (go early in the day--they're sold out by afternoon), gather to gaze at the bright *otsukisama,* and perhaps compose a few haiku poems. The Jido Kaikan (Children's Center) in Hoshima holds a moon-viewing party on the evening of the full moon, with stories, songs and cakes.

15   Ueno Hachiman Shrine Fall Festival features a *mochi-tsuki* dance in which costumed men pound rice into thick paste to the sounds of flute, drums and shamisen.

21   The hemorrhoid-curing Buddha is on display at Sanboji in Higashiyama.

Pounding rice at Ueno Hachiman Shrine.
(M.Imamura)

late   Autumnal Equinox Day. Celebrated in some way by all Buddhist temples. Graveyards at Utatsuyama and Nodayama are bustling with visitors.

OCTOBER

all month Autumn festivals are held at all local shrines. A special local feature is Kaga Shishimai, the lion dance performed by little boys. Annual exhibitions and recitals of amateur arts and performing arts around (See Exhibitions, in 'Things to Do' section).

2—4   Oyama Shrine's Autumn Festival. Liveliest on the fourth.

2—4   Festival at Kingengū shrine in Tsurugi features ribald songs and raucous parades through town, from noon to evening.

4—6   Festival at Naruwa no Taki, where Yoshitsune visited.

10   Memorial Services for poet Chiyo, at Nensaiji, attracts many haiku devotees. Begins at 1:00 p.m.

15   Festival at Shinmeigū in Hirokōji, famous for *aburi-mochi* cakes.

19—20 Festival at Gokoku Shrine, where shrine maidens perform stately dances.

NOVEMBER

early   *Yuki-tsuri* tree supports are erected in Kenrokuen. It's a fascinating process. Notice that there are more supporting strings on the north side of the tree.

7 or so Bidai Sai (Arts College Festival). Most high schools and colleges hold their annual Cultural Festivals in November, when they set up snack bars and hold concerts and exhibitions for the public. For tourists, perhaps the most

interesting would be the Bidai Festival, where student art works are on display.

all month *Hoonkō*. Ceremony at Jōdo Shinshū sect temples honoring St. Shinran, the founder. Parishioners visit their temples with flowers, and eat vegetarian meals together. The date varies with the temple so the priests can attend each other's party. Lectures and discussions are usually held at Higashi Betsuin between the 13th and the 18th.

15 Shichi Go San. Parents dress up children of ages 3, 5 and 7 for a shrine visit--colorful kimono and solemn faces. Oyama and Ishiura shrines are especially popular on the weekends surrounding the 15th.

23 Shinjōsai at Oyama Shrine. Annual rites of thanksgiving held at 10:00 a.m.

DECEMBER

early Plum trees bloom in private gardens and, most impressively, in Kenrokuen's Plum Garden. They last through February.

5 Aenokoto. A tradition of Noto farmers, who invite the gods into their homes for dinner, a bath and overnight, in thanks for the year's harvest. Held in the late morning at Edo Mura.

19 Seidensai. Oyama Shrine's annual housecleaning rituals. 10:00 a.m.

27 Mochitsuki. Pounding rice into cakes for the New Year at Edo Mura. Try swinging the hammer to the rythmic melody yourself. Best in the late morning.

30–31 Kenrokuen open for free, through Jan. 3.

31 Ōbarai semi-annual purification rites held at Oyama Shrine, 4:00 p.m.

31 Joya no Kane. 108 peals of the temple bells ring out all the evils of the world before midnight. Daijōji, where visitors may swing the clapper once themselves, or anywhere in popular Higashiyama, is recommended. Shrines like Oyama and Shirayama in Tsurugi attract thousands of visitors at midnight. Expect that most stores, and all museums and tourist attractions, will be closed for three or four days. During the holidays, it's best to stick to movies and kimono-watching at temples and shrines.

INNER-CITY BUS

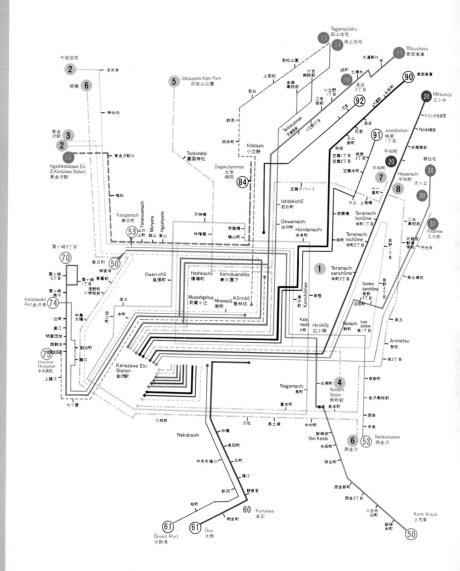

Kanazawa's wide Asano River lined with shiny black tile roofed houses.

SUBURBAN BUS

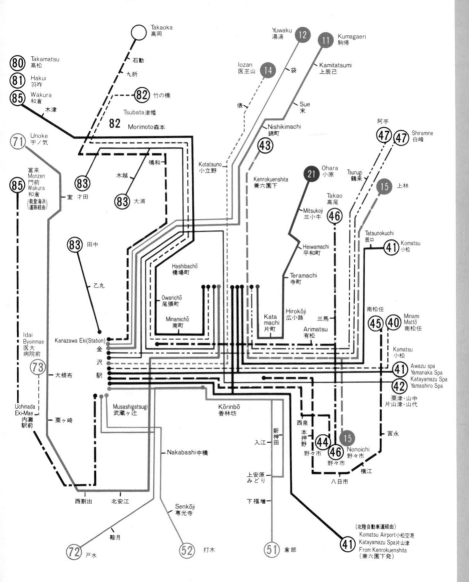

For further bus information, telephone 37-4831 (in Japanese).

9. Washing the paste from Kaga Yūzen silk.
10. The stained glass window of Oyama Shrine's gate.
11. Higashiyama's seven *jizōs*.
12. Kanazawa isn't all ancient.
13. Feudal town and country life recreated at Edo Mura.
14. Foreign trade thrives through Kanazawa Port.

Staying in Kanazawa

When you visit Kanazawa, a city preserving traditional surroundings, it is better to stay at a ryokan, a Japanese-style hotel, than at a western-style one. You can experience the traditional way of Japanese living, updated with clean, modern accommodations, and enjoy the wonders of carefully prepared Japanese cooking.

浅田屋 ASADAYA

a typical ryokan in Kanazawa

Jukkenmachi-Kanazawa:Phone(0762)31-2228

Our restaurants also run with   traditional warmth and hospitality of Kanazawa: **ROKKAKUDO**, a specialty steak house, **SEKITEI & ROKKAKUDO KATAMACHI-TEN,** a tempura and steak restaurant, **KAGA SEKITEI**, a Japanese reastaurant, and **SANJUKKEN NAGAYA**, specializing in pottery pan-broiled local cooking and local sake. **SHOGYOTEI**, a Japanese restaurant.

ASADA GROUP, INC:Phone(0762)64-2271

Areas

INTRODUCTION

In this section the city has been divided into 12 areas, so visitors may leisurely explore one neighborhood at a time. Each is discussed from three points of view: shopping, eating and drinking, and sightseeing. Nothing is actually very far from anything else in Kanazawa, so it is possible to make a wide circular tour in a day or two. For this purpose, the sights considered by most to be 'musts' have been starred.

A note about eating in restaurants: there are so many eating places and bars here that Kanazawa people often claim the national per capita record. Restaurants range from the most elegant Kyōto styles to the lowliest 'red lantern' hole-in-the-wall dives. This guide lists those of particular merit on the basis of at least one of the following criteria: great food, cheap prices, appealing atmosphere or singularity.

Prices and quality are subject to change--during the preparation of this book, at least three places under consideration went out of business. In many restaurants, the prices may seem high, but remember that half of the fun is the atmosphere, the valuable dishes and the graceful service, all of which you pay for. Particularly if you have a private room, be prepared for extra service and room charges.

Categorization is sometimes difficult. Coffee shops frequently turn into bars at night, and drinking places are often more famous for their food. Some Japanese restaurants have year-round fixed menus, and wax models in the window make ordering easier. But most adjust to the seasons, so the offerings change daily. At such places it's best to set a price, state your preferences and leave the menu up to the chef. When a reservation is required, settle the price over the phone in advance. Try the following phrases:

'*Hitori ____ en de tabesashite itadakemasuka?*'

'Can you feed us for ¥ ____ per person?'

'*Otaku no osusume ryōri kudasai.*'

'Please serve us your specialities.'

'*Watashi wa sashimi wa dame desu.*'

'I don't like sashimi.'

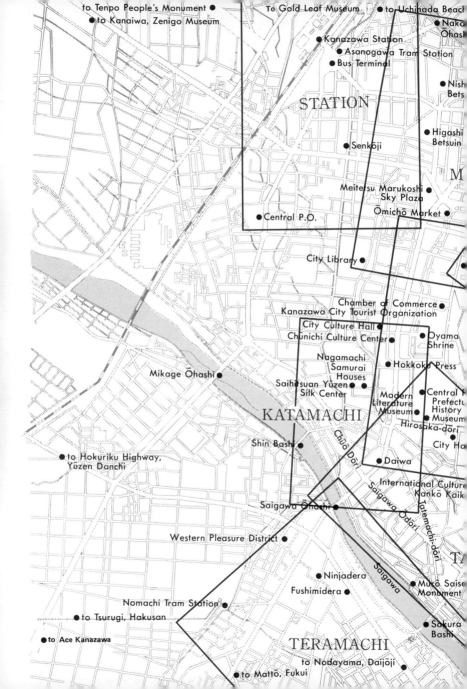

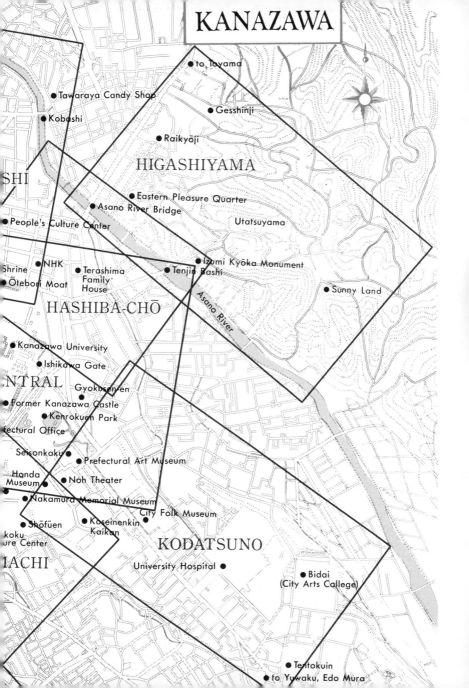

KANAZAWA

to Toyama

Tawaraya Candy Shop

Kobashi

Gesshinji

Raikyōji

HIGASHIYAMA

Eastern Pleasure Quarter

Asano River Bridge

Utatsuyama

People's Culture Center

Izumi Kyōka Monument

Shrine   NHK

Terashima Family House

Tenjin Bashi

Sunny Land

Ōtebori Moat

HASHIBA-CHŌ

Asano River

Kanazawa University

Ishikawa Gate

Gyokusen-en

NTRAL

Former Kanazawa Castle

Kenrokuen Park

ectural Office

Seisonkaku

Prefectural Art Museum

Honda Museum

Noh Theater

Nakamura Memorial Museum

City Folk Museum

Shōfūen

Koseinenkin Kaikan

koku
ure Center

KODATSUNO

IACHI

University Hospital

Bidai
(City Arts College)

Tentokuin

to Yuwaku, Edo Mura

SHI

KANAZAWA STATION 金沢駅

HELPFUL INFORMATION

Travel Information, reservations or anything else.

—JTB Travel Center inside the station, open 10:00—6:00, except Sundays and holidays.

—City Information Booth, just outside the exit towards the left, has all kinds of information, 8:00—8:00 daily.

—Travelers who arrive late in the evening or on holidays and find that regular information services are closed should try the train information booth beside the wickets, or the police box outside of the station and to the left.

Temporary Parcel Storage

Find coin lockers to the right as you leave the station, and in the station basement.

Railroad Express *(Chikki)*

A great way to send 'accompanying luggage' parcels (like an overload of souvenirs) anywhere in Japan. With the passenger's *jōshaken* train ticket, send packages up to 30 kilos, wrapped just in a box with string, to the station of destination or, for a small extra fee, to a home address. Outside on the right, just before the Parcel Storage Office.

Station Department Store

In the basement under the station, open 8:30—8:15 daily, this store has everything. Representative local souvenirs (famous cakes, lacquerware, Kutani, gold leaf, etc.), snacks, food, books for your trip, local sake, drugs--there's enough to keep you occupied between trains or to convince anyone at home that you spent weeks in Kanazawa. Across the street, on the first floor of the Miyako Hotel building, there are more 'famous products' shops.

THINGS TO DO

For people who have a few hours between trains, there are several interesting possibilities right near the station.

Movies. First-run foreign films (in the original language with Japanese subtitles) at the Roxy, second-rate porn or violence at the Bunka Gekijō. Both are in the basement shopping complex. All-night continuous showings on Saturdays.

Bath. The large Akame-yu public bath in the Ōkubo Hotel is just around the corner from the station and nice for a relaxing soak. 3:00−11:00, except Fri. The bath at the Green Hotel, across the street, opens at 5:00 a.m.

Restaurant. A short walk from the station takes you to Minori (美濃里), a lovely modern Japanese garden restaurant. The outer garden is visible through the glass walls, and even extends inside, in the form of waterfalls, greenery and rocks. Reasonable prices, Japanese and Western dishes, color photograph menu. 11:00−9:00, except Mondays.

Coffee and Bar. About 10 minutes walk from the station, Yellow USA is open 24 hours a day for coffee, drinks and food--perfect for midnight travelers with early connections to Noto.

Wandering Around. As is true in cities everywhere, the area immediately surrounding the station is rather run down, but if you get just a block away, you can begin discovering the charms of Kanazawa.

—Just outside the station stands a small statue of a character from a noh play, reminding visitors of the importance of this traditional art to the city. The Lions Club erected this figure, which is based on the eminent local teacher Sano Kichinosuke's portrayal of *Kakitsubata.*

—Buy a *bento* lunchbox for the next leg of your trip. The *ekiben* sold in Kanazawa Station haven't much of a reputation (although Toyama's famous Masu no Sushi, pressed rice and trout, is excellent). Better are the packets of Sasazushi, pressed fish and rice wrapped in bamboo leaves, sold at the Shibazushi shop across the street. Sasazushi will keep for 24 hours, so it makes a good souvenir, too.

—Saida's Tokobashira shop (オ 田) has rows and rows of

hewn and polished *tokonoma* alcove pillars all lined up for inspection. Most customers simply walk in and choose one for their new houses. There's also a selection of intricately carved *ranma* transoms and raw wooden table tops. Closed Sun. and holidays.

—Mosey on over to Rokumai street to look at the old fashioned shops--soy sauce, *geta* platform sandals, Japanese paper, tea. Also drop into IMC, a natural food store (自然食品店) specializing in pure cosmetics, organic vegetables and canned goods. Most are ingredients for Japanese cooking—there's no natural peanut butter. Open 9:30—6:00, except Sun.

VISITING

Yasue Kinpaku Kōgeikan--Gold Leaf Museum 安江金箔工芸館

Ninety percent of the world's gold leaf (and 100% of the silver leaf) is produced in Kanazawa. The best way to appreciate this traditional art is to visit 83-year-old Mr. Yasue's Kinpaku Museum, directly behind the station. (Facing the station, walk along the tracks to the right, cross under and backtrack.) Since age 7, Mr. Yasue has been working with gold, hand-pounding alloy into micro-millimeter-thin leaf and transferring it to lacquer, paper and, more recently, plastic. He will show you around the two-story hall, built with his own funds in 1977, explaining the details of his art and his fine collection. During his career, he has amassed gold leaf treas-

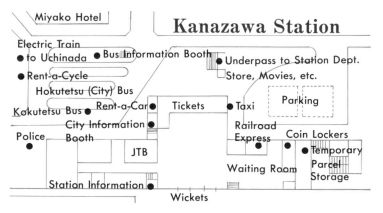

ures old and new, among them a gold threaded noh kimono, carved lacquer fish, *go* sets, screens, incense burners and a rare example of *kinpaku* on leather. Notice his Buddhist sanctuary, with 100% gold *umebachi* crests on the ceiling (most *kinpaku* is cut with cheaper metals), a gold leafed clay Inari God figure, and texts with gold leaf on the bindings to protect them from bugs.

After you wander around the spacious display rooms, Mrs. Yasue will serve you green tea with gold leaf floating in it and a dab of honey sparkling with gold powder (good for what ails you, especially rheumatism). If prompted, she'll describe her early days with her husband (How long does he work? 'As long as his eyes are open... Even during meals he wouldn't talk. Oh, it was a boring marriage!'), and perhaps demonstrate some of her own gold-work skills.

Open 9:30—4:30, except Tues. and Wed. ¥250. Tel. 33—1502

Kyūshōji 久昌寺

The building of the new Kanazawa railroad station in 1954 changed this whole neighborhood, and most affected were the quiet local temples surrounded by rice paddies. The railroad tracks run just behind Kyūshōji, bringing their dingy atmosphere right up to the doors of the temple. Inside, however, Kyūshōji does a flourishing business in *enmusubi,* or match-making. Dōgen, the 13th century Zen priest who founded the Sōtō sect and Eiheiji temple, came here and dedicated a statue of himself to this end. A mother looking for a nice girl for her son, a father trying to break up his daughter's unsuitable romance, the jealous party in a love triangle-- anyone with a problem in love and marriage may come here to get things settled.

Several methods are effective, such as writing the wish on white paper and tying it to the brass lantern in the dead of night, or writing names on little red and white dolls and hanging them from the rafters. The couple will be united if the dolls are tied facing each other, and the affair will end if the dolls are back to back.

Prayers are said to be most fruitful when said secretly, so the temple used to be open anytime. The local police, however, eventually got worried and demanded that the doors be locked at night. Visitors may use the door to the right.

Yasue Hachiman Shrine 安江八幡宮

The best time to visit this old Hachiman shrine is on the Day of the Dog, every 12th day according to the oriental zodiac. Since dogs are known for having easy deliveries, women in their fifth month of pregnancy pray here on that day, asking for a safe childbirth. Usually accompanied by their mothers, young wives offer for blessing a special white obi, which they then tie around themselves until delivery. This shrine is the originator of the famous roly-poly red doll, a talisman for a healthy baby kept by the grandmother (sold here for ¥1,000).

Established over 1000 years ago, this is the oldest Hachiman shrine (one of the 40,000 or so nation-wide) in Kaga district. It's not surprising that there remain such a raft of Shinto rituals and superstitions connected with the shrine. Its festival day, for example, is said to be always a rainy one. The priest explains that this is a result of the beneficence of the gods: the rain prevents fires at houses left unattended by all the festival participants in the neighborhood. In any case, there isn't a sunny April 15 in memory.

For all the pleasant ritual, the business of a shrine is business, and Hachiman-san has a thriving wedding industry. Especially on lucky days like *taian,* happy couples and beaming relatives can be seen promenading across the Heian-style arched bridge connecting the shrine and the hall.

Of note in the front grounds is a tiny shrine on the right housing a large stone statue. This is Yamato Takeru no Mikoto, the same mythic hero whose great statue is found in Kenrokuen Park. This statue was dug up nearby and given to the shrine for safekeeping, but no one knows its origin.

Senkoji 専光寺

Senkōji temple was influential in the 16th-century Ikkō Ikki peasants' rebellion. Its size and obvious prosperity today serve as proof of the Jōdo Sect's continuing popularity.

Among tourists, Senkōji is best known because of Japan's greatest female poet, Chiyo, whose parents were members of this temple. Her grave is in a lonely corner near the temple building--perhaps the butterfly of her famous haiku sometimes comes to rest there. *Chōchō ya nani o yume mite hanezukai.* ('Oh, butterfly--what are you dreaming that your wings flutter so?')

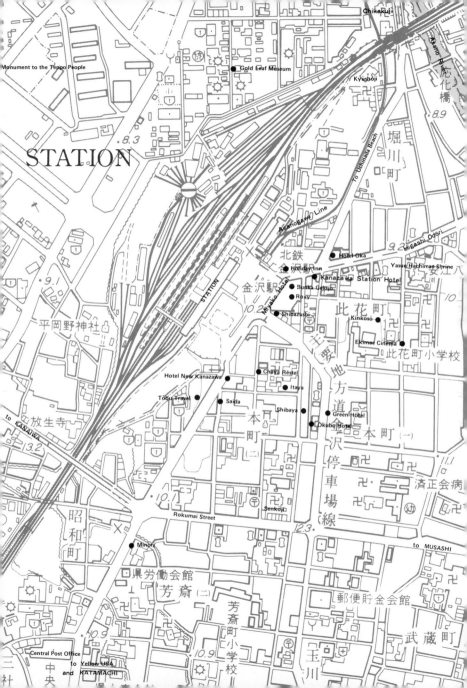

Monument to the Tenpo People 天保義民の碑

Near the end of the Edo era, poor weather and increased official corruption led to serious famine in the Kanazawa region. Particularly hard hit was the village of Sainen where, in 1838, tax officers refused to consider the blighted condition of the crops, demanding the usual tithes for the Maeda clan. Several peasant families protested, but in vain. They were exiled to the cruel mountain region of Gokayama, until they were pardoned eight years later. Their descendants still live in Sainen, and they erected a large stone monument to the brave victims. Visiting the monument itself would be most meaningful for those who have read Katsuo Kinya's novel about the incident, *People of the Tenpo Era* (see 'Before You Come').

Haiku poetess Chiyo.
(N.Aoki ; Prefectural Art Museum)

MUSASHI 武蔵ガ辻

SHOPPING

As a commercial area, Musashi has a long history. The influential west and east branches of Kyōto's Honganji temple are here, so Buddhist supply stores abound. Ōmichō market is Kanazawa's kitchen, as it has been since the 18th century. And the back streets at the end of Yoko Yasue-chō Arcade and behind Ōmichō are dotted with antique and junk shops. Although for shopping, Katamachi may be more efficient, the Musashi area has infinitely more charm. Try Ōmichō and the covered Arcade for a rainy afternoon's wandering.

Meitetsu Marukoshi—Sky Plaza (　名鉄丸越百貨店・スカイプラザ　　), a nine-floor department store and a three-story building of individual shops, dominates the Musashi area. All sorts of eateries, from international sandwiches to Kaga specialities are found in the basement, along side of an assortment of famous cake shops from all over Hokuriku. The wax samples look surprisingly delicious as you wander among the glass counters. The first and second Sky Plaza floors are crowded with fancy boutiques, more coffee shops and a gigantic fountain. A shopper can get easily, but happily, lost, only finding his bearings after going outside onto the street.

The department store has, of course, everything. Of cultural interest are the fifth floor gallery and the eighth floor hall where usually something artistic can be found. There are a tiny shrine dedicated to commerce and an outdoor playground on the ninth floor. At the very top of the department store is the Sky Hotel, and the view from the tenth floor lobby or the seventeenth floor restaurant section is the best in the city. Gaze out upon the university and consider how cleverly those Edo period lords chose their castle site. The whole complex is closed, as is most of the Musashi area, on Thursdays.

Ōmichō Market (近江町). As lively and bright as any market in Asia, the maze of covered arcades on the corner across from the Sky building shouldn't be missed. Crammed into the five or six intersecting alleys are nearly two hundred open shops, each with a hawker out front proclaiming the quality and low price of his wares. And it's true, the food is so plentiful, cheap and fresh at Ōmichō, it's madness to shop elsewhere. Conscious of a bargain, 30,000 Kanazawa shoppers jostle their way through the market on an average day, increasing to as many as 200,000 in the pre-New Year's rush. The shoppers today form a great cross-section of city people--housewives, restauranteurs, salarymen on their way home --but it wasn't always so. About 250 years ago there were two markets, one each on the Asano and Saigawa river banks. The Asano market, which served as the 'lord's kitchen' was right on the old North Highway leading out of the city, and as the population increased, it became difficult to serve the castle properly. The market was moved in 1721 to Ōmichō, where the Saigawa river market soon joined it. The tradesmen proudly continued supplying the castle for years, forbidding entry to women and other undesirables. In Meiji period, the market became public, and has continued to grow. In the name of sanitation, there are plans to modernize Ōmichō's construction within the next few years, but it is to be hoped that the bustling atmosphere and noisy charm will

Fresh produce and clever shoppers at Ōmichō Market. (Oasis)

be preserved.

'Kanazawa's kitchen' boasts 30 fish shops offering the most bewildering and mysterious variety of seafood, about 50 vegetable shops with the freshest seasonal roots and leaves, as well as 100 or so department-style and mom-and-pop provisions stores. The salespeople are so busy that a foreign shopper rates hardly a 'Hallo' or 'This is a pen.' Don't forget to take your own shopping bag.

They say that when you look down on the market from the Sky Building, the arcade roofs form the Chinese character for woman (女). But when you're inside the maze-like streets, such a concept doesn't help. The only way to figure out where you are is to exit--follow the light at the end of the tunnel and check your position with the Musashi intersection.

Tsuda Mizuhiki Shop (津 田). *Mizuhiki* are twisted strands of starched paper, woven into colorful, congratulatory shapes, to decorate gift packages. Mrs. Tsuda, a sweet, grandmotherly lady, has recently become nationally famous for her dedicated, imaginative work in fashioning *mizuhiki* cranes, flowers, tortoises, and other symbols of good luck. Despite her fame, she retains her charm, welcoming all visitors to her tiny workshop behind Ōmichō. She's there just about every day. Although there's not much on sale, the small dolls and miscellaneous shapes make good souvenirs.

Fumuroya (不室屋) specializes in Kaga wheat gluten, a local product used in soups and stews. A cheap, lightweight, thoughtful souvenir for Japanese friends or health food enthusiasts. *Sudarefu,* one type unique to Kaga, is rolled long and thin with a bamboo screen. 9:00−6:30, except Sun.

Nakashima Menya (中島めんや). Kanazawa's oldest toy shop, specializing in Kaga dolls and miniature lion heads, both very popular as souvenirs. Typical are the Kaga Tobi fireman doll and Hachiman Okiagari, the roly-poly doll which brings good luck to children. Open 8:30−6:00, except Thurs.

You can watch the dolls being made at the factory, which is geared for visitors. It's rather far away, about ¥4,000 by taxi, but there's also the bus to Hakui (#81, get off at Kahokudai Chūgak-kō), or the Nanao Line train to Unoke, where you take a ¥500 taxi to the factory.

Takahashi Antique Shop (高橋). The Musashi-Owari-chō area is crawling with antique shops, most either flea markets or elegant salons catering exclusively to favored customers. Takahashi strikes a happy medium, with well-displayed goods at a wide range of prices. 10:00–6:00, except Thurs.

Igarashi's Lantern and Umbrella store (五十嵐) is still an active workshop where visitors are welcome any day to watch the process of cutting and pasting. Splitting the bamboo ribs is the hardest part.

Hosokawa Nursery (細 川). Bonsai being chiefly a hobby of retired gentlemen, it's not surprising to find Mr. Hosokawa chatting amiably with his cronies at the front of his green and pleasant shop. He's been at this business for 60 years, about as long as it takes to create an excellent dwarf tree. Prowl around the back and up onto the balconies and roof, and marvel at the various bonsai, tray-arranged cacti and odd plants. Too bad it's so hard to take them to other countries as souvenirs. Closed Sundays.

Ishiura's Kamidana shop (石 浦) is one of the few speciality shops of its kind in Japan. Most families want a 'god shelf' to protect their homes as well as a Buddhist altar to revere their ancestors. The most popular shelf is around ¥12,000, of fine, pale wood with brass trim, but the cheapest begin at ¥6,500. Mrs. Ishiura weaves *mizuhiki,* twisted paper decorations, on the side. Closed Thurs.

Kurita's Brush shop (栗田) has the most amazing assortment of brushes, in all shapes and sizes, with the notable exception of the toothbrush. Closed Sun.

Meboso (目 細), in a narrow lane off Yoko Yasue-chō Arcade, makes Kaga Bari, the locally produced feather lures which have a national reputation for success in *ayu* (sweetfish) fishing. The shop began under Lord Maeda's patronage as a sewing needle business, and their original signboard with the lord's seal is on display. They changed to the tiny fishhooks in the early 1700's and still make them daily.

Sawada Butsudan Shop (沢 田). One of the best-stocked of the numerous Buddhist supply stores in Yoko Yasue-chō, Sawada's also has an impressive assortment of representative Kanazawa Buddhist altars. They range from 'cheap' (¥1,500,000), incorporating much plastic, to 'reasonable' (¥4,800,000), decorated with real gold leaf and fine *maki-e* lacquer. Notice that they are displayed in a fire-proof storeroom. Old Mr. Sawada will be glad to show you his workshops in the back, where various stages of the process are under way. (Say: *'Tsukuru tokoro o misete itadake-masenka?'*) 9:30—7:30, except Thurs.

Hayashiya (林 屋). Well-stocked tea store with a counter for tea-based drinks. The cream soda is good. 9:30—7:30, except Thurs.

Morohashi Tōfu (諸橋). Although largely mechanized by now, Morohashi's retains the atmosphere of an old-time bean curd shop. The whole family is involved in the process most of every day, soaking the soy beans in the afternoon and rising at 5:00 to produce the famous *kinugoshi* curd. Visitors are welcome to watch, but since the most interesting time is between 5:00 and 8:00 a.m., Mr. Morohashi gets few takers. He's the fifth generation in the business, which has been going since 1804--the oldest in Ishikawa Prefecture. The original equipment is on display at the City Folk Museum in Kodatsuno.

Ichimatsu Tea Shop (一松). Friendly Mr. Okamura runs this spacious and attractive tea utensil shop and lives in the old section upstairs. Every morning he puts up a distinctive red umbrella out front and waits for customers, mainly tourists on their way to Tawaraya candy shop. Open daily, 9:00—7:00.

Tawaraya Candy Shop (俵 屋) has become a great tourist attraction because of its 160-year-old building, typical of Kaga shopkeepers, its friendly old grandmother and its boldly-stroked hanging cloth sign. But even more significant is its unique product, *ame,* a sticky honey-like candy, made of rice and barley with neither sugar nor preservatives. Its sweetness comes naturally from the barley, making it a traditional health food, perfect as a gift for *byōki mimai,* visiting a sick friend. It's also used in cooking and makes a good coffee sweetener. 9:00—6:00, except Sun.

EATING

Jimbei (甚 平). Kaga cooking in reasonably priced, set dinner form. Easy to order from the plastic models in the window. Sky Plaza basement, closed Thurs.

Maison de France (メゾン・ド・フランセ). Famous coffee and chocolate mousse, good salad Nicoise and pizza. Meitetsu Department Store, near fountain on 2nd floor.

Takanoha (鷹の羽). Hiding in the sub-basement outside the department store, this tempura speciality shop is known for good set dinners and tempura *soba*. Try the unusual *matcha-shio* (green tea-coated salt) on your batter-fried shrimps. 9:00−11:00, except Thurs.

Toritsuji (とり辻). Noisy, lively and cheap. They'll grill any of the fish, meats and vegetables laid out on baskets around the counter. Try the delicious *yaki-musubi,* grilled rice balls, with some draft beer. 5:00−11:00, except Thurs.

Kadochō Honten (加登長). For 70 years the Yoshidas have been serving good *soba* and *udon* at their original shop. While waiting for your noodles, get a taste of the personalities of Qwari-chō with some people-watching in the high-ceilinged dining room, or take a look at the private rooms upstairs. The third generation Mr. Yoshida at the cashbox recalls fondly the days when the soldiers stationed in the castle grounds before the war used to come for merrymaking on Sundays. Closed Thurs.

Kotobuki-ya (寿 屋). At first, Kotobuki-ya seems like a quiet, unassuming restaurant specializing in *shōjin ryōri,* the vegetarian, Buddhist-inspired cooking. Most Japanese associate this food with funerals and thus leave its pleasures to the rest of us. The 100-year-old merchant's house is magnificent, as are the lacquer utensils, the exquisite service and the dainty but filling dishes. Take a dictionary along to help figure out what you're eating. Reservations are necessary, tel. 31−6245. About ¥4,500 a person, a bargain for such a serene experience. 11:00−6:00 daily.

Tsuruko (つる幸). Elegant Kyōto-style cooking, lovely garden and careful attention to details. Very expensive at dinner, but a *bentō* lunch for about ¥5,000 a person is available. Worth the investment for an exquisite taste of Japan's best. Reservations necessary, tel. 64−2375.

Fuku Wa Uchi (福わ家). Famous for cook-it-yourself *udon* noodles. First you are brought green tea and cakes to enjoy while you choose between plain, fish, mushroom, beef and tempura *udon*. When your individual pot comes, you cook it on a small flame, eat the noodles and make a rice stew from the leftover soup. This set dinner, with tea and pickles, is around ¥1,000, high for *udon,* but good fun. Open 11:00–8:30, except Wed. A new *soba* shop, *Oni Wa Soto,* is next door.

DRINKING

There's a curious dearth of interesting drinking places in the Musashi area. Katamachi and Tatemachi's lively variety is more fun.

Akane (あかね). Tiny hole-in-the-wall shop with cheap food and drink served by friendly Ms. Itō. She knows more English than she lets on. Popular with Kanazawa University professors. Open 5:00–1:00, except Sun.

Jupiter (ジュピター). Kanazawa's only 'gaybar,' meaning that the charming hostesses are transvestites. Open daily from around 8:00 p.m., the place only begins to swing past midnight. Relaxed and friendly for uninhibited. The girls may do some erotic dancing upon request.

Kagayaza (加賀屋座). Low down strip joint. 1:00 p.m. to 9:30 or so. Later on Sat. About ¥3,000 per person.

Mr. Donuts. The usual cheap coffee and familiar donuts. Open 24 hours.

Plaza Miki (プラザ樹). Quiet coffee shop combined with a gallery of local crafts, pottery, flower arrangement, whatever, on the second floor. Exhibitions change weekly. 10:00–7:00, except Sun.

VISITING

People's Culture Center　　町民文化館

Much of Kanazawa's cultural heritage centers around the feudal aristocracy (Seisonkaku, Honda Museum, etc.), but recently an attempt has been made to preserve evidence of Edo-era merchants' life as well. A 1908 former bank building with dark woodwork, high ceilings and marble counters now houses a People's Culture Center, in the heart of the feudal merchants' district. Exhibitions change four times a year. The permanent collection emphasizes the lion dance typical of neighborhood festivals. ¥50. 9:00–4:00, except Thurs. Receptionist Ms. Satake speaks English.

Ichihime Shrine 市媛神社

This tiny shrine across from Ōmichō market was originally the worship place of the market tradespeople. Dedicated to Ebisu, the lucky god of hardworking fishermen and shopkeepers, the shrine moved here from Kansai when the people of Ōmi (around Lake Biwa) followed the great priest Rennyo here during the 16th century. But there's a great turnover at Ōmichō, and less than one percent of the present shopkeepers descend from the early settlers. Most of them now live elsewhere and go to family shrines near their houses.

Shōenji 照円寺

Shōenji is at the end of Yoko Yasue-chō Arcade on the edge of a wide intersection where no fewer than eight roads intersect. The surrounding area is packed with antiques shops, temples and children playing on quiet streets under grandmother's watchful eye. Right across the street is a shop specializing in repair and restoration of old family Buddhist altars. You can watch the old man out in front, polishing and hammering rusted and bent parts while his assistant coats pieces of wood with black lacquer.

Shōenji itself has had an uneven history. It has burned down three times, most recently in 1967 when some children were playing with matches. In former days the garden boasted an elegant teahouse, but it had to be sold when the temple fell upon hard times. Despite fire and poverty, the priests have been able to preserve intact some great treasures. Best known is the series of 18 scrolls, 13 of which depict grisly but fascinating scenes from Buddhist hell, and four of which show heaven. Every year at spring equinox, parents bring little children for a look, an impressive reminder of the perils of bad behavior. Neighborhood adults still remember the terror they felt as small children when they saw the scenes of bloody, dismembered corpses being devoured by demons, only to come back to life again for more torture, and so on into eternity.

Now that prosperity reigns again, the temple will show the scrolls, displayed in the new treasure hall, at any time, for ¥200. But it's best to call (21−4785) or drop by in advance. No one knows who painted the scrolls or how they came into Shōenji's

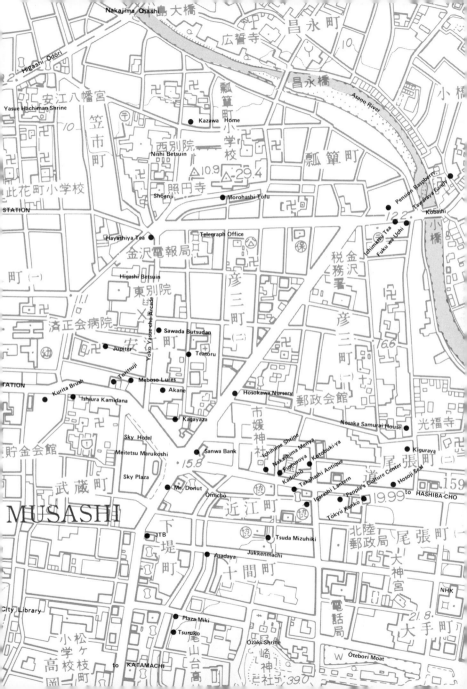

possession, except that they are based on a description of hell by Genshin, a Tendai sect monk of Hieizan. But the pictures themselves are self-explanatory. Pleasant dreams!

Higashi and Nishi Betsuin Temples 東・西別院

The center of Musashi is new, due in part to the great Hikoso Fire of 1927, which leveled most of the area. (The Japanese are accustomed to fires, and they rebuild quickly, trying to get things back to normal as soon as possible.) Along the edge of Musashi, however, the oldest buildings still remain. The Nishi (West) Betsuin temple is at their center. Although the grounds are crawling with kids (the nursery school is a major source of the temple's income), Nishi Betsuin retains a unique flavor of the 16th-century days when the Buddhists controlled Kanazawa, and the Jōdo Sect temples were political, as well as religious, centers.

The children's baseball diamond marks the main temple points: the catcher squats on the steps of the gate; first base is one of the gnarled pines; second is the steps of the old main hall; and third is the six-sided revolving library for sutras--all written in a classical language no one can read anymore. The temple's history is the subject of controversy, with the theoretical dates of its origin ranging from 1334 to 1546. In any case, the Nishi and Higashi Betsuins are direct branches of the West and East Honganji temples of Kyōto.

The Higashi (East) Betsuin, down the street, burned to the ground in 1963, and the replacement, although very impressive, hasn't yet developed much character. But the Higashi temple organization is extremely active--religious lectures, exhibitions and services are held constantly. They are attended mostly by the elderly, who have the time and a natural inclination toward spiritual matters, but anyone is welcome to any event, including the daily lectures at 8:00 a.m. and 1:00 p.m.

Nishi Betsuin's revolving sutra library. (H.Ikeuchi)

HIGASHIYAMA　東山

About 50 temples dot the Higashiyama hillside. Their over-abundance is evident in the large proportion which has fallen into disrepair--parking lots, playgrounds and nursery schools abound. Visitors will probably wish to limit themselves to choosing among the 20 or so active temples, described below. Most are of the Nichiren sect, assembled here by Lord Toshitsune in the early 1600's.

Temple buildings are generally closed up during the year. Other than in the summer *obon* grave-visiting season, at the spring and autumn equinoxes or on other special holidays, visitors must ask at the door of the adjoining house for permission to see whatever statue, grave or garden is of interest.

Higashiyama is not all temples, however. Some of the oldest shops and the windiest roads, as well as the largest geisha district, are here. The best time to visit is in the afternoon, when the sun hits the hillside and the *tofu* man pulls his cart around the streets. He rings his bell, and the housewives run out to buy the fresh silken bean curd that is a Kanazawa speciality.

Kanazawa City's walking tour course provides a convenient route for seeing most of the major spots. But it's also fun to let yourself get lost wandering in the hills. You can always get reori-entated by walking back down to the main street and finding a bus stop. Higashiyama is actually part of Utatsuyama, but because of the road system, they have become separated into two distinct areas.

SHOPPING

Fukushima Shamisen (福 島). The only shamisen maker in Kanazawa is ensconced in an attractive, high-ceilinged shop on Kannon Machi Street. Herè Mr. Fukushima pastes catskin on the square boxes, while his eldest son makes the wooden parts upstairs in the back. Visitors are welcome to watch both processes. It takes weeks to make one instrument, so the prices are high. Even a plectrum of tortoise shell can cost ¥50,000. But it's pleasant to drop in for a look anyway.

Yonezawa Tea Shop (米 沢) was begun in 1876, by the Yonezawas' Meiji ancestor, Kiroku, a man of wide interests and great local influence. Tea itself is sold downstairs, but if you go up to the second floor, you are welcome to inspect their wide variety of utensils, lacquer and pottery. 8:00–7:00, except Sun.

Takagi Kōji Shop (高木糀店). This old shop's facade is well-known in town for its picturesque rope *noren* curtains covering the sales area. Glance in and see the shallow wooden trays stacked up in the back. *Kōji,* malted rice, is used in pickle-making.

EATING AND DRINKING

Shōgyotei (松魚亭) is a Japanese restaurant specializing in fresh fish. A great view with excellent service. 11:00–10:00.

Rokkakudo (六角堂) across from Shōgyotei specializes in steaks. Dinner runs from ¥3,300; special luncheon steak ¥1,000. Relaxing spacious interior. 11:00–10:00 daily.

Birds House (バードハウス). Tastefully nestled in the Utatsuyama mountains. A varied Western menu at moderate prices. 10:00–10:00, except Mon.

Lennon (れのん). Hand-written menu changes daily. Enjoy your coffee or drinks with the geisha from nearby Higashi, who often visit Lennon after their evening engagements. 5:00–1:00, except Mon.

Circus (サーカス). Student hangout-type coffee house, with cheap drinking in the evenings. 11:00–11:00, except Wed.

Goriya (ごりや) has been serving river fish, particularly the tiny *gori* famous in Kanazawa, for over 200 years. Guests stroll to each room through the quiet garden on the Asano River bank. First-class prices (¥7,000 and up), and reservations recommended (tel. 52–2288). Lunch and dinner daily.

VISITING

Asano River Bridge 浅野川大橋

Pause as you cross the Asano River to notice the view of Utatsu-yama and far-off Iōzan upstream, and a gracefully curved pedest-rian bridge downstream. On the left, there's an ancient willow tree with a sign appealing to citizens to treat it with care. Beyond the police box is an old house with vertical wooden slats, and horizontal inside screens of narrow bamboo strips. This is a typical example of Kanazawa architecture, allowing people inside to see out, while their privacy is protected from the view of passers-by.

Down the street to the left of the old house are many old-style merchant families selling such·items as Chinese herb medicines, tatami mats, kimono fabric—just one of several old neighborhoods remaining in the Higashiyama district. Another is Kannon Machi Street (観音町通り), the second right after you cross the Asano River Bridge. This narrow road is lined with soy sauce and rice dealers, a shamisen maker, a pawnshop, and a tatami maker--evidence of its former status as a craftsmen's town. On the right, notice a curious jumble of straw hanging under the eaves of an old sake shop. The grandmother explains that it's a keg stuck with straw bits, and it has served as their trademark for the last 200 years.

Seven Jizōs' Temple (Jukyōji) 寿経寺

In the late Edo period, although crops were poor, the feudal government was still demanding heavy taxes of the farmers. One summer evening in 1858, about 1000 starving farmers dared to make a protest, yelling from Utatsuyama in the direction of the castle, 'Rice is too expensive! We're hungry!' Their bold move set off riots all over the city. Peasants broke into storehouses, stealing rice in frenzied, if short-lived, exultation. But when the riots were quelled, seven of the ringleaders were beheaded for their crime, particularly unforgivable because commoners were forbidden to climb Utatsuyama, where one could boldly look down on the castle.

In the early Meiji period, memorial *jizō* statues were erected to console the martyrs' spirits. The seven statues, decorated with caps and capes, and holding the rice ears they were denied in life, are visible through a fence in a shed in front of the Jukyōji temple. Their common grave is to the right.

Kannon-in 観音院

At the end of Kannon Machi Street, up a long flight of stone steps, is a temple to Kannon, the goddess of mercy. Panting climbers should pause for the view--the city, the Higashi geisha district, the fast-developing suburbs and the Japan Sea in the background-- and then resort to their imaginations. This now closed-up temple was once powerful, graced by a three-story pagoda and an outdoor noh stage. Under Maeda patronage, annual plays were performed here for 250 consecutive years, and Kannon-in was a central influence in the development of Kanazawa's Hōshō noh school. But the theater was abandoned in the Meiji period, and the pagoda was accidentally burned down by a vagabond's campfire. The temple still houses the famous 11-faced, wooden Hase Kannon statue, supposedly commissioned by Imohori Tōgorō and his wife. It's displayed once a year, when the whole temple comes back to life during the Corn Festival in August. Buy a sacred ear and hang it in your entryway, for a year's good fortune. One visit to the temple on this day is worth 46,000 visits on regular days, more than making up for a year's dereliction.

★ Eastern Pleasure Quarter (Higashi) 旧東廓

The Higashi district was set aside in 1820, by the Kaga feudal government, as an entertainment quarter. A high-class area, it boasted talented and beautiful geisha who provided amusements for wealthy customers and patrons.

Notice the picturesque, wooden slatted facades. At dusk, you can still see geisha walking by, bound for their appointments in the few 'tea houses' which are still in business. Many houses are now *minshuku,* inns and restaurants. But the old atmosphere comes alive in the evenings when the strains of shamisen and singing penetrate the thin walls and entertain wistful passers-by. It is not possible to attend a geisha party without an introduction, and even then it's outrageously expensive. The company of one geisha runs about ¥4,000 per hour, plus food, and room charges.

Higashi is the site of a nationally famous novel, *Toki no Haka* (The Grave of the Ibis), written by Itsuki Hiroyuki, about a geisha's love affair with a Russian officer after the turn-of-the-century Russo-Japanese War.

The dignified charm of Higashi, the Eastern Geisha District. (S.Bishago)

Shima 志摩

This elegant former geisha house offers tourists a rare chance-- a visit to its interior: a charming enclosed garden, entertainment rooms and a tea room. At the *irori* open hearth near the entrance, you can rest with a cup of tea. Notice the dancing performance room between two private entertainment chambers on the second floor.

Shima is the fifth house down on the left as you enter Higashi's main street. Although their official holidays are Mondays and at New Year's, operation is erratic, so it's worth calling to check before going (tel. 52−5675). ¥200.

Utasu Shrine 宇多須神社

Utasu is one of many old shrines which still shows signs of Buddhist influence. It was originally dedicated to Bishamonten, one of the Seven Lucky Gods of Buddhist folklore. At the Meiji Restoration, Utasu shed the Buddhist part of its heritage, took over the Shintō elements of Raikyōji temple, and became a full-fledged shrine.

Utasu lies just behind the Higashi Quarter, so in the old days it was popular with geisha. One could see them every evening, all dressed and coiffed, saying a prayer here before going out on their appointments. Utasu is also known as the rallying ground for the rice riots of 1858.

Hōsenji 宝泉寺

This temple is also known as Gohon Matsu, because of its striking pine tree--five trunks extend from a single base. The original Gohon pine, said to be a giant one visible to fishermen out in their boats, was lost in a landslide. The present tree is its 'child.' The expansive view of the mountains, the city and the sea is excellent from here.

The front garden is crowded with small stone figures, a statue of Kōbō Daishi, and a little shrine which somehow escaped the Meiji directive that Buddhist and Shintō places of worship must be separated. You can also say a prayer before each of the 88 Kannon statues, to help you on your way to enlightenment and to avoid making the pilgrimage to the 88 temples of Shikoku.

Hōsenji's history revolves around a tiny gold statue of Marishiten, the Buddhist god of war. The 6-cm. figure became famous in the 14th century for its active influence in improving its owner's martial skills. Since most Buddhas offer only passive assistance, the Marishiten was highly coveted and was admired by such prominent militarists as the Ashikaga shōgun, Yoshimitsu. But its owner and his family carefully kept control of it, until one descendent became a Maeda retainer. The statue was then kept in Kanazawa Castle, where Lord Toshiie built it a small house, and wore it on his helmet into battle, where it protected him admirably. His son Toshinaga designated some land out of the northeast gate of the castle (the gate where evil enters and departs) as a site, imported the priest, Hōsenbō, and built a temple for the statue. It was visited by the faithful from all over the country--samurai seeking martial skills, merchants praying for prosperity and householders after general good fortune. Recently, politicians seeking election success have been making the long climb up the temple's stone steps. The statue is still temple property, but only on display every 33 years; the next time is 1994.

In the back is another temple, Higashiyama Gobō, boasting a great statue of Rennyo Shōnin, the 15th-century missionary of the

Jōdo Shinshū sect. (A similar statue can be found on the hill behind Daijōji.) The road from here continues up into Utatsuyama.

Renshōji 蓮昌寺

There was a great fire in Higashiyama in 1736, and over 3,000
homes were burned. As a memorial to the victims, in 1759 a
magnificent statue of Buddha was commisioned. Five majestic
meters of bug-resistant camphor wood, it stands in the left-hand
hall of Renshōji. Since it's only half visible through the door's
glass window, it's best to ask the grandmother living at the right
side to let you inside (*'Daibutsu o misete kudasai'*). Along with
those of Hōshūji and Genmonji, this is one of the three Great
Buddhas of Kanazawa.

Up in the mountains behind the temple is the grave of the
Shimada family. Their black sheep, Ichirō, killed Meiji statesman
Ōkubo Toshimichi.

Raikyōji 来教寺

Firm metal-studded wood and earthen walls surround this small,
attractive temple. The well's dragon-shaped water spout and the
large Buddha statue (notice how young he looks--this is in
Gautama's pre-enlightenment, princely days) are both Toyama's
Takaoka ironwork. Brightly clothed *jizō* statues welcome visitors
at the temple's entrance. The architecture is unusual, dating from
before the Meiji-era decision to separate Buddhism and Shintōism.
The sloping front roof and abundant stone lanterns indicate Raikyōji's shrine-influenced past.

The main interest here, however, is the priest, Mr. Kawai Chikai,
who is known for his fortune-telling abilities. Twenty-fifth in the
priestly line, he uses various Buddhist sooth-saying devices, I Ching,
and phrenology, in his consultations with visitors from all over the
country. The prices are posted, and Japanese-speakers or others
with translators may wish to ask his advice (tel. 52—2056). Try a
manjū bean cake at the shop across the street, or a hot soak at the
old bathhouse beside it.

Genmonji 玄門寺

Although mainly devoted to its new occupation as neighborhood nursery school, Genmonji also houses one of the three Great
Buddhas of Kanazawa. Standing nearly five meters, made of wood
with gold leaf and bright paints, it's an impressive sight. Now the

temple is built like a fireproof storehouse, with dried mud walls, but in the old days, to protect the statue, there was an enormous hole dug directly underneath. In case of fire, the Buddha could be dropped into the earth and covered, while the wooden temple burned above.

Kishimōjin--Doll's Temple 真成寺（人形寺）

Kanazawa women praying for a baby or for safe childbirth often visit this temple. When the goddess Kishimōjin answers their prayers, they gratefully place a picture or figure of the healthy child on the altar. Kishimōjin, also known as the Indian deity Hariti, was originally a protective mother who thought only of her own babies. When she took to stealing innocent children and giving their blood to her children to drink, the lord Buddha decided to teach her a lesson. He hid one of her beloved 500 babies, and the stricken Kishimōjin reformed and became the protectress of all children.

The outside yard, dotted with 'see-no-evil' monkeys, is charming in itself, but the colorful insides of the temple shouldn't be missed. Call 52−6060 in advance, and ask for an appointment. They will be glad to show you around the halls, overflowing with statues and symbols of children. On April 29, a Ningyōkuyō festival is held to dispose of old and broken dolls by burning them. The grave of the first Nakamura Utaemon (1714−1751), of the famous Kabuki family, is in the grounds of this temple.

Kishimōjin's steep front steps.
(S.Bishago)

Sanbōji 三宝寺

Sanbōji's speciality is a discreet, effective cure for a difficult affliction--hemorrhoids. The temple found itself in the business in the Edo period when a dying parishioner dedicated himself as a Buddha to helping fellow sufferers of the then-untreatable malady. His five-tiered grave, in the far right-hand corner of the front garden, was visited by an increasing number of people plagued by piles. As their prayers were answered and the word spread, the temple began dispensing medicines and incantations. For those who call in advance (tel. 52−3380), the priest will chant the sutras and hand out a soothing salve and a packet of red pills, made of shredded paper brushed with holy words. The altar on the left, inside the temple building, is decorated with the photos of satisfied patients.

The altar on the right is crowded with pictures of grateful people cured by Sanbōji's other service, a general-purpose Buddhist exorcism, in which a mysteriously gifted person takes on the ills of the supplicants. Until she recently became ill herself, the exorcist was a spiritual old woman whose success was legend among local Nichiren temples.

Ryūkokuji 竜国寺

At this mountain temple, somebody recently discovered the inconspicuous gravestone of Miyazaki Yūzensai (1682−1707),the painter who developed the Yūzen silk dying technique. Like most Edo-period craftsmen, he died quietly and wasn't fully appreciated until years later. But the Yūzen dyers of today have gone to great lengths to make up for the lapse. Their association has built an excellent tea house, where they hold a memorial tea ceremony on the 17th of each month. The May ceremony, which includes a Buddhist prayer service, is particularly interesting, but visitors are welcome to come and watch any month. The dyers group has also erected a monument inscribed with Yūzensai's nostalgic poem, *Kyō no koto mata kuchi ni deru yokan kana,* expressing his longing for Kyōto in a spontaneous complaint against Kanazawa's lingering winter. Although it's not clear where Yūzensai was born or why he came to Kanazawa, most explanations agree that he spent most of his life in Kyōto, and in Kanazawa he was employed by the Maeda clan to introduce the silk painting art to Kaga dyers.

Miyazaki Yūzen-sui's modest grave
at Ryūkokuji. (Oasis)

Zenshōji 全性寺

Also known as Akamonji because of its unusual red-painted gate,
this is the site of the grave of Kaga Hōshō school of noh's founder,
Shisetsu. The gravestone, along with that of Izumi Kyōka's mother, is through the small gate at the left side of the temple grounds.
Around July 10, many students of Hōshō noh gather here to pay
their respects. Because Shisetsu was a teacher of the Maeda family,
permission was given for the gate to be painted a lordly red. Hanging on the gate are the curious giant *waraji* straw sandals given by
local farmers and laborers in thanks for strong legs. On the roof of
the red gate, notice the *onigawara,* tiles in the shape of a monster's
face, which are rare in Kanazawa.

Myōtaiji 妙泰寺

In early Edo period, a certain princess had a toothache. She
found relief through prayer at the then newly-built Myōtaiji temple.
When she died in 1615 (tragically young, of course), she vowed to
help other toothache sufferers from beyond the grave. For the rest
of the Edo period, and most of Meiji, the temple flourished as,
chopsticks in hand, people came seeking relief. When dentists were
trained and gradually became available to all, the temple fell upon
hard times. But still standing in the dilapidated temple grounds is
the princess' five-tiered grave, surrounded with mossy lanterns and
vases left by grateful recipients of her prayers.

Renkakuji 蓮覚寺

Renkakuji's claim to a place on the tourist route is the lonely
grave of Itaya Heishirō, the genius who constructed the vital
Tatsumi Yōsui canal which supplied Kanazawa Castle with water.
According to the legend, when the project was completed in 1636,
poor Heishirō was killed in order to keep the technique a Maeda
secret. His mossy grave is the last on the left in the third alley to

the right.

In the back of the graveyard stands a typical *muenzuka,* a collective grave of all those stones and jars of ashes whose identities have been lost over time. Most temples have such a grave, often built of the ancient illegible gravestones, and prayed over regularly by the priest, and by any visitors who care to.

Gesshinji 月心寺

In back of this lovely temple is the immaculately kept grave of Sen Sōshitsu, an Ura Senke tea master who came from Kyōto at the invitation of the fifth Maeda lord, Tsunanori. Sōshitsu taught tea ceremony to the third, fourth, and fifth lords, for 50 years, before dying at age 76, in 1698. Due to his early influence, Ura Senke is still the dominant tea school in Kanazawa. Sōshitsu brought along *rakuyaki* potter Ōhi Chōzaemon, who set up shop in Kanazawa, and provided the bowls necessary for tea. The first Chōzaemon's grave is also here.

You are free to walk around the gardens and graves and insp ct the two tea houses. But the best time to go is on the 23rd of the month, when a public tea ceremony is held in Sōshitsu's memory. You can participate in the ceremonies for regular and thick tea, for ¥3,000 (the high price is to keep the crowds down), or simply walk through the temple and grounds, soaking up the tea atmosphere.

Shinrensha 心蓮社

Behind this old temple is a lovely, little-known garden of the Enshū school. Its pond is in the distinctive *kokoro* shape of the Chinese character for spirit (心). Although you can stroll through the garden by walking around behind the temple at the right, the scenery was designed for appreciation from the inside porch. Try entering at the left door and asking for permission (*'Oniwa o haiken sasete itadakemasenka?'*). Notice the mossy rocks on the pond's back-right bank. They are carefully placed to divide the one waterfall into three dainty streams, giving an impression of coolness and preventing stagnation in the pond.

The other feature of the temple, described at great length on the sign outdoors, is its treasured scroll. The ancient painting is tenuously connected with a complex legend of duty, honor and motherly love. The friendly priest will happily explain the details.

but it turns out that the scroll is actually now in Nara for safekeeping, and the story itself has nothing to do with the temple anyway. Stick to garden-viewing.

Kōkakuji 光覚寺

Another lovely, undiscovered Enshū-style garden can be found at Kōkakuji. Abundant maples make the autumn scene especially attractive. The temple's first priest founded it in Takefu, in 1580. He later won the confidence of Lord Toshiie, who gave him a plot within Kanazawa Castle. Eventually, castle expansion projects forced the move to the Higashiyama area.

The temple is known locally for its Candy-buying Ghost (curiously enough, similar stories are found in nearly every Japanese town). In the late Edo period, a woman's figure was noticed leaving her grave behind the temple to visit the sweet shop across the street. Brave neighbors investigated and found an infant boy in the grave, where he'd been born after his pregnant mother's death. This expression of motherly love became legendary, and a *jizō* statue was erected on her grave. It's the red-bibbed one on your right as you stroll around the mossy stones behind the temple.

Naruwa no Taki 鳴和の滝

Legends of the handsome 12th-century hero, Yoshitsune, can be found all over Japan, but one of the most popular and credible is that of the Ataka Barrier Gate, near Komatsu. According to the noh play, *Ataka,* Yoshitsune and his retainer Benkei continued on into the hills near Kanazawa, where there is a fresh, natural spring. In the meantime, Togashi, the sympathetic Ataka Barrier guard, decided to follow them with some gifts. He caught up with them here, and they all sat down near the gurgling spring to eat and drink. Since Togashi was still ostensibly their enemy, clever and slightly drunken Benkei devised a plan to help Yoshitsune escape again. He made up a song and performed a charming dance for the rapt Togashi, and Yoshitsune and the others made their way off into the mountains. The song begins, *Naru wa taki no mizu...* (The waterfall is ringing...), and the name Naruwa has stuck.

A shrine was built at the site of the party, where the revellers' chopsticks were left sticking up in the front grounds, until they were washed away, according to the neighbors, in a typhoon a few years ago. This last bit reduces somewhat the credibility of the story. Anyway, the lovely, cool waterfall and the shrine are there for imaginative visitors to create their own versions of the tale. A good time to visit may be at the festival in early October. Notice the bold little ferns and mosses growing out of the characters carved into the shrine's new stone purification basin. The place is a little hard to find: pass the Royal Hotel, turn right at the eyeglasses shop, jog right, then left, and go all the way up the narrow road.

Matsu Mon 松門

In Edo period, travelers along the old roads from the east (Niigata) or the west (Kyōto) had to pass through the gates of the city to be checked by a guard. At that point, the rural area officially ended, and the dusty traveler was required to change into urban dress--no more kimono tucked up into the belt, no protective leggings, no bundles dangling from the shoulder. Remains of the west gate have completely disappeared, but in Ōhimachi, along the old North Country highway, a signboard attached to a low-hanging roof indicates the spot of the eastern Pine Gate.

This old street, beginning at Kasuga Machi, is worth a stroll. Everything needed in Edo-period life seems available here--a fishmonger, a wicker craftsman, *miso* shop, inns, baths--most of them preserving the atmosphere of this road in its heyday. The road eventually passes through the Ōhimachi Valley, famous for *Kaga renkon*. All summer the lotus plants grow, catching rain in their basket-like leaves, until early fall, when the roots are harvested, and the ground turned over for the winter.

Hasudera 蓮寺（持明院）

Lotus flowers, sacred to Buddhism and producing a crisp, tasty root, are cultivated and worshipped all over Asia. But here, in Kanazawa, grows a unique, seedless lotus, with as many as 2,000 petals per flower and several blossoms to each stalk. The eminent priest, Kōbō Daishi, is said to have brought this special *tatōren* back with him from his studies in China, over 1,000 years ago, but according to the chief priest, Mr. Yoshiyama, no such flower has been found in China either. (Hasudera has generously donated live samples to two other temples, in Fuchū, near Tōkyō and in Shiga, near Kyōto.)

The flowers bloom from mid-July through August. Then, instead of forming a normal seed pod, they simply wither and die on the stalk. Dried flowers and those pickled in alcohol are available for believers to take home. Caring for the flowers is a delicate and time-consuming job, but Mr. Yoshiyama and his ancestors have also found time to cultivate the tea ceremony. Around 300 years ago, an understated but worthy tea house was built here, under the instructions of Ura Senke master Sen Sōshitsu. A new tea house, mercifully equipped with chairs as well as tatami, adjoins the temple, and tea is served monthly on the 27th, between 10:00 and 3:00. A donation of ¥1,000 should be wrapped up and left at the door. Taxi is the most convenient transportation.

UTATSUYAMA　卯辰山

During Edo period, access to this mountain was forbidden to commoners. Now it's almost overdeveloped, with housing creeping up the edges, and vast graveyards spilling over the summit. But except for crowded Sundays, the quiet narrow roads through the woods are inviting to strollers, cyclists and drivers. Afternoon, when the sunlight strikes the hill, is the best time to go. Especially beautiful are the cherry trees in April, which bloom slightly later than Kenrokuen, and the orange and hot-pink maples of autumn. Utatsuyama is the perfect place for monuments. Everyone—inventors, martyrs, literary figures—seems to be memorialized here by some stone or signpost.

The orthodox route, described below, begins at Tenjin Bashi bridge and continues back to Kenmin Park, the deepest point on the mountain. It is also possible to enter the Utatsuyama road from the Higashiyama temple area, past Gesshinji or Utasu Shrine, and from the Tokiwa Bashi bridge upriver.

Izumi Kyōka Monument　泉鏡花句碑

This great stone slab stands right in the hairpin turn outside the Shōgyotei restaurant. Kyōka's mother died when he was eleven, and the theme of his loneliness for her runs throughout his works, often in the form of a yearning for the Eternal Woman. The poem inscribed on this monument is typical: *Haha koishi yūyama sakura mine no matsu* (I miss my mother, cherry blossoms on the evening mountain, pine trees on the ridge).

Toyokuni Shrine　豊国神社

Around the next bend is a gourd-shaped lake in the center of Miya no Mori, or Shrine Woods. There are three shrines right near the lake. The biggest, Toyokuni, is reached by the long stone stairway going up to the right. It was a Maeda family shrine, dedicated, strangely enough, to Toyotomi Hideyoshi. Although the Maedas were allied with Ieyasu, Lord Toshiie wisely remained friendly with Hideyoshi, the challenger. The small shrine beside Toyokuni is a Tenmangū, dedicated to the god of learning, and now frequented by students who invest hopefully in the ¥300 scholarship charms. On the left is an old well, covered with moss and ferns, and identified with a signboard explaining that it is the well figuring in the ghostly noh play, *Izutsu*.

The third shrine in this area is the tiny Atago altar, which survives in the Tenmangū building. A branch of Kyōto's main Atago Shrine, it fell on hard times in the Meiji period and is now virtually forgotten. There is a back exit to Toyokuni Shrine, over an arched bridge, which offers a glimpse of the valley and promises even greater scenery to come. Down to the right is Momijidani, or Maple Valley, with a walking path.

Tsuda Yonejirō Monument 津田米次郎の碑

The statue overlooking the valley from the top of a stone stairway is of the inventor of Japan's first automatic weaving machine which replaced foot pedals. Textiles are one of Hokuriku's major industries, so it's not surprising that Mr. Tsuda is thus honored.

Two hairpin turns away, beside Kakurinji temple, is a stone monument dedicated to Shimizu Makoto, the 'Father of the Match.' Whether he invented matches or not is unclear--apparently he was involved in popularizing their use--but the tall, thin monument makes a suitable memorial.

Kakurinji 覚林寺

This temple is notable for its statue of Nichiren, which makes the militant, ambitious priest look like anybody's jolly old uncle. Out front of the temple is a gravestone sales lot, which serves as a reminder of the realities of temple finances.

Tokuda Shūsei Monument 徳田秋声文学碑

Literature buffs make pilgrimages to the memorial to novelist Tokuda Shūsei, behind a souvenir shop at Utatsuyama's first plateau. The inscription on the back of the mud wall quotes from author Kawabata Yasunari, who wrote that Shūsei was one of the three greatest novelists in Japan. On the front, a plaque in Shūsei's hand proclaims the perils of going three days without reading a book. The path behind the monument, with a magnificent view of Kahoku Lagoon and Uchinada Beach, is a popular lovers' lane.

Christian Monument　長崎キリスト殉教者碑

Around the bend past the Tokuda Shūsei Monument, a tiny sign points down the hill to the right. A few minutes' descent leads to the Nagasaki Christian Monument. Its base is built of rocks from the original dungeon here, where 500 Japanese Christians were incarcerated from 1869 to 1873. When the new Meiji government named Shintō the national religion, another wave of religious persecution began in Japan. As many as 3500 Christians in Kyūshū were sent in exile around the country, and a portion of them suffered four lean years on this mountain, before the government relented.

On the other side of the playground, across the arched bridge, are more monuments. The great stone hulks, lined up in rows five deep, memorialize the thousands who donated their bodies over the years to the Kanazawa University medical school. The staff and students hold an annual service for them here at the end of June.

Shiunsan-en　紫雲山苑

Shiunsan-en is a natural Japanese garden, rather wild and unkempt, but decorated with labeled rocks, lanterns and statuary. Fine for a civilized nature walk, it also has two grassy plateaux, which would be good for picnics. The best thing is that it's deserted, even on Sundays. Find it on the right, past the University medical school graveyard.

Kanazawa Sunny Land

When this family amusement complex opened 20 years ago, there is no doubt that it served Hokuriku well, giving parents the chance to watch shows and movies or soak in the enormous bath, while the kids ran around freely, visiting the zoo and the aquarium. But today the difficulties of maintaining the place as a private business show up clearly. The entrance fee (¥2,000) may be beyond the means of budget-minded tourists. 8:00—9:00 daily.

Sumō Stadium and War Monument　相撲場

The circular outdoor amphitheater is mainly used for the National High School Sumō Championships in June, but rock and

Avid fans and energetic wrestlers at the National Sumō Tournament. (Hokkoku Press)

folk concerts are sometimes held here in the summer.

On a rise behind the stadium is a solemn monument to 52 Ishikawa girls who were killed when the Aichi naval plant, where they had gone to work, was bombed on August 7, 1945. Their deaths were particularly tragic because of the date--the war ended a few days later.

Kenmin Park 健民公園

Because it was originally a golf course, this park has the largest expanse of grass in Kanazawa--one of the few places where one feels comfortable running around barefoot. It has beautiful scenery and a play area, planted with trees donated by Kanazawa's Belgian sister city, Ghent. The park gates are open between 9:00 and 7:00 from April to September, and 9:00−5:00, October to March. At the far end is a 'Field Athletics' obstacle course. A complete run through the 38 imaginative trials costs ¥300. Closed

Dec.—March.
Stupa   仏舎利塔

As a good-will gesture, in 1954, Indian Premier Nehru presented Kanazawa with a fragment of Gautama Buddha's bone. Donations were collected, and soon a great stupa was built at the back of Utatsuyama to house the relic. Just as the white dome is visible from all over the area, the view from here is magnificent and makes a suitable hiking destination.

Ningyōkuyō doll ceremony at Kishimōjin. (Oasis)

to Naruwa no Taki
Matsu Mon
Prefectural Budokan
Hasudera
Toyama

Circus

Yonezawa Tei

ano River Bridge

Dr. Nakamura
Genmonji

Renkakuji
Myotaiji

Kōkakuji

Hashimoto Bamboo

Zenshoji

Shinrensha

Fukushima Shamisen

Takagi Koji

Yogetsu

Raikyoji

Geshinji

Shima

Kannon Machi Street

Eastern Pleasure Quarter
(Higashi)

Utatsu Shrine

Renshoji

Kishimojin

Sanboji

Taki no Shiraito Monument

Yama no O

Ryukokuji

Asano River

Seven Jizos Temple

Hosenji

Higashiyama Gobo

Ladies Hotel

Kannon-in

Tenjin Bashi

Rokkakudo

White House

Izumi Kyoka Monument

Miya no Mori

Tsuda Yonejiro Monument

Toyokuni Shrine

Shimizu Makoto Monument

Shigosan-en

Maple Valley

Utatsuyama

Medical School Graveyard

Kakurinji

Playground

Christian Monument

Tokuda Shūsei Monument

Tokiwa Bashi

Goriya

Health Center

Kanazawa YH

HIGASHIYAMA

Sumō Stadium

War Monument

to Kenmin Park
Stupa

Toge Jaya

Field Athletics

HASHIBA-CHŌ 橋場町

When Maeda Toshiie moved here from Nagoya (called Owari in those days), he brought with him many excellent merchants and craftsmen, to insure the prosperity of his new domain. He set them up along the main street of present-day Owari-chō, not far from the castle entrance, and the neighborhood became the commercial center of Edo-period Kanazawa. The area is still heavy on traditional shops, some run by the descendants of the original Owari folk. There are also many antique shops concentrated around here, both the junky kind and first-class businesses catering to wealthy collectors.

Hashiba-chō, along the Asano River, is even older. It was the center of early settlements in the Kaga region. A tall wooden monument to that effect stands across the street from Morihachi cake shop, beside the pedestrian crosswalk. The center of Kanazawa City is now in Katamachi and Kōrinbō, but Hashiba still retains its dignity and riverside grace.

SHOPPING

Morihachi (森 八). Kanazawa's most famous cake shop has a history of over 300 years. Browse and drool over the dry pink and white sugar wafers and the heavy sweet-bean 'Chitose' dumplings. Try a cup of *matcha* green tea and a sweet cake in the tea room to the left. And notice the ancient gate from Izumi Kyōka's birthplace, set into the facade of the modern Morihachi building. Open 9:00–7:30, except the first and third Sun. of the month.

Tsukuda (佃). An unpretentious, but well-known *tsukudani* shop, which sells a delicious cake, called 'Hakuchō,' of walnut *tsukudani,* tucked into walnut-shaped rice wafers. They keep forever and make fine souvenirs. Tsukuda will let you have a taste of any of the other *tsukudani* flavors on sale. 8:30—8:00 daily.

Kamiya Asunaro Craft Shop (かみや). For twenty years, Mr. Kamiya has been carving tiny earrings, unusual jewelry and amusing figurines of Ishikawa's prefectural tree, the *asunaro*. 8:30 —8:00 daily.

Kiguraya (木倉屋). The Kigurayas have been making Yūzen wallets and silk tea-caddy bags for so long, at least 15 generations, that they've lost track of how long they've been in the business. The fascinating shop has rows of antiques on exhibit and garrulous Mr. Kiguraya to show off his skills. 9:00—5:00 daily.

Hosoji Hanko Seal (細 字). Hosoji is the last family of craftsmen which came to Kanazawa from Owari with Lord Toshiie, still working at the same business in the same place. The eleventh Mr. Hosoji still carves chops on the tatami in the front office daily, except Sundays.

Kuroda Incense (黒 田). The Kuroda family has been in business about 400 years. Originally a Maeda-sponsored Chinese medicine dealer, they specialized in Gibamanbyōen, a remedy for palsy and high blood pressure, and Shisetsu, a general pick-me-up, which is still on sale. Their much-admired wooden signboard, carved by the same artist who did the transoms in Seisonkáku, dates from those days. Now its gold leaf is peeling, and the graceful phoenix perched on top looks a little peaked, so the sign is kept inside the shop. Over the years, the Kurodas' business has moved increasingly towards incense, as is evident as soon as you walk in. They mix their own, from plum pits and other fragrant natural materials. Mrs. Kuroda is happy to demonstrate everything—and it needs some explaining. The range of shapes, scents· and burning equipment seems endless. Closed Sun.

Matsuda Calligraphy (松 田). The Matsuda family has been in the calligraphy equipment business for ten generations. They are still making writing brushes and mixing inks by hand in an old-style shop. Closed Sun.

Sōbi Woodcarving (創美). Transoms, trays, saucers and tea caddies from Inami, the famous woodcarving town in Toyama. Sōbi is only a sales outlet. Try Mr. Ishizaki in Teramachi for a look at the carving process. 9:00—6:00, except Thurs.

Inamura Lantern (稲 村). Times are changing fast for old Mrs. Inamura. She and her husband used to make 300 paper umbrellas a month to sell to local hot spring hotels, and lanterns for all kinds of shops were in great demand. Now Mr. Inamura has died, and Gifu Prefecture's cheaper machine-made lanterns have made their hand-measured, cut and pasted product non-competitive. But she keeps the shop open, taking some orders and staying busy. The workplace is there in the front. Visitors may watch or place an order. It takes about a week, and hand-made lanterns begin at ¥10,000.

Ōhi Chōzaemon Pottery (大樋長左衛門). The original, and outrageously priced, tea ceremony pottery made by the 9th Chōzaemon and his son. The pleasant showroom and garden are good for a wistful look, anyway. Open daily.

Chōami Ōhi Pottery (大樋長阿弥). For real shoppers for Ōhi pottery, this place is a better bet. Eighty-two-year-old Chōami and his daughter are at work in the back, and his wife tends to customers. The daughter is experimenting with some new Ōhi pottery colors and designs. 8:00−6:00 daily.

EATING

Tarō (太 郎). A famous *nabe* (stewpot) restaurant, set among geisha houses along the peaceful Asano River. Reasonable *teishoku* set lunches from 11:30−1:30. *Nabe* is served only in the winter, but Tarō is open daily year-round.

Tamura (たむら). Really cheap *yakitori, ramen,* grilled vegetables and fish (try the little ones in the aquarium). Open 5:00 p.m.− 4:00 a.m., except Sun.

VISITING

Kuboichi Ototsurugi Shrine 久保市乙剣神社

Although the Chinese characters have long since changed, this shrine was named for the Kubo Ichi market, Kanazawa's first, which existed here in the 14th century. Hashiba-chō was the center of civilization in these parts, and the Kubo Ichi Shrine was the guardian of its heart, the marketplace.

More recently, this shrine has taken on a new claim to fame as the site of a monument to Izumi Kyōka (1873−1939), the novelist, who was raised nearby. If Saigawa is associated with Murō Saisei, the Asano River is Kyōka's. He played on its banks and in the grounds of this shrine and frequently drew on these memories for his stories' themes. At the right through the *torii* gate, stands a monument engraved with his words, *Utsukushiya uguisu ake no myōjō ni,* 'The exquisite nightingale at the morning star.'

Kazoemachi 旧主計町

The riverside road to the left, before the Ōhashi bridge, is lined

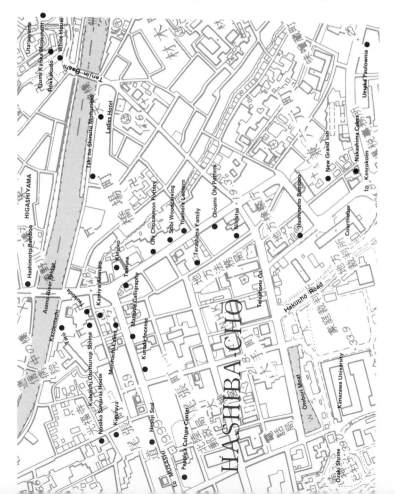

with cherry trees and old geisha houses. The *chaya* can be distinguished by the discreet white signs, brushed with a few black characters giving their poetic names. This is Kanazawa's third geisha district, after Higashi and Nishi.

Taki no Shiraito Monument　滝の白糸碑

Because Tenjin Bashi bridge is the stage for the meeting of two lovers in Izumi Kyōka's romantic novel, *Giketsu Kyōketsu,* a memorial stone has been erected nearby. Shiraito, a traveling magician, fell in love with a young man on the road between Takaoka and Kanazawa. In later years, when she was unjustly charged with a murder, the presiding judge turned out to be her former lover. Although not much read these days, the novel is set in the Meiji era, written in a style typical of the Taishō and a classic of modern Japanese literature.

Terashima Family House　寺島応養邸

Although there are several middle-level samurai houses remaining in Kanazawa, Terashima is the only one open for public tour. What makes a visit particularly worthwhile is the fine explanation given by the 16th generation Mr. Terashima, a retired school teacher. (The details are available in an excellent English pamphlet.) His ancestors came to Kanazawa at the time of the fourth Maeda lord and took up the life of a 450-*koku*-a-year samurai in a neighborhood not far from the castle. But it was the 12th Terashima, Ōyō (1776–1837), who made a name for himself in Kaga history. An artist and intellectual, Ōyō dared criticise the feudal government for its policies during the years of famine. Furthermore, he questioned the government's anti-foreign, isolationist stance. As a result, Ōyō was banished to Noto Island, where he soon died. Three generations later, in the Meiji period, he was officially forgiven by the 15th Maeda lord, who recognized his honor and brilliance.

Architecturally, the Terashima house is noted for its slate roof, in a city of tiles. Mr. Terashima also points out the lack of corridors (to discourage attackers) and of a *tokonoma* pillar (to provide space for unavoidable sword fights). For 300 yen, you can enjoy a cup of tea and cakes in the peaceful, five-mat tea room (no swords allowed) and view the garden, designed by Ōyō about 150 years ago. Open 9:00–5:00, except Thurs. ¥200.

CENTRAL 中央地区

SHOPPING

Nakaya Medicine Co. (中 屋). After a long night of drinking in Katamachi or wolfing down *yakitori* and *oden,* you may be ready for some medical advice. Drop into Nakaya, describe your problem, and they'll give you something suitable from their nine unique remedies. Most famous is Kongentan, a natural drug which is made of plants and herbs, like ginseng, plum blossom and Chinese bellflower, and which is said to cure just about anything. If so, it's a bargain at ¥1,150 for 36 packages of tiny red pills, a 12-day supply. Nakaya has been in business for 400 years, selling Chinese medicines and others devised by their own ancestors. The business began to flourish when the fifth Maeda lord lent his support to various scholarly researches, including medicine. Nakaya prepared concoctions for the use of the castle, and slowly their products spread to national fame.

The building itself dates from late Edo period and remains a fine example of local architecture. The Meiji Emperor stayed here in 1879, in a gold leaf-paneled room in the house behind the gate to the right of the shop. The tall stone monument at the right calls attention to the celebrated event, but unfortunately, the room is not open to visitors. Why didn't the Emperor stay at the castle? Meiji Restoration politics is the answer--reformist Meiji ministers were not on the best of terms with the traditional Maeda family. 8:30—6:00, except Sun.

Chōraku Ōhi Pottery (大樋長楽). Chōraku offers the famous brown tea ceremony pottery, mainly vases, bowls and tea caddies, at reasonable prices. 8:30—8:30 daily.

Nakashima Cakes (中 島). Nakashima's delicious, sugary Setsugetsuka, made of walnuts and white beans, will keep about a month. 9:00—7:00, except alternating Sun. and Mon.

Hashimoto Bamboo Craft (橋 本). While customers putter around among the vases and boxes on display, Mr. Hashimoto serenely keeps busy on his worn-out cushion, cutting, weaving and polishing bamboo. He won't make things for order. All his work comes from his own creative ideas. Look in the cases, unwrap or unbox some of his masterpieces, and sigh--the prices reflect the time and experience that went into them.

Uesaka Paulownia (上 坂). The best selection in town of this local woodcraft, including *hibachi,* coffee cups, vases, ashtrays and cake dishes. 9:00—6:00, except Sun.

Kankō Bussankan (観光物産館). A complete sampling of all Kanazawa's products, arts, crafts and food, in a modern, convenient building. 9:00—6 00 daily. (See p.152.)

EATING

Iketen (いけ天). Known as the best tempura shop in town. Daily 'set course' runs around ¥2,500. Small, friendly shop run by the Ikeda family for the last 33 years. Evenings only, irregular holidays.

Nakaya Medicine Co.stands as it has for centuries. (H.Ikeuchi)

Akiyoshi (秋吉). *Yakitori* chain known for its thick sauce and low prices (¥40 a stick). Noisy and cheerful. 5:00–12:00, except Sun.

Ōtomorō (大友楼). The last Maeda clan-sponsored family of cooks still in the business. They specialize, of course, in Kaga dinners, from ¥4,000 a person, served at their lovely old restaurant. Reservations are necessary at noon or evening. Tel. 21–0305.

Miyoshian (三芳庵). Miyoshian has been in business inside Kenrokuen for 100 years. A reasonable *bentō* lunchbox sample of their excellent Kaga cooking is available for ¥1,000. Closed Tues.

Takanoha (鷹の羽). On the second floor of Kankō Bussankan. A variety of set meals including Kaga dishes, from ¥1,300–3,000. 10:00–9:00 daily.

VISITING

★ Prefectural History Museum   県立郷土資料館

This Meiji-era red brick building was originally the schoolhouse of Shikō, the national Fourth Higher School. Cool, stone-tiled corridors and high, panelled walls strike a nostalgic note, and we marvel that such a building was created in 1891, only 28 years after the battling-samurai, isolationist days of Edo period ended. The building has been preserved as a museum since 1968, with a permanent exhibition of local history, from potshards to Occupation-era English newspapers. Some of the most appealing exhibits include a pre-erosion chart of Noto peninsula, several *haniwa* figurines and a relief map of Edo-period Kanazawa, with pushbutton lights to show the locations of Carpenters Town, the Matsu Mon entryway to the city, Falconers Town and the Honda family's vast holdings. Other vivid displays are the scale model of the colorful, tri-annual daimyō procession to Edo, and a morbid chart of local disasters, with the casualty lists and the number of houses destroyed. There are also three special exhibitions a year. An airy, well-organized museum, it's a bargain at ¥100. 9:00–4:00, except Mon.

Out front are some old stones from the Tatsumi Yōsui waterway, with the joints, originally set with pine pitch, clearly visible. There are also some Shikō memorabilia, a bust of the first head-

master and a monument engraved with the school song. A large percentage of Kanazawa's elite attended Shikō; loyalty and fond feeling for the old school pervade the town.

Central Park 中央公園

Spacious, green Central Park is so accessible and pleasant that it seems to have been here forever. But on the site where now frisbee players frolic and families stroll, once stood the home of tragic Ōtsuki Denzō, the Edo-period genius who was too bright for his own good. At the height of his favor with Lord Yoshinori, Denzō was invited to live right beside the castle. But the lord was powerless to stop the vicious slander by envious samurai, which toppled Denzō from his position as valued economic advisor, and resulted in his banishment.

In Meiji period, Central Park was the campus of Shikō, the famous Fourth Higher School. Shikō developed as a direct descendent of the Maeda clan's school, an unusually far-sighted institution, which had added a 'foreign learning' department in the first year of Meiji. In Shikō's 62 years of existence, more than 20 foreign teachers introduced English, Christianity and western technology to the youth of Kanazawa.

Along the Prefectural Office side of Central Park runs a line of trees, each identified by a small sign. These are the official trees of 15 of Japan's prefectures, presented to Ishikawa.

Prefectural Office 石川県庁

This cavernous office building is worth a visit, if only to pick up some of the color posters of the city and Ishikawa Prefecture available at the Tourism Section (Kankō Bussanka, on the right rear of the third floor). But notice the typical Taishō-era architecture of the monstrosity on your way up. The art deco touches are almost in fashion again. It was built in 1924. Out front are two great pasania trees, said to be 300 years old and moved here from poor Ōtsuki Denzō's mansion in Central Park.

Modern Literature Museum 石川近代文学館

This museum is to be recommended on a rainy (or, more likely in Kanazawa, snowy) afternoon. One of the city's greatest sources of pride is the profusion of poets and novelists born here between the Meiji period and World War II. Many are nationally famous, and although now somewhat old-fashioned and difficult to read, local interest in them remains high. Some of the better known works are available in English translation (See 'Before You Come'), and a few can be rented to read here for another ¥200. Punctuate your cosy read on the third floor with a look around the museum's fine exhibition of materials on notable native sons. The emphasis is on the three greats: Murō Saisei, Tokuda Shūsei and Izumi Kyōka. Several cases of memorabilia, manuscripts and photos are also devoted to architect Taniguchi Yoshirō and others. A replica of Saisei's beloved Karuizawa garden is on the second floor. The cubic, tree-shaded building was the library storeroom of Shikō, as evidenced by the leftover book-elevator pole. This is reputed to be the best local museum of its kind in Japan. 9:30—4:30, except Mon. ¥200.

★ **Oyama Shrine** 尾山神社

The magnificent, three-story gate of this shrine, with its stained glass window and layered *tomuro* stone construction, symbolizes an early European presence in Kanazawa, and gives a Continental touch to the city skyline. The tower was built in 1875, 8 years into the Meiji period, with the help of some Dutch instructors at the medical school. Rumors that the stained glass itself was smuggled in during the late Edo period by progressive, but nevertheless outlawed, traders cannot be confirmed, but such stories lend further romance to the tales of Kanazawa's role in Meiji Japan. The tower originally served as a lighthouse, but these days, it is surrounded by tall buildings and is no longer visible from the sea.

Oyama Shrine is dedicated to Lord Maeda Toshiie. It was built in 1873 on the site of the Maeda villa, Kanaya Goten. Parts of the villa were used in the shrine's construction, including the ornate ceiling, leafed in gold and painted with the imaginary Indian flowers *udonge,* or plantain, which only bloom once in 3000 years. Fifteen years ago, the shrine was expanded to the left to make space for the booming wedding business (as many as 16 ceremonies are squeezed in on an auspicious Sunday in the spring). Rather than cut down a majestic *toge* tree (hemlock spruce), however, shrine officials decided to build around it--the tree stands now in the center of the corridor. Visitors who inquire at the office may be shown around the inside halls, the grounds and possibly up into the tower itself. (Say, *'Annai shite itadakemasenka?'*)

The garden, also preserved from Kanaya Goten, is designed on a musical theme. The somewhat oversized signs indicate the *biwa* (lute) shaped island, the koto bridge, and the *shō* (panpipe) stretch of rock. The garden is best in the snow or during May, when the wisteria is in bloom.

To the left of the garden stands the East Gate, which is one of the few structures salvaged from the fires which destroyed Kanazawa Castle. The carvings under the gate's roof represent two dragons, which were not doing their job--dragons are supposed to have the power to provide water when fire threatens.

Other points of interest are the noh stage, now unfortunately out of use, and the hillock to the right where pre-war priests used to pray in the direction of the Grand Shrines of Ise. Oyama Shrine is popular with both Kanazawa citizens and tourists, so it is never deserted, but the most lively times are New Year's, Shintō-related holidays and the Hyakumangoku Festival in June, when outdoor flower exhibitions and tea ceremonies are held here.

Jinuemon Slope　甚右衛門坂

The quiet castle entrance just to the right of Ozaki Shrine is known as Jinuemon Slope, in honor of the brave warrior Hirano Jinuemon who died here in 1580. Jinuemon was a masterless *rōnin* in the temporary but honorable employ of the Ikkō-shū religious fanatics who were occupying Oyama Gobō (later to become Kanazawa Castle and now Kanazawa University). The legend of Jinuemon was created during the fierce, and ultimately successful, attack by Sakuma Morimasa. As Sakuma's troops pressed closer and closer, the Ikkō-shū peasants were forced to retreat to the slopes of the temple itself. Jinuemon fought for hours, single-handedly defending his small patch of hillside as warrior after warrior attacked. But eventually, enemy arrows bristling from his body, he succumbed, Kanazawa's own Horatius at the Bridge.

Ozaki Shrine 尾崎神社

Ozaki Shrine, lying just outside the castle walls, is known as a miniature replica of Tōshōgū in Nikkō. Unfortunately, it is now run down, the red paint is peeling and the grounds are used as a parking lot. Those who visit Ozaki with visions of Nikkō's splendor will be disappointed. Ozaki Shrine's fascination lies instead in the lessons to be learned from its history.

For much of the Edo period, the Maedas ruled over the most prosperous fief in Japan. Although political power was centered firmly around the Tokugawas in Edo, provincial economic strength could be interpreted as a threat. The Maedas constantly felt the need to demonstrate their loyalty to Edo. What better way than to spend some of their resources on a shrine dedicated to Ieyasu, the founder of the Tokugawa Shōgunate? The fourth Maeda, Lord Mitsutaka, called skilled carpenters and craftsmen from Edo and built this Tōshōgū in 1642. The cleverest scheme of all was his choice of a site: the north section of the castle grounds, near a particularly vulnerable gate. If the Tokugawas ever were to attack, they'd think twice before violating a shrine dedicated to their patriarch.

In the early Meiji period, the shrine was moved to its present site, just on the other side of the castle wall. Perhaps its deterioration since then is symbolic of the shallowness of Kanazawa's early, fair-weather allegiance to Edo.

Ōtebori Moat 大手堀

In its heyday, Kanazawa Castle was surrounded by two protective moats, fed from the upper reaches of Saigawa river through the Tatsumi Yōsui canal. The outer moat has been converted to everyday use in the form of regular *yōsui*, the waterways which flow through town. But, with a little imagination, the inner moat is still recognizable. One section, Ōtebori, has been preserved as is, and, lined with cherry trees, it is now a sleepy fishing spot, popular with little boys. The rest of the inner moat circled the castle via what are now the shady Hakuchō (Swan) Road behind the Courthouse, and the Hyakkenbori main street running between Ishikawa Gate and Kenrokuen park. It continued on around to the right, through the present-day Kenrokuen tennis courts and the roads surrounding Oyama Shrine.

Kankō Bussankan 石川県観光物産館

A fine one-stop building for an instant, if somewhat sterile, shopping and crafts tour of Kanazawa has been built near Kenrokuen by a shopkeepers' association. Every possible 'famous product' is available in the basement and first floor sales area (9:00−6:00). Restaurants and a Japanese tea shop are open on the second floor from 10:00−9:00. And on the third floor, visitors may watch, for a ¥200 entrance fee, artisans crafting lacquer, Kutani pottery, Kaga Yūzen silk, gold leaf, tea cakes, paulownia wood--each of the major local specialities. An English pamphlet is available. Open daily.

Gyokusen-en Garden 玉泉園

Although Kenrokuen is Kanazawa's most famous tourist attraction, many true garden enthusiasts prefer Gyokusen-en, the gently terraced stroll-garden of the Nishida family. Gyokusen-en 'borrows' next-door Kenrokuen's expanse of greenery as a backdrop, but retains the intimacy of a small-scale private garden. Ask for the English pamphlet. Don't be put off by the ¥350 entrance fee--it's worth it. Open 9:00−4:00 daily, except in winter, around mid-December to early March. Tea and cakes are served between 9:30 and 3:30 for another ¥300.

★ Kanazawa Castle and Ishikawa Gate 金沢城と石川門

This strategic spot is the central focus of Kanazawa City. In the days when the Kaga region was ruled by militant Buddhists, their temple-fortress was here. At the height of the Edo period, political and cultural influence emanated from the Maedas' castle. Its grandeur was surpassed only by the Tokugawa fortresses at Edo and Ōsaka. And today, when Kanazawa's self-image is of an educational center, the national university's main campus occupies this coveted position.

Little remains of the Oyama Gobō temple--perhaps a few mossy stones scattered around the science department's botanical garden. But the castle is very much in evidence--the massive stone walls, gate, armory and moat. The first Maeda, Lord Toshiie, began building the castle in 1583, when he took over Kaga from Sakuma

Morimasa. Successive Maeda lords made improvements, despite periodic fires, and as peace and prosperity continued, they devoted increasing consideration to the aesthetics of the spot. But the Maedas were a warrior family, and conscious of the importance of military precautions. The attractive white tiles on the roof of Ishikawa Gate, for example, are actually made of lead, ready to be melted into ammunition in an emergency. And the attractive windows protruding from the castle wall are designed for dropping boulders on approaching enemies.

The castle's last fire, after which it was never rebuilt, was in 1881. Army barracks occupied the space until World War II, and the university was established in 1950. The university architects made efforts to keep the school buildings in harmony with the castle atmosphere. The 'Thirty Compartment Armory' is preserved as a library storehouse. The classroom buildings are decorated with

Hyakkenbori moat, then and now.
(Prefectural History Museum)

the distinctive, gray *namako* stone tiles, which were also used in the interior castle walls and are now found around Seisonkaku villa. The height of all structures has been limited, to preserve the castle's original skyline. But this last consideration has finally spelled doom for the whole set-up. The university cannot expand, and the decision has been made recently to move eventually to the suburbs.

Ishikawa Gate, which now symbolizes Kanazawa Castle and the city itself, was originally merely a rear gate to the grounds. And even such a monolithic, impregnable-looking structure is vulnerable to fire--it burned to the ground in the mid-1700's and was rebuilt in 1788.

The central location of the castle encourages visitors. Kanazawa citizens pass through on their way across town, and students stroll around the botanical gardens and along the paths among the stone walls. Despite a small sign to the contrary, tourists may wander through, inspecting the progressive series of fortified rises, and examining the stonecutters' hieroglyphs on the *tomuro* rocks.

★ Prefectural Art Museum 石川県美術館

The new art museum is a fine example of the prefecture's long-term plans for the cultural development of the area around Kenrokuen. The permanent collection, housed on the second floor, offers works by contemporary artists who are connected in some way with Ishikawa. Oils, sculpture, Japanese painting, and traditional crafts each have a room, as does the distinctive pheasant-shaped incense burner, a National Treasure, made by the Kyōto potter Ninsei. The pride of the museum is its collection of Ko-Kutani, which is unrivaled anywhere in the world. All displays are changed monthly, and the second floor entrance fee is ¥300.

Traveling exhibitions and other temporary shows are displayed on the ground floor, and entrance fees vary. Several parts of the museum, including the coffee shop, may be entered freely. A small library offers books on Western and Japanese artists, and exhibits may be previewed on the videotapes prepared by the museum staff.

The museum closes while exhibits are being changed, so a call (tel. 31−7580) is recommended. 9:30−4:30.

★ Kenrokuen 兼六園

Famous places are categorized all over Japan, be they Eight Views or Forty-four Temples, and parks are no exception. Kenrokuen falls into the Three Gardens classification (along with Okayama's Kōrakuen and Mito's Kairakuen), and has become Kanazawa's best-known tourist attraction. Thousands of tourists pour into the park every day. Groups sweep through to the tune of their guide's loudspeaker, and individuals mosey along, nose in a guidebook.

Foreigners are more likely to favor a leisurely inspection of the park. Perhaps the best approach is to divide your visit into two stages. First, just wander around, exploring dark grottoes and enjoying broad vistas, noticing the shapes of the trees, streams and rocks, and giving free rein to adventure and imagination. Then, perhaps on a second visit, tackle the park systematically, considering the historical significance of that mound or the romantic tale behind this tree.

According to Mr. Shinkura Tadashi, the master of Miyoshian restaurant and resident expert on Kenrokuen, eight hours are necessary for an explanatory tour of the park's famous rocks, and a description of only the most notable of the 11,800 trees takes at least one and a half hours. This guide is limited to a few details about the major attractions. Those with further curiosity should petition Mr. Shinkura directly.

First a historical note is appropriate. Because of its proximity to the castle, Kenrokuen was an outer garden used by the early Maeda lords to lodge visitors. It wasn't until the time of the fifth lord, Tsunanori, in the 1670's, that work began on creating a spacious stroll-garden to surround his pleasure villa on the crest of the ridge. Work continued slowly, hampered variously by a fire in 1759 and perhaps a general policy of austerity, until the early 1800's when the 12th lord, Narinaga, and 13th lord, Nariyasu, completed the park. They bestowed on it a name from a famous Chinese garden of the Sung Dynasty. Kenrokuen means Combined Six, referring to the park's ideal size, seclusion, artificiality, antiquity, fresh water and views. In 1872, Kenrokuen became public property, operated by the prefecture, and in 1922 it was designated a national 'Famous Spot.'

In 1975, despite the protests of Kanazawa citizens, many of whom enjoyed a stroll through the park on their way to work or school, the prefectural assembly closed most of the park gates and instituted an entrance fee system. The ostensible reason was to cut down the number of tourists and repair long-neglected damage. Curiously enough, the number of visitors actually increased after new system was put into effect. But considering that it costs 166 million yen annually to keep up the park (each tree is groomed twice a year--and imagine keeping 100,000 square meters of moss and gravel swept), it's hard to complain.

Everyone has a favorite season for visiting Kenrokuen, and certainly each season has its unique beauty. Flowers are always in bloom--even in winter the plum trees blossom, and the leafless trees are decorated with *yuki-tsuri* supports. Each branch is tied with a straw rope from a central pole, creating a striking picture of pale yellow umbrella-like shapes against the gray skies and white snow. Some Kenrokuen lovers even feel that a rainy day, when the moss glistens and the stones become smooth, enhances their enjoyment.

A 19th century artist's view of Hisago Pond. (Kenrokuen Office ;
Prefectural History Museum)

The peak visiting hours at Kenrokuen are between 11:00 and 1:00. A mob of school children or a bus guide's portable amplifier goes a long way toward diminishing one's appreciation of the park's beauty. For visitors with flexible schedules, early in the morning or late in the afternoon are times to be recommended.

People who are really flexible, that is, who can make it out of bed before dawn, can join the Hayaoki-kai. This is a group of early risers, mainly elderly gentlemen, who get together every day to watch the sunrise. They gather at Kanazawa Shrine at around 4:00 a.m. in summers and 7:00 a.m. in winters to drink tea and chat. All are experts on Kenrokuen, and at least one of them, Mr. Baba, speaks English.

The park is open 6:30 to 6:00, except Nov.–March, 8:00–4:30. The gate between Seisonkaku and Kanazawa Shrine is opened much earlier. Entrance fee is ¥100.

1. Higurashi no Hashi--Day Spending Bridge 日暮橋

This unusual bridge is made of *tomuro* stones, the long-lasting, highly valued rocks dug from Tomuro Mountain out by Iōzan. (Kanazawa Castle walls are made from *tomuro,* which are also common as gravestones of high-ranking samurai and lords.) The top of Higurashi Bridge is the blue type *tomuro* stone, and underneath is the red type. The stones are laid out in a diamond pattern and held together with pine pitch. The name signifies that a person can spend a whole day there without finding it tiresome.

2. Midori Taki--Green Waterfall 翠滝

   Hisago Ike--Gourd Lake 瓢池

The scenery around gourd-shaped Hisago Lake was designed with colorful maples, each one of a different variety, to remind the viewer of the Takao and Arashiyama areas of Kyōto.

The Midori Waterfall is famous more for its sound than for its visual beauty. Over the years, the position of the rocks has been adjusted six times by various lords to create a perfectly pleasing splash. Whenever arranged just right, the waterfall-viewing window in Yūgaotei tea house would be closed, and those inside would enjoy their tea in the dark, with the falls supplying background music instead of setting the mood with a pretty picture.

Although Kanazawa is overcast and wet most of the winter, the temperature rarely falls very low. Midori Waterfall freezes to a stop only once in about ten years.

3. Kaisekitō--Korean Lantern 海石塔

The six stone pagoda-like roofs of this lantern are said to have been brought back by Toyotomi Hideyoshi from his abortive Korean campaigns in the late 16th century. Hideyoshi presented the lantern to Lord Maeda Toshiie.

4. Shidare Zakura--Weeping Cherry 枝垂桜

In mid-April, the Weeping Cherry beside the Korean Lantern begins to bloom at the uppermost branches. It then takes fully eight days for the blossoms to reach the low-hanging tips. It is one of the more famous of the 50 or so kinds of cherry trees in

1. Forever-intwined Married Pines. (H.Ikeuchi)
2. The Seven Gods of Fortune watch over Kenrokuen.
   (H.Ikeuchi)
3. Yugaotei teahouse. (Oasis)
4. Imohori Tōgorō's legendary sacred well. (H.Ikeuchi)
5. Raised Root Pine

Kenrokuen.

5. Yūgaotei--Moonflower Pavilion 夕顔亭

Yūgaotei is the epitome of a Japanese tea house--designed to look like a humble peasant dwelling, it is actually a masterful design of rigid refinement. Notice that under the two roofs there are actually three rooms, and see if you can find all seven entrances. Their use, as well as that of the hand basins, was strictly prescribed, for example, one basin (the massive round one) was for the lord only. For his wife and children was the lower bamboo root-looking basin to the right, said to be petrified bamboo brought from Thailand by Edo-period smuggler Zeniya Gohei. The paper window in the front room is designed for a clear view of the waterfall. Yūgaotei was built in 1774 in accordance with the taste of the great tea master, Kobori Enshū.

6. Miyoshian Restaurant 三芳庵

Excellent Kaga cooking is served in Miyoshian, the small restaurant with a wisteria-shaded view of Gourd Lake and the waterfall. Reservations are necessary for such a special treat; tea ceremony groups are the most frequent guests. But a less expensive sample can be had at the Miyoshian branch behind Yūgaotei. Try a cup of green tea and a cake or a *bentō* lunchbox and examine the unusual souvenirs on sale.

7. Renchimon--Lotus Pond Gate 蓮池門

All that's left of the castle's equestrian training fields is the wide staircase which served as a kind of front gate to Kenrokuen. When horses presented to the lord by the shōgun were displayed for the first time, they would be paraded several abreast up these stairs. Young samurai also practiced their horsemanship by riding up and down.

Renchimon was only one of the 35 gates built by the fifth lord, Tsunanori. Only its steps remain. Stand at the top, with the traffic just out of sight, and you can imagine the great moat that lay between the castle and garden.

8. Furō Zaka--Longevity Slope 不老坂

At the base of wisteria-shaded Furō Zaka stands a row of tea shops which now offer mainly souvenirs. When the Tokugawa daughter Tama-hime came to Kanazawa at the age of three to marry the third lord, Toshitsune, her retainers and nursemaids were housed here. It was then known as Edo Machi. During cherry blossom season, the shops specialize in delicious 'flower-viewing' rice cakes (*hanami dango*).

The area just behind the first few shops was originally a terrace of 66 tiny rice paddies used as an agricultural experimental station. Seed-rice samples from all over Japan were planted separately, and the seedlings most suited to local soil were distributed to the peasants.

9. Funsui--Fountain　噴水

This is Japan's first fountain, built 120 years ago as part of the Tatsumi Yōsui system channeling water from the upper reaches of the Saigawa river into the city. Passing through 10 kilometers of streams and tunnels, the water arrived at the top of Kenrokuen. It flowed down through the park in several streams, emptying into the outer moat. At the bottom of the park, just down the slope beside the Kotoji Lantern, a syphon device lifted the water up through the inner moat and into the castle itself. The height of the fountain's spurt depends on the amount of water in the mountains. No mechanics, only natural pressure causes the short, fat burble or a graceful, three-pronged stream. The fountain shoots its highest in the June rainy season.

10. Kōmon Bashi--Yellow Gate Bridge　黄門橋

　Shishi Iwa--Lion Rock　獅子岩

This six-meter-long curved bridge is made of one piece of blue *tomuro* stone. Notice that the bridge rests on the corner of the supporting platform, rather than the middle--a typical expression of Japanese feeling for the beauty of dissymmetry. The surroundings suggest a mountain path, with dark, heavy growth. The narrow stream and rocks are imitative of the upper reaches of Tedori River. One of these rocks, in the shape of *shishi,* the fanciful Chinese lion, is just visible from the middle of the bridge. Until 1964's disastrous typhoon felled several great trees, this bridge was never struck by sunlight.

11. Tokiwa ga Oka--Evergreen Hill　常盤が丘

This mound to the left of the fountain is known as a splendid moon-viewing spot. Tea and haiku parties were enjoyed here by lords and ladies of the castle on the night of *meigetsu,* September's full moon.

12. Sakura ga Oka--Cherry Hill 桜が丘

There are 38 cherry trees on this ridge behind the Edo Machi souvenir shops. Most bloom in April, when Kenrokuen is open to everyone free of charge, and people stream in morning and night for revelry under the fluffy blossoms. The Edo-period lords enjoyed the unusual cherry varieties in a more dignified manner. Dressed in special flower-viewing kimono, they surrounded themselves with cultured attendants, to compose haiku poetry and sample seasonal delicacies.

13. Tora Ishi--Tiger Rock 虎石

The shape of this rock nestled into the base of a tree is reminiscent of a crouching tiger. Along with Lion Rock and Dragon Rock, it was brought here from Noto Peninsula.

14. Kasumi ga Ike--Misty Lake 霞が池

At the edge of Kasumi ga Ike is Kenrokuen's most famous landmark, the two-pronged Kotoji Lantern, which Kanazawa has taken for its city symbol. Perhaps when standing on the koto-shaped bridge, gazing at the lantern which looks like a koto string's fret, the lords and ladies could hear koto melodies in the water flowing below. The bridge is a single five-meter slab of red *tomuro* stone, this one particularly treasured for its deep red color after a rain.

The ridge at the left of the lake is known for its view of the three provinces of old, Noto's flat curve extending out into the Japan Sea to the left, Mt. Tateyama in Etchū (Toyama Prefecture) to the right, and Kaga in between.

Kasumi ga Ike was designed with eight special viewing points in mind, each recalling one of the nationally famous Eight Views of Lake Biwa. Across the pond is Uchihashitei tea house, which is now too fragile for use.

15. Hōraijima--Tortoise Shell Island 蓬莱島

In the center of Kasumi ga Ike is a small island resembling a fat turtle, with a rock for its head and a lantern for its tail. For a time, the island served as the resting place for a flock of swans which graced the lake. When they died of natural causes, however, there was no effort made to replace them. It was agreed that foreign birds were somehow incompatible with a pure Japanese garden.

16. Karasaki Pine 唐崎の松

This tree, greatly admired for its sprawling branches, was

planted by the 13th lord, Nariyasu, with a seed from the shores of Lake Biwa. It's especially beautiful when supported by a snow umbrella in winter.

17. Hime Komatsu--Princess Pine　姫小松

　　　Asahi Zakura--Rising Sun Cherry　旭桜

Poor crippled Princess Pine formerly had six major branches, but recent typhoons have reduced her to a single shoot, propped up by three logs. In this century, two major typhoons have destroyed many of Kenrokuen's greatest trees. There is, however, the one small consolation that the way a tree falls in a storm tells much about the garden's history. Original growth and later transplants will topple over differently.

Asahi Zakura, the park's oldest cherry tree, is lovely in any season. After it blossoms in the spring, the green leaves slowly change to a pale yellow. And even when they fall, the naked shape of the branches seen against the snow makes a compelling picture. It was planted from a Mt. Hakusan cherry seed and is famous among cherry specialists for the long stamen of its flower.

18. Karigane Bashi--Flying Geese Bridge　雁行橋

Another of Kenrokuen's famous landmarks, this bridge is made of 11 tortoise-shaped red *tomuro* stones, appealingly laid out to look like geese flying in formation. This combination of two symbols of longevity is said to ensure the long life of those who pass over the stepping stones. But we are now denied the chance, for the bridge itself is suffering from old age.

19. Koshi no Ishi--Carriage Block　輿の石

The two low rectangular stones near Karigane Bridge serve as reminders of the decadent aspects of Edo-period castle life. Residents of Seisonkaku Villa at the other side of the park would board a palanquin and be carried to these rocks. Here they would alight, slip on their zōri sandals and take a stroll around the garden before returning home in like fashion.

20. Takezawa Goten--Takezawa Villa　竹沢御殿

In the clearing across from Karigane Bridge there once stood a great mansion called Takezawa Goten. It was built in 1819 by the 12th lord, Narinaga, and constituted the height of Kenrokuen's opulence. From the second story rooms the lord and his entourage enjoyed views of Mt. Hakusan to the south, the Japan Sea and

Noto Peninsula over the entryway, and Mt. Tateyama out front. Unfortunately, when Lord Narinaga died in 1824, his luxurious plaything was dismantled by order of the disapproving Tokugawas.

The site of the lord's bedroom is now occupied by two ancient statues of *jizō* deities in their own tiny house. At the *jizō*'s right front stands the famous Otowa Pine (乙葉松) which was originally a tiny bonsai and the prized possession of Lord Nariyasu. Although now fully grown, it still retains the distinctive bonsai shape.

21. Shichi Fukujin Yama--Seven Lucky Gods 七福神山

Tucked in among the azalea bushes on this slope are seven stones of odd, but natural, shape. Each represents one of the Seven Gods of Fortune. See if you can pick out fat Ebisu with a fish slung over his shoulder or gracious Benten whose flowing robes and lute are an inspiration to artists and musicians.

22. Shiogama Zakura--Salt Pot Cherry 塩釜桜
   Kumagaya Zakura--Bear Valley Cherry 熊谷桜

In the vicinity of the *jizō* house are two famous cherry trees. The Shiogama Zakura in the back was presented 300 years ago by Date Masamune, the lord of Sendai. The tree is highly valued for its thick eight-layered blossoms, which come out ten days after the other cherries in the park have bloomed—a delightful postlude to the season.

The Kumagaya Zakura also blooms a week later than the rest and is known for the deep red color and peony-like shape of the petal clusters. This tree was the gift of the lord of Mito.

The beauty of the cherry season inspires joy and revelry, but its brevity causes regret. Haiku poets compose verses about impermanence and mortality, and party-goers nurse a week's worth of hangovers. Such late-blooming trees as these provide a respite from the sadness and an extension of the pleasures of flower-viewing.

23. Kenrokuen Kiku Zakura-- Chrysanthemum Cherry 菊桜

Cherry aficionados generally agree that this is the most gorgeous tree in Kenrokuen. As it blooms—about one month later than the others—the flowers change color from red, to greenish and then pink. At its peak, each blossom holds some 340 petals; on a windy day they fall like snow flurries. Kenrokuen Kiku Zakura is the second generation of a tree brought here 300 years ago from the Imperial Palace in Kyōto.

日本武尊の銅像

24. Yamato Takeru no Mikoto--Prince Yamato Takeru's Statue

This striking copper monument is in the likeness of Yamato Takeru, the legendary fourth-century prince who bravely conquered barbarian tribes in the south only to die tragically young, lonely and misunderstood. Such appealing heroes are still the subject of TV dramas and cartoon epics today. And the die-hard Kyūshū samurai who clamored for the invasion of Korea in the 1870's are thought of in this way--as the classic 'noble failure.' This statue is dedicated to them.

Built here in 1880, the figure itself is notable as the first outdoor statue erected in Japan. The base is made of natural stones, cleverly layered to rest without any concrete adhesive--fortunately Kanazawa is not an area prone to earthquakes.

25. Neagari no Matsu--Raised Root Pine 根上松

This unusual pine showing more than 40 roots looks as though it's about to rise off the ground and fly.

26. Hanami Bashi--Flower Viewing Bridge 花見橋

In May and June, anyone standing on this bridge can be a successful picture postcard photographer. The bright purple iris plants, nestled in their green stalks and lining both sides of the stream, are reflected in the clear waters which flow between them--a scene so perfect that one gladly pays the entrance fee day after day for a glimpse.

27. Sekirei Jima--Wagtail Island せきれい島

Sekirei Island is named for the small bird in the Japanese creation myth who taught the first god and goddess, Izanagi and Iganami, how to make a child. The island is dedicated to fertility and decorated with discreetly symbolic rocks. The 'male' rock is inscribed with a poem declaring that men's and women's shapes have been thus since Izanami's time and will always be so. If these rocks symbolize birth, then the two slender pine trees suggest marriage, and the lantern of five tiers, a typical gravestone shape, represents death.

28. Ryūseki--Dragon Rock 龍石

On the corner of the path beside Sekirei Jima is the third of Kenrokuen's animal rocks, a Chinese dragon which somehow looks more like a mossy frog. It acts as a charm against evil spirits.

29. Yamazaki Hill 山崎山

This small rise in the eastern corner of Kenrokuen is especially pleasant in autumn. Stroll up to the resthouse on the summit for a view of the pink and orange maples which set off the deep green moss and pine background. The water flowing from the cave is channeled from the Tatsumi Yōsui canal and runs all the way through the park to the castle side.

Yamazaki Hill is famous as the site of the *himuro* icehouse, which is now a small pond behind the hill. In the Edo period, winter ice was placed in a deep straw-lined hole, then thick camellia bushes were planted on the top for shade. In the heat of the summer the castle could enjoy cold drinks, and every year the Maedas made a present of the coveted ice to the Tokugawa shōgun. Four men made the annual run to Edo, carrying great chunks of ice, which must have melted into cube size during the five-day trip. July 1st is still celebrated as Icehouse Day in Kanazawa.

In the back corner stands a great tree encircled with bamboo slats to discourage bugs. The oldest tree in the park, it looks every bit of its 750 years.

A small monument to poet Bashō's haiku, *Akaaka to hi wa tsure naku mo aki no kaze,* was erected at the base of the hill by one of his Kanazawa disciples:

> Red, red is the sun,
> Heartlessly indifferent to time,
> The wind knows, however,
> The promise of early chill.

30. Seisonkaku Villa　成巽閣

This majestic villa, typical of Shoin architectural style, was built in 1863 by the 13th lord, Nariyasu, for his mother's retirement residence. Unfortunately it costs an extra 300 yen to see the interior, but such a rare treat is worth the price. Seisonkaku's *ranma,* transoms carved from single blocks of wood, are especially famous.

An English pamphlet is available, but note too the display cases at the back of the first floor. In one is a fascinating scroll map of the long road from Kanazawa to Edo which was traveled constantly on such official business as transporting hostages and delivering gifts.

The back porch is famous for its unobstructed view of the 'Fly-

ing Crane Garden'; the roof was constructed without supporting posts. The floorboards are laid according to the famous 'singing nightingale' technique, to warn the residents of intruders. On the second floor, the surprising art deco-like designs fit in well with the bold cobalt blue, red and purple walls. Visitors may not enter the tea rooms except at the June 15 public tea ceremony. Closed Wed.

31. Meoto Matsu--Married Pines　夫婦松

The two intertwined pine trees standing just behind the lake are said to symbolize marriage. Just to the right stands another gnarled pine whose branches twist and curl wildly in every direction. This is called the third party, usually identified as a female, who regards the happy couple with jealousy and frustration.

32. Sazaeyama--Shellfish Hill　さざえ山

This is the highest point in the park, favored by sunrise strollers and autumn moon-viewers. When the full moon rises over Utatsu-yama and the Karasaki Pine and is reflected in Kasumi Lake, Sazaeyama makes a perfect lovers' lane.

The name Sazaeyama comes from the path winding around up to the top of the hill like the spiraling back of the *sazae* shellfish. A massive *tomuro* stone-roofed pagoda stands at the summit.

At the base of Sazaeyama are two small mud-walled buildings.

Uchihashitei, the tea house extending out over the lake, is no longer open to the public. But at the small restaurant beside it, visitors may enjoy a cup of tea or a bowl of noodles, sit on the tatami mats and gaze out over the water.

To the left of the tea house, along the edge of the lake below Sazaeyama runs a narrow, rocky path. It was designed in imitation of Oyashirazu, the treacherous coastline in Niigata, where the old North Road ran. Travelers had to be so cautious when crossing the rocks that parents forgot the welfare of their children and vice versa--it was every man for himself.

Around the corner, behind Sazaeyama, is another branch of Miyoshian restaurant. Out front stand two 'Christian lanterns,' with crosses clearly carved on them. Both are said to have come to Kanazawa with Takayama Ukon, the "Christian daimyō" who left

Edo after Hideyoshi's anti-Christian edicts, for safety under the protection of his friend Maeda Toshiie.

33. Hase Lake 長谷池

This small lake is in an obscure corner of the park and frequently ignored by tourists. It is known for its male and female waterfalls--and with Japan's traditional attitudes toward women in mind, it's not hard to figure out which is which. Each is decorated with an impressive stone lantern.

34. Plum Garden 梅林

During the time of Takezawa Villa, this area was occupied by ladies-in-waiting. Marking the spot now are 280 plum trees, of 24 different varieties, collected here from all over Japan. They bloom in late winter.

35. Kanazawa Shrine 金沢神社

The southwest section of Kenrokuen, including Kanazawa Shrine and the Plum Garden, falls outside the area requiring the 100 yen fee. Kanazawa Shrine was built by the 11th lord, Harunaga. In keeping with the Maedas' support for education, it is dedicated to Tenman, the god of learning, and thus popular with students. No doubt most of the hundreds of *ema,* votive tablets sold for 200 yen, are inscribed with the prayers of examination candidates or their parents. The *ema* are gathered up on December 25 and ritually burned on January 15.

Kanazawa Shrine was built in imitation of the head Tenman Shrine in Fukuoka. On the inside ceiling of the main shrine are many square panels picturing the most unlikely assortment of animals and insects, everything from centipedes to badgers. A striking bronze phoenix, enveloped in flames and with wings nobly spread, stands on the roof. Out in front of the shrine, half hidden in the bamboo grass, is the Ibotori Ishi, a rock which will remove warts. But there's a trick. The sufferer must rub the warty place against the stone when no one else is watching, or the cure won't work. It certainly appears effective; the black stone is well worn away.

36. Kinjō Reitaku--Sacred Well 金城霊沢

Hōōsan--Phoenix Hill 鳳凰山

Here is the well where Imohori Tōgorō came to wash his legendary potatoes. Gold rose up from the water's depths, and the name

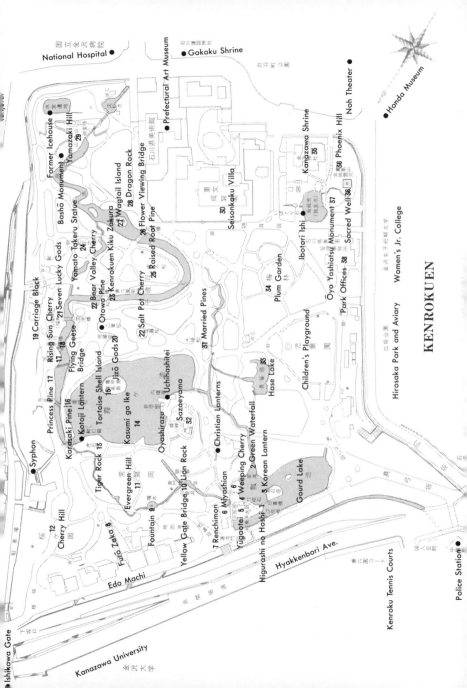

KENROKUEN

National Hospital ●
● Gokoku Shrine
Prefectural Art Museum
● Honda Museum
Noh Theater ●

Former Icehouse ●
Bashō Monument ●
Yamazaki Hill 29
Yamato Takeru Statue 24
27 Wagtail Island
28 Dragon Rock
26 Flower Viewing Bridge
Kanazawa Shrine 35
36 Phoenix Hill
19 Carriage Block
21 Seven Lucky Gods
Rising Sun Cherry 18
17 11
22 Bear Valley Cherry
23 Kenrokuen Kiku Zakura
Otowa Pine
25 Raised Root Pine
Seisonkaku Villa
30
Ibotori Ishi
Ōya Yoshiatsu Monument 37
Sacred Well 36
Princess Pine 17
Flying Geese Bridge
16 Kotoji Lantern
15 Iizō Gods 20
Tortoise Shell Island
14 Kasumi ga Ike
Uchihashitei
31 Married Pines
34 Plum Garden
Park Offices 38
Karasaki Pine 13
Sazaeyama
32
Christian Lanterns
Hase Lake 33
Children's Playground
Syphon ●
Tiger Rock
Evergreen Hill
11 Lion Rock 10
Oyashirazu
Green Waterfall
2 Green Lantern
Hirosaka Park and Aviary
Cherry Hill 12
Fountain 9
Yellow Gate Bridge
7 Renchimon
6 Miyoshian
Yūgaotei 5 4 Weeping Cherry
3 Korean Lantern
Women's Jr. College
Futō Zaka 8
Higurashi no Hashi 1
Gourd Lake
Kanazawa Women's Jr. College
Ishikawa Gate ●
Edo Machi
Hyakkenbori Ave.
Kenroku Tennis Courts
Kanazawa University
Police Station ●

Kanazawa (Marsh of Gold) was born. Some gold has in fact been found in local rivers, so this story may not be as dubious as it sounds. It is unusual for a well to be found on such high ground. But even more curiously, this well has never dried up. The water is also valued for its fine taste by tea lovers and restaurant cooks who make special trips here for it. The same water runs into the purification basin at Kanazawa Shrine where anyone can sample it. In the winter, the water turns to steam as it hits the cold air, lending an eerie feeling to this corner of the park.

Next to the well is Phoenix Hill, built of stones from the demolished Takezawa Villa. At first the hill was in the shape of a phoenix, with wings spread and neck raised high, but successive typhoons have battered it beyond recognition. The dark cave contains a stone tablet written by Lord Nariyasu, explaining the story of the well.

37. Ōya Yoshiatsu Monument　大屋憕欨の標

For a well-entrenched feudal family, the Maedas were surprisingly quick in adapting to the Meiji Restoration and the opening of Japan to the West. The Kaga government encouraged foreign studies, importing teachers schooled in the new subjects and sending young scholars to the capital. One of these local boys was Ōya Yoshiatsu, who headed the clan's school and compiled an English-Japanese dictionary and numerous works on world geography and history. Ōya Sensei picked up some foreign ways in Nagasaki and was known to take pleasure in the people's open-mouthed amazement when he strolled around Kanazawa with a western umbrella. The tall monument in front of Kanazawa Shrine is dedicated to him. Behind it is a squat rectangular monument. This and the one on the back right side of the shrine memorialize other early western scholars.

38. Park Offices　兼六公園事務所

This former samurai house is the perfect sightseeing spot for sword movie fans. The ceiling of the enormous entryway (facing away from the street) is stained with blood spattered by Tsuda family ancestors in a vicious vendetta. The family decided to preserve the spots to remind descendants of the value of calm and reason. The Tsuda family of Maeda retainers lived in Ōtemachi. Their house was moved here in 1922.

KODATSUNO 小立野

Kodatsuno is the student center of Kanazawa. The shopping potential is limited, but the atmosphere is relaxed, the tiny restaurants cheap and good, and the sightseeing spots just waiting to be discovered.

SHOPPING

Kaga Musubi (加賀むすび). Open daily 9:00−5:00 for great rice lunchboxes (*bentō*), suitable for trips to Kenrokuen or Edo Village or for a stroll by Saigawa riverbank.

Takasagoya (高砂屋). This local cake maker has no connection with the famous Kobe cookie company. Here the specialities are 'Makiginu' (Folded Silk) and 'Hanayūzen' (Flowered Silk). The names alone are enough to induce you to buy, but take a few for yourself only--they only last about five days and don't ship well. 8:30−7:00, except Sun.

EATING

Donsuki (どんすき). All kinds of *udon* noodles, with some unusual combinations, displayed in the window. 11:00−8:00, except Sat.

Kazue Tail Shop (可寿栄). Popular with doctors and med students from the nearby University Hospital. Known for Korean barbecue, individual *nabe* stews, great pickles and spicy oxtail. Smoky, garlicky, but warm atmosphere. 5:00--11:00, except Mon. The owner's son speaks English.

New Tanuki (ニュー狸). Everything is delicious and reasonable, especially the salmon steak dinner. Western food, menu in English, counter style. 11:00−10:00, except Fri.

Wakaba (若 葉). Really cheap *oden,* with one of the widest selections in Kanazawa. The friendly master speaks some English. Draft beer. 12:00−2:00, except alternating Sun. and Mon.

Hachi-ban Rāmen (8番ラーメン   ). One of the modern branches of·this large noodle chain, it looks like a slick McDonald's. Famous for serving lots of vegetables with the soup noodles. 11:00−9:00, except 2nd and 4th Wed.

Dai Nana Gyōza (第7ギョーザ   ). Cheap, dirty and good. Chinese dumplings can fill you up for less than ¥300. Don't wait for your tea or beer; it's self-service. Open 4:00 p.m.−2:00 a.m., except Wed.

DRINKING

Gironbo (ジロンボ   ). Offers a great bargain, a delicious, fancy cake and coffee for ¥350. Also famous for order-made birthday cakes (same day service). 8:00−8:30, except Sun.

Fūgetsudō (風月堂), a few doors down, has great cakes but no place to sit down.

Joe House (じょーハウス   ). Cheap food and drinks in a student atmosphere. Lots of records, mainly jazz. 11:00 a.m.−12:00 p.m. daily. Good while waiting for your laundry at the coin-op across the street.

Joe no Ie (じょーの家   ). Another student hangout, centering around folk music and cheap drinks. Their rice dishes, like *ocha-zuke* and *omusubi,* are popular. 6:00−12:00, except Thurs.

VISITING

★Honda Museum 藩老本多蔵品館

The greatest of the Maeda family minister-advisors was Honda Masashige who was invited from Edo by Lord Toshinaga in 1602. Honda soon became Toshinaga's and later Toshitsune's, respected confidant and was granted 50,000 *koku* of rice and an enormous spread of property near the castle. The intimate relationship continued throughout the Edo period, and although things have changed considerably since the Meiji Restoration and World War II, the present Mr. Honda, Masakazu, still visits Mr. Maeda frequently in Tōkyō.

Mr. Honda now runs a fine museum of his family treasures, with particular emphasis on lacquer and chinaware. The trousseaux and dowries of Maeda daughters who married into the Hondas, gifts sent from the Tokugawas in Edo, and colorful uniforms of the family's personal firefighters are special points of interest. Well-known locally is the rare equestrian military equipment used by the second Honda. After the third generation, when peace was showing signs of permanence, the family turned to cultural pursuits, especially tea ceremony.

The museum is on the former site of the 300-room family mansion, the grounds of which included the present Plum Garden of Kenrokuen and the Noh Theater spot. A pleasure villa, equipped with a pond for boating, was located by the garden behind MRO. And in the present Honda Machi lived the family retainers, some of whose houses and mud walls remain. Museum open 9:00−5:00 except Thurs. ¥500.

Just beside the Honda Museum stand three low red brick buildings. Originally armories, in 1946 they became the campus of the Municipal Art College (Bidai), until it was moved recently to its new site behind the University Hospital. Kanazawa people feel great affection for the three, in part because they are fine examples of Meiji architecture, and in part because of a wave of nostalgia for fast-disappearing red brick.

Noh Theater　能楽文化館

Kanazawa is dominated culturally by the Noh Theater. Most theaters in Japan are privately run, but the enlightened Ishikawa Prefecture built this magnificent structure in 1972, and rents it for a nominal fee to professional and amateur groups. Not only noh, but also classical dance and music, whether rehearsal or recital, can be enjoyed here almost every day. There is also a full-scale professional noh production on the first Sunday of the month.

First time visitors are temporarily confused by the building. Its sleek, modern, yet clearly Oriental exterior offers no preparation for a glimpse of the traditional polished wood stage set up inside. The new Noh Theater is a worthy symbol of Kanazawa's interest in traditional culture. The original noh theater stood beside the City Hall. There were no seats in the drafty hall; the audience knelt, shivering, on the tatami, and tried to glean some warmth from feeble *hibachi*. But at least the cold was stimulating. The new theater is so comfortable, with plush chairs, fine lighting and heating, that even the most dedicated noh fan can become drowsy. The observer must concentrate on the tension underlying the gentle dance, or muse over the beauty of the inner stage (salvaged from the old theater). When all else fails, take along a sushi *bentō* lunch and nibble at it to keep from nodding off. Closed Mon.

The surprising Taishō-style buildings beside the Noh Theater are a former military headquarters and officers club, one of which was originally built in Kenrokuen when soldiers were stationed in the castle. They are now prefectural offices.

Gokoku Shrine 護国神社

During World War II, one great shrine was built in each prefecture, in memory of the dead from all wars since the first year of Meiji, when many died in the upheaval of revolutionary modernization. All known war dead are registered in the shrine of their family seat (now nearly 44,000 in Ishikawa). A few days before the *meinichi,* anniversary of death, the shrine sends a letter of reminder to the family, who will visit or send a contribution. At 11:00 a.m. every day, visitors may watch, or join, the services for the dead of that day. Throughout the year several general services are also held.

But the system is controversial. Whereas supporters say the shrine reminds us of the evils of war, critics claim that it serves to glorify those who died on the battlefield. The issue of separation of church and state is also frequently raised, and the participation

Kyūdo archery range at Gokoku Shrine. (Hokkoku Press)

of politicians in the services is questioned. Most devoted to the memorial services seem to be rural Noto families, who come in groups by bus and spend the night at the shrine. City people perhaps find it easier to forget after 30 years.

Also of interest here is the old prefectural archery hall to the back of the shrine. Visitors may quietly enter and watch students and teachers practicing this Zen-inspired, spiritual sport.

Tatsumi Yōsui and Ishibiki-chō 辰巳用水と石引町

Tatsumi Yōsui was one of the greatest engineering feats of the Edo period. After Kanazawa Castle burned down in 1634, Lord Toshitsune realized the necessity of water, for both defense and firefighting purposes. He commissioned a Komatsu man, Itaya Heishirō, to work on the problem. The ingenious result was a four-kilometer underground conduit, bringing fresh water from the mountains, through the town, to the foot of the castle and lifting it into the fortress with a unique syphon gadget. Originally the conduits were hollowed-out pine logs, but later they were replaced with stone joints, secured with pine pitch.

At certain places in Kanazawa, like along Ishibiki-Dōri and throughout Kenrokuen park, the stream is exposed, giving a clean, fresh feeling to city dwellers. There are now several *yōsui* streams transporting water through town, cooling the hot pavement in summer and washing away snow in winter.

This neighborhood just above Kenrokuen is known as Ishibiki (stone-pulling) town. The great *tomuro* stones from the mountains near Iōzan were dragged through here on rollers, destined for use in the castle walls or for aristocratic gravestones.

City Folk Museum 市民俗文化財展示館

While most folk museums show only crafts, Kanazawa's displays in this well-preserved, 1899 Meiji school building, the tools and processes used by the city crafts people themselves. Every imaginable artisan is represented--makers of musical instruments, *tabi,* chopsticks, candles, and lanterns, as well as the more famous Kanazawa cake, silk, gold leaf and lacquer makers. The photos of artisans' faces are fascinating. The display of tools and processes is more or less self-explanatory, but going with an interpreter may be helpful. 9:00—4:00 except Tues. and several periods during the year when the exhibits are changed. The city is to be congratulated for providing that this museum be free. It's unfortunately one of the very few that are.

Hōenji 宝円寺

Hōenji was the Maeda family's first personal temple established in Kanazawa, the priest having followed Lord Toshiie, via Fukui and Nanao, through his various campaigns for Nobunaga. The temple is now best known as the gravesite of Tawaraya Sōtatsu, the great 17th century, Momoyama painter who was said to be born in Noto. His remaining works are few, but they can be found in the Freer Gallery in Washington, the Ueno Museum in Tōkyō and the National Museum in Kyōto. In Kanazawa, it turns out that most works held privately and thought to be by Sōtatsu are actually by his student, Sōsetsu, who used the same chop signature. Several authentic Sōtatsus are held by the Prefectural Art Museum and are on display there in January. The mistakes were discovered when some research was done during a special exhibition a few years ago. At that time, it was proved that not only was Sōtatsu not from Noto, but the 'grave' is actually a monument, erected relatively recently by his admirers in Kanazawa.

Those who wish to have a look anyway, should walk out the back gate and down a street until arriving at the graveyard on the edge of the Kodatsuno plateau. (The cemetery is now separated from the temple by houses which have sprung up on shrinking temple property.) Sōtatsu's 'grave' is the largest one off to the right in back. A large public tea ceremony is held in his memory on a Sunday early in September.

In the front yard of Hōenji, there is a linden tree said to have been grown from a sprig of the original tree under which Gautama Buddha found enlightenment.

Umazaka 馬坂

If you leave Hōenji and turn left at the gaudy castle of a love hotel, you will come to Kōgenji (高源寺) with its rows of *jizō* statues in the front yard. Perhaps these are to protect those continuing on down the steep, zigzag slope to the left. This is Umazaka, or Horse Slope.

At the second turn is a *fudō* statue, standing below a thin water spout. Passersby stop to say a prayer, fill up a ladle with fresh, clear water and pour it over the *fudō*. Although this ritual is meant

City Folk Museum in a Meiji schoolhouse. (Hokkoku Press)

to purify the statue, it seems to be more for the *fudō*'s soft covering of moss. The water has a reputation for curing eye trouble. After your eyes are taken care of, you may wish to pray for long life to the colorful *enmei jizō*, in his newly improved house, across the way. Then pause for a view of Utatsuyama (here it's easy to understand why it's also called Mukaiyama--Over There Mountain) and the sea.

Kyōōji 経王寺

Kyōōji is another of those temples whose story is more interesting than the actual visit. Down the street, in the graveyard now separated from the temple, lies Shinnyoin, the unfortunate victim of Kaga Sōdō, the biggest of several unsuccessful attempts to overthrow the feudal Maeda clan government. The story centers around Ōtsuki Denzō, a brilliant young man who gained the confidence of the sixth lord, Yoshinori. In thanks for his sound advice, Denzō was raised astronomically from a lowly apprentice priest to the 3800—*koku* treasurer of the clan (his estate included what is now Central Park). Envious samurai, pressed by his strict and practical economic policies, started false rumors that Denzō was carrying on a love affair with the Lord's mistress, Shinnyoin. Furthermore, they charged that her son was actually by Denzō, and that together the lovers were plotting to poison Yoshinori and replace him with the boy. Denzō was banished to a dungeon off in Gokayama, and Shinnyoin is said to have been tortured to death with snakes. Perhaps her grave does deserve a sympathy visit.

Bidai -- Kanazawa Arts College 金沢美術工芸大学 (美大)

In keeping with the city's Edo-period tradition of support for the arts and education, in 1946, Kanazawa City opened an arts college. Perhaps the citizens felt an urge to invest in peace and culture the resources that other Japanese cities were at the time spending on rebuilding after the war's destruction. In any case, Kanazawa Bidai is one of only two municipally supported arts colleges in Japan--the other is in Kyōto.

The first campus was, significantly, in the old armory buildings at the top of Kenrokuen. The school moved to its beautiful new campus in 1973, attracting students from all over the country to its courses in fine arts, traditional crafts and industrial design. The Bidai students add a fresh, avant-garde atmosphere to an otherwise conservative Kanazawa.

Although visitors are not officially permitted without some sort of introduction, they may wander around the campus discreetly. The lobby gallery shows a range of student work. Except when a class is in progress, it's also possible to peek into the studios and watch the students at work.

Geba Jizō 下馬地蔵

The city's attempts to widen main streets have had mixed results in Kodatsuno. Here the street accomodates 4-lane traffic (or two moving lines and two illegal parking spaces) until the end of Ishibiki-chō, where it narrows again for a while before widening in the outskirts. The road finally becomes narrow again out toward the mountains. Perhaps one cause of the suddenly narrowed section is the *geba jizō*, which signifies the point where Edo period travelers were expected to get off their horses and proceed through town on foot. The *jizō* statues are lovingly cared for by people in the neighborhood, with regular supplies of candles, fresh flowers and incense.

Tentokuin 天徳院

Lord Toshitsune built this temple as a memorial to his beloved wife, Tama-hime, when she died at age 42. Most of the buildings have been destroyed by fire and rebuilt, but the original two-storied gate, built in Chinese style by a master carpenter, dates from 1694. Visitors may enter the broad front garden through a sliding door to the right of the gate. Tama-hime's grave is actually in Nodayama at the Maeda family burial ground.

Ueno Hachiman Shrine 上野八幡神社

Noh is usually thought of as an amusement of the moneyed leisure classes, but in Kanazawa, enthusiasm at the grass roots level gives the theater its vitality. Noh teachers, students and audiences are found all over town, and amateur performances are frequent. One such group gathers regularly at the Ueno Hachiman Shrine--a visiting teacher and local housewives, young married couples and old grandfathers, notably the shrine priest. He will proudly show visitors the impressive wooden slabs which line the walls inside the shrine. They list the plays and performers in annual gatherings since the Meiji period.

Also on the walls are photos of the shrine festival, centering around a large *mikoshi* float, housed most of the time in a small hut in the front grounds. The parade looks like fun--young, white-kimonoed men jostling down Kodatsuno's streets with the *mikoshi* on their shoulders. But it's disappointing to discover that the festival is held only once every 33 years--please come back in 2010! The photos are from 1911 and 1977 (the war prevented celebrations in 1944).

The other item of tourist interest is a memorial stone inscribed with a haiku attributed to Bashō, and several curious, small holes bored in a horizontal line across the characters. The origin of the poem about the cold and lonely mountains, and the monument itself, remains a mystery. *Yama samushi kokoro no soko ya mizu no tsuki.*

Eianji 永安寺

Eianji is a paradox--a normally conservative Shingon temple, with a colorful conglomeration of gaudy, almost Southeast Asia-like statues, altars and shrines. The explanation is simple. The former priest was troubled by the rising crime, divorce and general godlessness of twentieth-century youth, and he decided to do something about it. Perhaps concluding that more is better, he assembled every imaginable deity and then set about attracting followers. There's a god for every taste or trouble. The 3-eyed (he can see the past, present and future) and six-armed (one hand is empty, free to assist worshippers) giant Niō is the deity representing love. The bright red and orange hillside temple is occupied by Benten, patroness of the arts. And one altar, decorated with radishes in gold relief, seems to cover just about everything else, scholarship, business, health, safety. (The radishes were a mistake on the part of the sculptor. He was commissioned to engrave an auspicious flower pattern, but he got confused.) Around the corner stand 33 Kannon goddesses of mercy, just in case.

The priest's policies seem to have been successful--if not in re-forming the world, at least in keeping the temple well supported. It was moved to this breezy suburban hilltop at great expense (the new main building is all *keyaki,* a rare and precious hardwood), and the grounds are always immaculate. Although the winters are harsh here, it's a popular spot for 'first worship' at the New Year. For the tourist, the scattered gods and the lovely view give Eianji an atmosphere as well suited to hiking as to sightseeing.

Eianji's fearsome Niō.
(M.Nakamura)

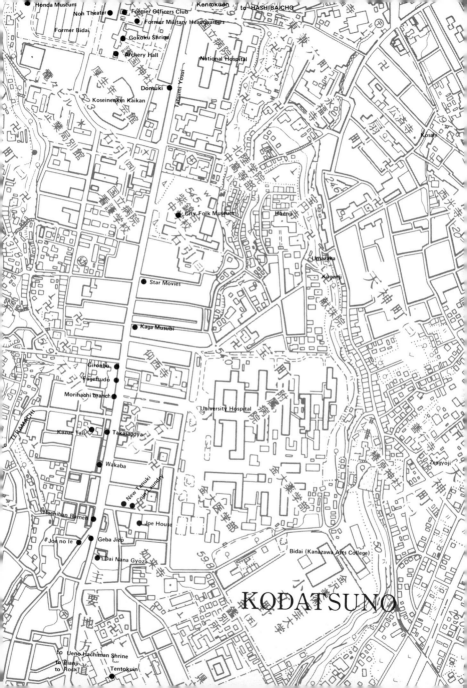

Honda Museum
Noh Theater
Former Officers Club
Kenrokuen
to HASHIBA-CHO
Former Bidai
Former Military Headquarters
Gokoku Shrine
Archery Hall
National Hospital
Domuki
Kosahi
Koseinenkin Kaikan
City Folk Museum
Hōenji
Umazaka
Kōgenji
Star Movies
Kaga Musubi
Girōabo
Fugetsudo
Morihachi branch
University Hospital
Kazue Tail
Takasagoya
Zengyoji
Wakaba
New Tanuki
Coin Laundry
Hachiban Ramen
Joe House
Joe no le
Geba Jizo
Dai Nana Gyoza
Bidai (Kanazawa Arts College)
TERAMACHI
KODATSUNO
to Ueno Hachiman Shrine
to Eianji
to Rock!
Tentokuin

KATAMACHI 片町

The Katamachi district behind Daiwa Department Store is focused on amusements--shopping, bar-hopping and dining. But there are several cultural attractions mixed in with the fashionable boutiques and packs of prowling hot-rodders. Most of the shops, including many restaurants and bars, close on Wednesdays.

SHOPPING

Ishikawaya (石川屋). Cakes in great variety, to suit all kinds of drinks, teas and coffees. Just tell Mrs. Uchida (she speaks English) what you're planning, and she'll suggest the perfect sweet accompaniment. 9:00−8:00, except Wed.

Elle (エ ル) building is packed with boutiques that somehow manage to stay in business. Good English book section on the sixth floor. Variety of restaurants and bars on 7th and 8th floors, open until 9:00. Building open 10:30−7:30, except Wed.

Daiwa Department Store (大 和). The oldest in Kanazawa; it has everything. Just by riding up the escalator, you can get a good summary view of Kanazawa shopping. Foreigners particularly appreciate the imported foods in the basement. 10:00−6:00, except Wed.

Shibazushi (芝寿し). Famous Kaga pressed sushi, in *bento* boxes, from ¥320 to elaborate 3-tiered wonders. 9:00−7:00 daily.

Utsunomiya (うつのみや). Best book and stationery supply. English magazines on the first floor; English books on the third floor. Great variety of illustrated coffee table-type books on every Japanese subject. Guidebooks and books on local subjects on the first floor, back left. Ask for *Furusato Saihakken,* a color photo essay on Ishikawa. 10:00−7:30, except Wed.

German Bakery (ジャーマン・ベーカリー). Best bread, French and dark styles. 9:00−8:00, except Wed.

Sumita Fan Shop (寿美田). Fans for tea, noh, dancing, decoration, or simply for a hot day. Also purses. 9:30−8:00, except Wed.

Hanamasa Florist (花 正). International FTD delivery--English catalogue, Japanese prices. 8:45−7:00 daily. Visitors are welcome to watch the flower arrangement lessons on the 2nd floor.

Hokkoku Shorin (北国書林). Some English paperbacks in the back of the 2nd basement. 10:00−7:30 daily.

Mizuochi Sudare (水落すだれ店). This family has been making finely split bamboo blinds since the Meiji period. These days it's mainly by special order, but the shop has some lovely examples. Mizuochi is the only *sudare* hand-crafter left in Kanazawa. 8:00 −6:00, except Sun.

Maruzen (丸 善) has a selection of English books, but it is a disappointing cousin of the national chain. 10:00−5:30, except Sun.

Sakao Cake Shop (坂 尾). The best-known product of this charming old store is Kaga-sama, a pie-like waffle shaped like the Maeda *umebachi* crest and divided into 5 different sweet-bean wedges. 9:00−6:00, except Sun.

Shimazaki Wig (島 崎). The last wigmaker in Kanazawa, they use only real hair to create the cumbersome traditional hairdos. How is it that when brides or dancers put them on, they look so graceful and delicate! The workshop is right out in front, and clearly visible from the window. Or you can go inside and perhaps discuss your own requirements--hairstyles vary widely among matrons, maidens and geisha. Prices vary between ¥100,000 and ¥180,000. Open daily.

EATING

Tamazushi (玉寿司). One of the best, especially for *temaki* sushi rolls. See if you can figure out the *kana* in their logo. Closed Sun.

Gesshōtei (月祥亭). Out of 60 possible *tōfu* dishes, lively, English-speaking Ms. Ōmura has at least 15 on hand every day.

Kansai style *tōfu* cooking in a 150 year-old house. Lunch by reservation, tel. 63—8338. Dinners daily, except Sun.

Wan-san (王さん). Best Chinese food in town, prepared before you by Mr. Wang. He left Shanghai during the war and came to Japan 20 years ago, via Taiwan. Counter only, but it's fun to watch him cook. 5:00 p.m.—2:00 a.m., except Mon.

Tamae (玉 栄). Great atmosphere, excellent trimmings (vegetable, salad and fruit), average steak. Choice of sirloin and tenderloin. Less than ¥5,000 a person. Best to call first, tel. 63—3833. 4:30—1:30 a.m., except Mon.

Hideyoshi (秀よし). Larger cousin of the tiny Hideyoshi on Saigawa Ōdōri. Good fish, any style, but ask what they recommend. 5:00—1:00 a.m., except 1st Sun.

Midōen (味道園). Korean barbecue lovers recommend Midōen. Good sauce, meat and pickles. It's tiny and often full, so call in advance (tel. 62—4411), or you may have to wait at a nearby coffee shop for a seat to open up. 5:30 p.m.—3:00 a.m., except Wed.

Irohanihoheto (いろはにほへと). Cheap, Japanese-style pub with photo menu. 5:00 p.m.—4:00 a.m. daily.

Zeniya (銭 屋) is one of Kanazawa's best *kappō*, where excellent seasonal food is served at a counter. Its quality is well-known --reservations are a good idea, tel. 33—3331. Reasonable lunches (from ¥1,000) between 11:30 and 2:00. Dinners, between 5:00 and 10:00, run from ¥8,000. Closed Sun. Leave the menu up to Mr. Takagi, the jovial master.

Sanjukken Nagaya (三十間長屋). Although named for the samurai longhouse still standing in the Kanazawa Castle grounds, this place is best for Kanazawans who wish they were elsewhere. Under a giant Mt. Fuji mural, customers cook *nabe* hot pots, and down local sakes from all over Japan. Open daily, 12:00—11:00.

Umihiko Yamahiko (海彦山彦). Japanese food from both the mountains and the sea, in a basement restaurant styled like a country house. Long wooden counter and box seats. Reasonable prices, popular with tourists. 12:00—10:30 except Wed. The name comes from a children's story about two brothers, a fisherman and a mountain peasant, who exchanged jobs for a while.

Kanekyū (金 久) ain't cheap, but it's known for its sliced, raw

beef sashimi, as well as other steak and sukiyaki dishes. Some reasonable *teishoku* at lunch. The sister place in the basement, Takanoha, also has first-class Japanese food. 11:00−3:00 and 4:00−11:00. Alternate Sun. closed.

Ippei (一 平) is a rarity--a cheap and good sushi shop. It's a tiny place, on the left in an alley marked with a purple sign. Run by Mr. Ishizaki. 6:00−2:00, except Sun.

Dosanko (道産子). Great for rice balls, soup and pickles after a long drinking evening. Or good *onigiri teishoku* set course at lunch, ¥500. 11:30−12:00 a.m. daily. Till midnight on Sat.

Kitama (きたま). Restaurant-style Japanese food, with a nice little garden. Try the Kaga set dinner or the *Kōjitsu bentō* lunch-box. 11:30−9:30 except Wed.

Yakitori Yokochō (焼鳥横丁) is a narrow, covered alley of tiny, cheap *yakitori* shops. Open late afternoon till late at night, except Sun. Point to anything that looks good.

Ōzeki (大 関). Cheap, good *oden,* sashimi, tempura. 4:00−11:00, with 2 unscheduled holidays a month. Closed in summer.

Sekitei-Rokkakudō (石亭・六角堂). The small, downtown branch serves great luncheon set meals of tempura upstairs and steak downstairs (¥1,000), 11:30−2:00, weekdays. Dinner, from 5:00 to 10:00 on weekdays and all day on weekends, is much more expensive.

Keizel (恵是瑠). Run by the amiable Ken Kosaka, who used to be with Benihana in Philadelphia. Keizel's speciality is using fresh local ingredients in European dishes, like *baigai* cooked with garlic and butter, in place of escargots. Cheap lunches and slightly expensive dinners. 11:30−10:00, except Wed. Second floor.

Kikuichi Oden (菊 一). Cheap, good and convenient. The master speaks a little English, but he may rush off in the middle of pouring your sake, in his capacity as a volunteer fireman. Little wooden chits pile up as you order. 5:00–12:00, except Tues.

Katsuki (かつ喜). *Tonkatsu* speciality shop for pork cutlet lovers. Cheap 'service lunch.' 11:00–9:30.

Tenryū (天 龍). About Chinese food, they say the dirtier the restaurant, the better the food. By these standards, Tenryū should be good, and it is. Try *wantanmen, tantanmen,* or anything. 11:00 –8:00, except Fri.

Parvati. The best, and the only authentic, curry in Kanazawa. Made by Ōiwa Yutaka, who was in the Japanese Peace Corps in Malaysia for several years, and speaks English. The atmosphere is relaxed, open late for cheap drinking in the evenings, and a very leisurely opening around lunchtime. Don't forget his yoghurt drinks, chutneys and pickles (sometimes).

Sanuki (さぬき). Fun to watch the noodle-making. Great *udon,* unusual toppings, from ¥300. The entry is small, the sign is red, and the friendly guy has been at it for 8 years. Don't confuse him with the young upstart who opened another 'Sanuki' right next door. 5:00–2:00 a.m., except Wed.

Chūbei (忠 平). Good *soba* noodles. Try the unusual *soba jibu* (Kaga-style stew) or *norimaki sushi* (*soba,* rolled up and sliced). 11:00–9:00, except some Sundays.

Shiogama (しほ釜). Good beef and vegetable Shiogama-yaki, for ¥1,700 at the counter. Dinner in a private room is much more, with many added expenses for the same food. Reservation necessary for a room, tel. 21–0738.

DRINKING

Moonlight / Aurora (ムーンライト／オーロラ). Both are typical of the infamous, astronomically priced hostess clubs. Bright, attractive, English-speaking girls work at both. Best to negotiate the price as you enter, but don't expect to get out for less than ¥10,000 a person. Both open around 6:30 to 11:30 except Sun.

York has loud jazz (records) and frequent poetry readings. 11:00– 2:00, except 1st and 3rd Wed.

Escargot (えすかるご) is one of the older European-style bars, in operation for 15 years. Coffee from 9:00 to 6:00 and drinks from 6:00 to 2:00 a.m. daily.

Vie Vogue. Loud, good, up-to-date rock music. Dark brick and copper interior. 10:00 a.m.–3:00 a.m., except Wed.

Hayashiya Green Shop (林屋みどり). Every imaginable use found for green tea: sodas, toast, cakes, ice cream, as well as the regular whipped and brewed tea. Tiny counter next to a tea utensils shop (try browsing upstairs). 9:00–6:30, except Wed.

Chevalier (シュバリエ). Reasonably priced bar run by the handsome and friendly Mr. Seki. Popular with young working women. 6:00–2:00, except 1st and 3rd Wed.

Savoja (サボイヤ). Long European-style basement bar, reasonable drinks and food. 6:00–2:00 a.m. daily.

Banana Beach (バナナビーチ). A disco popular with the young teenage set. Go early for lower prices. Open from 6:00 daily.

Manhattan 21 (マッハンタン21). In the basement of the Elle building, this disco attracts a twenty-ish crowd. Average bill runs ¥2,700. From 6:00 daily. (Tel. 67–3653).

Laurence (ローレンス) looks like someone's slightly shabby Victorian livingroom. Famous as an early haunt of literary types like Itsuki Hiroyuki, its present-day appeal lies in the charm of its faded elegance and its low prices. Noon to 9:00 daily.

Mugonka (無言歌). Great classical record collection and good speakers. Customers may make requests. 8:30–9:30 daily for coffee.

Nikore (似故礼). Mrs. Mori and her son bought an old samurai house three years ago and opened the garden and living room as a tea house. You can sit on the veranda, inspect the old painted screens and enjoy the various tea-based drinks or coffee, from 8:30 to 6:00 every day.

Kaga No Niwa (加賀の庭) is another samurai house-turned-tea shop, right around the corner from Saihitsuan Yūzen Center. The 300-year-old garden is the central attraction. 10:00–6:00, except Thurs. and all winter (Nov.–March).

VISITING

Yōchi-in　養智院

Yōchi-in still sits proudly, as it has for 1100 years, in an area now the center of Kanazawa's shopping and amusement district. The creeping neon and traffic have encroached heavily on the land surrounding the temple, which once extended all the way to the Saigawa river. But Yōchi-in retains hints of its past glories in the multitude of *jizō* and Kannon goddess statues lined up in the cramped front yard. The present head priest, a sweet and grandmotherly poet, keeps up the temple's long tradition as a haiku center. As her ancestors have done since the lively Genroku era (late 17th century), she holds a monthly poetry party, where amateur haiku makers gather to create, criticise and share ideas.

Yōchi-in is most proud of its ancient, wooden *jizō* statue, carved in 825 by the great Kōbō Daishi, when he passed through Noto. Since it became temple property, the statue has been shown only once every 33 years. It next comes out of its airtight case in 1992. On an inside wall, however, hangs a small photograph for those who visit between times.

In one sense, it is appropriate that Yōchi-in find itself smack in the amusement area. The temple's main Buddha is Kankiten, the god of pleasure. The haiku people are a small minority, in fact, compared to the number of visitors from the entertainment business.

★ Saihitsuan　Yūzen Silk Center　彩筆庵

Several years ago, some Kaga Yūzen kimono painters set up a workshop designed to explain Kanazawa's famous silk techniques to the public. For ¥500, visitors have the opportunity to watch the artists daub in the colorful patterns at their low tables, inspect the architectural details of the Meiji-era tea master's house, and listen to a full explanation of the 18-step Yūzen process over a cup of tea and cakes. A complete English pamphlet is available. Although guests can wander freely through the house and garden, because it is an actual workplace, decorum is maintained--on the front door there is even a sign forbidding entrance to children and drunks. Those who know Kyōto Yūzen will welcome the comparative explanation: the patterns, painting techniques and *nori* paste differ slightly. Green tea is offered for an extra ¥300. Until recently, Saihitsuan offered visitors a chance to try painting their own silk, but it became too popular, and they had to stop. But ask about it if you like, because they promised to start up the program again in the future. Those with further interest may wish to visit the main factories at Yūzen Danchi. Saihitsuan is open 9:00 −12:00 and 1:00−4:30, except Thurs.

Kibunesha 貴船社

This diminutive house, sheltered by sprawling pine branches, enshrines an extremely jealous Edo-period woman whose despair at her husband's philandering ruined her health and brought about her early death. Vowing before she died that no woman should again have to bear such agony, she pledged to intervene from the spirit world in cases of marital discōrd. Although Japanese divorce laws have been greatly modernized, she still gets a lot of business.

1 Enjoy Nikore's old garden over a cup of tea.

2 Tiny Kibunesha answers the prayers of women in distress. (K.Motoya)

Women who want to break up their husbands' affairs, or even their own marriages, visit frequently, rinsing their hands and mouth in the small basin and tying a slim paper, brushed with their wishes, on the small tree to the right. And the shrine appears effective -- limousines carrying a bride to her new home strictly avoid using that street.

Nagamachi Samurai Houses　長町武家屋敷

In Nagamachi stand many of Kanazawa's samurai houses, surrounded by tile-roofed mud walls and exuding an austere charm, at once intimidating and relaxing. Some have special windows in their gates, curtained with bamboo slats, for unseen inspection of visitors. Most have quiet gardens of brown dirt and sparse greenery, which can be glimpsed by passers-by or enjoyed fully at one of the several recently opened tea shops. Strollers in this neighborhood of narrow streets and dead ends can develop a sense of life in a castle town in an age when the size, style and location of one's house were specifically prescribed according to one's rank.

Many of the houses in Nagamachi, although old, are actually from the Meiji period, and not real samurai houses at all. There are only a handful of authentic ones left, and they, too, will soon be torn down and replaced by convenient, modern dwellings--chairs and tables, heating and plumbing. Everyone loves the old structures, but few are willing to live in them.

One man who is willing, is Mr. Yonekawa Hiroshi, a junior high history teacher who lives at 3-1-47 Nagamachi. His family came to Kaga 400 years ago, long before the Maedas took over, to serve as Imperial retainers. As well as being a virtually unretouched architectural wonder, the Yonekawa house is full of ancient lacquer, letters from various dignitaries (the less they are legible, the more the calligraphy is admired) and other museum-pieces. If you happen to catch Mr. Yonekawa at home (a Sunday is the best bet), he will show you his treasures and explain, in English, the layout of the house.

Onikawa　鬼川（武家屋敷跡）

Samurai may have enjoyed the comforts of prestige and lordly favor during much of the Edo period, but by the time of the Meiji Restoration, economic realities had become inescapable. In Kaga, many samurai were already deeply in debt to the merchants, and

Nagamachi samurai district in the winter. (C.Matsui)

when their stipends were cut off, the samurai were helpless. Thousands of unemployable, destitute warriors set off to Tōkyō and Hokkaidō to seek, poorly in most cases, their fortunes. Those who remained behind did their best to survive, often becoming craftsmen or farmers. Some even sank to the ignominy of business.

A typical case is Nomura Denbei, who first attempted to turn his vast, 1000 *tsubo* (3305 square meters) estate in Nagamachi into an apple orchard. For a time, Kaga *ringo* were very popular in Tōkyō, and the business flourished. But the center of apple production gradually shifted to the Tōhoku district, and Nomura began selling off his land. The last piece of property was bought in the early Shōwa period by a local industrialist, who moved a beautifully constructed old house here from Daishōji town. The house and garden are now open for inspection from 9:00 to 5:00 daily (8:00 to 6:00 in summer), for ¥300. Tea is served for ¥200 in the excellent tea room overlooking the Enshū-style garden.

The name Onikawa comes from the *yōsui* waterway running by the house and through the garden. The *'oni'* is now written with the Chinese character for 'demon,' but originally it was written 'honorable luggage,' indicating that the river was used to transport supplies from the sea to the castle.

TATEMACHI 竪 町

The diagonal Tatemachi-dōri, decorated with a green vine painted on the asphalt, is the center of Kanazawa's shopping district. It's worth a window-shopping stroll, beginning from the entrance opposite Daiwa Department Store, and continuing down into some older neighborhoods of Kanazawa. Old stores, like a doll shop, family groceries and a *tōfu* maker, are mixed in with stores displaying the latest fashions and fads. The excitement begins to die down at the far end of the road, but keep walking, across the Saigawa Ōdōri main street, and into Shin (New) Tatemachi-dōri.

Notice the Tengu Meat Store on the corner. It's one of the first foreign-inspired businesses in Hokuriku, and it took, ironically enough, the long-nosed, red-faced Tengu demon as its symbol. Shin Tatemachi is a slightly modernized version of an Edo-period Kanazawa market street. It is lined with antique dealers and unusual speciality stores like seaweed, calligraphy equipment and a koto maker. The road again crosses a main street, with a sprawling, wooden sake shop on the corner. Eventually, Tatemachi peters out into a Kanazawa-like dead end.

SHOPPING

Moroeya (諸江屋) Kutani shop has a museum-like third floor, a bargain basement and everything in between--a wider selection than most. They'll pack and ship medium-sized boxes overseas. 9:00–8:00, except Wed.

Itō Shoyūdo (伊藤尚友堂) is devoted to local Kaga crafts, particularly tea-related items. Flower exhibitions are often held on the 2nd floor. 9:30–7:00, except Wed.

Goshuin (御朱印). A Komatsu cake company famous for chocolate covered bean paste confections--cross-cultural enthusiasm gone berserk. 9:00—7:30 daily.

Nosaku (能 作) carries a good line of several local lacquerware styles, including outrageous Wajima and more reasonable Yamanaka. Prices reflect the recent boom in lacquer's popularity. Most people come to gaze at the second-floor display of exquisite artwork, and end up with inexpensive chopsticks as their souvenir. 9:00—7:00, except Wed.

Inachū (稲 忠). Lovely Wajima lacquerware sold by the delightful Mrs. Sakajiri. There's also a Shibazushi sales outlet in the front, popular with the Kenrokuen-bound who want to take along a lunchbox. 10:00—7:00 with irregular holidays.

Pied Piper House directly imports the latest records, and sells them at a few hundred yen below the usual inflated prices. 12:00 —9:00 daily.

Disk 33 (ディスク33). Imported classical recordings and audio parts. Mr. Yokoi's college-day dreams have been realized in this speciality shop. 12:00—6:45. Closed Wed.

Tōkyō Store. Good variety of foreign foods in three supermarket floors. Popular with night-owls. 10:00—10:00 daily.

Miyanaga Tabi (宮 永). One of the few remaining *tabi* makers in Japan. Mr. Miyanaga will measure every irregularity in your feet and sew up a pair of perfectly-fitting (but tight) white *tabi* socks for ¥1,600. If you want colors or patterns, take your own cloth, but be sure it's 100% cotton, because he refuses to work with synthetics. Mr. Miyanaga has such a back-log of work that it may take a month or more, but he can mail your *tabi* to you, or perhaps give a tourist's order first priority.

Satō (さとう). Delicious *manjū* (sweet bean cakes) made every morning around 7:00. The old lady is happy to have visitors watch. Sales until 9:00 p.m. Closed Wed.

Erihana (ゑり華). A favorite place for souvenir shopping—Yuzen purses and ties, paper goods, knick-knacks. Also elegant kimono fabric and accessories for gazing. Friendly, English-speaking clerk, Mukai Mamoru, is a great asset to the place. 9:00—7:00 daily. Closed Wed.

Ishida (いしだ) lacquerware is downright reasonable for some items, and worth the attention of comparative shoppers. Also some paulownia and Yūzen silk products. 9:00−7:30, except Wed.
Matsumoto Paper (松 本). From a wide variety of *washi* (Japanese paper) goods from all over the country, you can choose lightweight souvenirs, like boxes, calendars, dolls and wall decorations. Don't forget locally made Futamata paper goods--'cloud' paper sheets, muted purses, and postcards of Hakusan alpine flowers. 9:00−6:00, except Sun.

DRINKING

Mr. Donut. Cheapest coffee and best donuts in town; open 24 hours, it's a great place for midnight munchies or a sobering rest on the way home from Katamachi barhopping.

Mokkiriya (もっきりや). Popular jazz place with frequent evening concerts, usually featuring foreign jazz and folk musicians. The shop's own group often holds jam sessions. A folk-rock place, Last Summer, occupies the third floor. 8:00 a.m.–midnight daily.

Mon Ami is run by Mr. Kura, a unique character who began this shop in 1934 and is the last 'master' left over from the days when there were only 10 or so coffee shops in Kanazawa. He's full of information about the history of Japan's enthusiasm for coffee and stories about the Shikō boys who gathered in the hall upstairs to listen to classical music on victrolas. Things aren't what they used to be, with TV and home stereos taking over, but Mr. Kura still has the ancient gramophones on display in a cozy back room, coffee for only ¥250 and 20,000 records on request. Coffee-flavored soft ice cream and pudding are good. Another entrance to the same shop from behind City Hall is called 'Mozart.' 7:00–7:30 daily.

Saisei (犀せい). Excellent coffee, friendly people, English menu, good music. There are many books and magazines (notably a volume of reproductions from ancient Kanazawa screens) for browsing. Saisei becomes a bar in the evening. In the basement. 11:00–11:00, except Wed.

Mon (もん). Japanese style tea room above the *manjū* shop, Satō. Sweet bean confections, *mochi* rice cakes and green tea. 12:00–7:00, except Wed.

Seiyō Kojiki (西洋乞食). Strobe-pulsing, ear-splitting disco, in the basement. 6:00 p.m.–3:00 a.m. daily.

London-ya (倫敦屋). An English pub never had such a low ceiling, but the atmosphere is good and the prices reasonable. 4:00–12:00, except 1st and 3rd Sun.

Newspaper. Rock and folk and Budweiser beer in cans. Open 11:00 a.m. to 1:00 a.m. for pizza, spaghetti and unusual potato dishes. Wide range of whiskey prices.

Ichibankan (一番館). The newest of Katamachi's all-bar buildings. Just wander along the corridors and gasp at the fantastic variety. Some are very elegant (and exorbitant) like Charade (4th floor).

Some are cheaper and more relaxed, like Bottom Line (1st floor) and Sawarabi (3rd floor). Emperor on the top floor has a Filipino band, a big dance floor and lots of space for watching the slightly self-conscious line dancers. Most places are closed on Sun. Penthouse on the 4th floor has disco dancing.

Wonderland, on Ichibankan's 2nd floor, has a large copper bar in the front and a live band and comfortable couches in the back. Reasonable prices. Attractive Ms. Wajima, the manager, speaks English. 5:00−11:30 daily.

EATING

Gyohan (魚 半) is a bit of nostalgia left over from 1929. It used to be popular with Shikō students, and the Old Boys still gather here to reminisce. The place is scheduled for relocation in the new building on the same spot. 11:00−10:00 daily.

Unashin (うな新). Good, inexpensive food, especially *fugu* blowfish and *unagi* eel. The slightly run-down building has been around awhile, recalling the days when Katamachi was quiet and eating out a rare treat for Japanese. 11:00−10:00, except the 3rd Thurs. After dinner, try going up to the 5th floor *go* parlor to watch the men concentrating over the black and white stones.

Toichi Shokudō (ト一食堂). Best deal in town are the *teishoku* set meals of tempura, sukiyaki, *tonkatsu* pork or sashimi, each only ¥400. Everything else is cheap, too. 11:30−3:00 and 4:00−9:30, except 2 Sundays a month.

Sunaba (砂場). The most famous *soba* shop hardly lives up to its reputation, but the dark wood interior gives it a nice atmosphere. 11:00−7:45, except Wed. Especially mobbed on New Year's Eve for *toshikoshi* ('ring in the new') *soba.*

Uchūken (宇宙軒) has cheap food and beer, between 11:00 a.m. and 5:00 a.m., in a counter-style hole-in-the-wall somehow reminiscent of the Bowery. Closed Wed.

Lili Marlene (リリー・マルレーン). European food and late-night drinking to the strains of the Hungarian musicians' melodies. 5:30−2:00, except the 3rd Mon.

Hideyoshi (秀よし). Small and friendly, delicious fish at the counter or on the tatami. Ask them what's best that day. 12:00−11:00, except Sun. One of two Kanazawa branches of a Nanao restaurant.

Sekitei (石亭) specializes in the Japanese dishes thought most suited to foreign tastes: tempura, sukiyaki and *shabu-shabu.* The price rises considerably for a private room, so a cheap way to enjoy the excellent food is to stay in the dining room. Lunchtime is a bargain, when *teishoku* set courses cost from ¥900−1,800. Especially popular is the *godan bentō,* a five-tiered lunchbox which varies every day. Sekitei is also famous for *nagashi sōmen,* cold noodles running down a bamboo trough in the lovely garden, between May and early Sept. Reservations are not necessary, but a good idea. Tel. 31−2208. Open daily 11:30−10:00 (be in by 8:00).

Hyōtei (瓢亭). Strange and wonderful combination of western and Japanese cooking, like eel *en croute* and beef cooked with *miso.* The view of the Honda's garden makes it more special. 11:30− 9:00 daily.

Mizuguruma (水車). Everything is available, from sashimi, *nabe* hot pots and *tōfu* to *yakitori,* at a large U-shaped counter around the kitchen. Inexpensive lunches and raucous evenings. Mon.− Sat., 4:00−11:00. Lunch on weekdays between 11:30 and 1:30.

Botejū (ぼてぢゅう) has the best *okonomi-yaki* savory pancakes. Cooked, and kept warm, in front of you on a grill. 11:30−8:30, except Wed.

Ron (ロン). First-rate steaks cooked before you at the counter. Filet steaks are half-priced on the 29th, a homonym for meat. Spumoni available. Try the garlic rice. 11:30−1:30, 5:00−10:00.

Closed 10th, 20th, 30th. (Tel. 22—6688).

Kinkōrō (錦江楼). Chinese food, dressy atmosphere. 11:30—9:30 daily.

Pilsen (ぴるぜん). Long, German beer hall-style counter. Draft beer and good food to go with it, at reasonable prices. Just glance up and down the counter to see what's available. 5:00—1:00 daily.

Robe (炉 へ). Good Japanese-style grill. Try the *yudōfu* bean curd and *robe-mushi,* steamed shrimps and vegetables. Or ask Mr. Tagawa, who speaks English, for his suggestions. Then admire the photos of him and his wife, winning various local ballroom dance championships. They took up the hobby in late middle age and are still going strong. Robe also offers a nice souvenir: tea mugs and sake cups decorated with erotic *ukiyo-e* prints are on sale. 4:00—1:30, except every other Sun.

Ofuji Chaya (お藤茶屋) across from the Murō Saisei monument, has a dark, old-fashioned interior and reasonable prices. A pleasant walk from downtown by the Saigawa riverbank. 11:00—8:00, except Thurs.

Uogashi (魚河岸). Friendly atmosphere, and delicious food, at as reasonable a price as you can get for good sushi. Some grilled foods and soups also available. 12:00—12:00, except Thurs.

Goendama (五円玉). A tiny place open 24 hours for light food, drinks and coffee. Popular with students by day and the after-hours crowd at night. Closed 6:00 a.m. Sun. to 6:00 a.m. Mon.

Hiyoko (ひよこ). Best steak in town, low overhead, friendly master, Mr. Hayashi. Call ahead--it's a small place. About ¥4,000 for the works. Tel. 63—4054. 4:00—9:00 or so, except Sun.

VISITING

Hirosaka Catholic Church カトリック広坂教会

In the hall to the left of the sanctuary is an unusual collection of local Christian memorabilia. In the early 1600's, when Christianity was banned by Ieyasu and the Tokugawa shōgunate, the religion went underground. Some of the results are on display here: Madonna statues in the shape of Kannon, the Buddhist goddess of mercy, discreet crosses on everything from sake cups to ceremonial hats, and a well-preserved, if unpleasant, example of a *fumi-e,* the carved cross on a board, to be trodden upon by apostate Christians in symbolic proof of their recantation.

Ishiura Shrine 石浦神社

This is the oldest shrine in Kanazawa, dating back 1200 years, when shrines and temples were mixed together. In early Meiji period, when division was effected by Imperial decree, Ishiura became a shrine, managed by the prefecture. After World War II, the policy changed again. MacArthur ordered complete separation of church and state, so Ishiura became independent. There was an attempt to erase the characters for 'prefectural shrine' (縣　社) at the top of the signposts, but ironically enough, the engraved symbols were filled in with a darker stone. They attract the eye more than ever. But Ishiura is the most popular shrine in the city, and particularly lively at New Year's, autumn and spring festivals and the Shichi-Go-San festival in November. Every evening the shrine grounds are softly illuminated by stone lanterns. Out front, notice a little house containing some ancient pieces of fire-fighting equipment, one of which came from Holland.

★ Nakamura Memorial Museum 中村記念美術館

Nakamura Eishun (1908−1978) was a prosperous sake brewer and tea lover who devoted himself to collecting tea ceremony utensils. He hoped to protect Japan's national treasures, particularly Kanazawa's Ko-kutani, from dispersion and damage. In 1974, he moved his old home to Hondamachi, filled it with his valuable collection, designed a neighboring garden and teahouse, and donated the whole thing to Kanazawa City. On display in the lovely building are paintings, lacquerware, gold inlay work, pottery, and every kind of tea utensil imaginable, including some famous Sung porcelains. Notice the carved transoms on the second floor. The exhibition changes with the season, four times a year, and the unused portion is kept in the attached white storehouse. The ¥250 entrance fee includes tea and cakes, served in a tea-room alongside of the garden. 9:00−4:00, except Tues. & holidays.

Honda Garden (Shōfū-en) 松風苑（旧本多庭園）

The Hondas, a family of influential ministers to the Maedas, were granted a great chunk of property near the castle, where they built two villas, an enormous garden and homes for their own samurai retainers. Most of the holdings are now broken up, but behind MRO lies the best part of the original Enshū-style garden.

A mere one-third of its former size, it still retains the elegance of former days, surrounded by tiny, humble tea houses and one large Shoin-style mansion, Shōfūkaku. A restaurant attached to MRO provides a nice view of the garden, but it was originally designed as a strolling garden--the perspective is equally lovely from any point around the edge of the pond.

The former storehouse is now the Hokkoku Culture Center's pottery studio. Visitors are welcome to browse around inside. Around the corner, behind MRO, lies Hondamachi, where several of the early samurai houses still stand, their mud walls marked by graffiti, and their gardens shrunken by the press of population.

Suzuki Daisetsu Memorial　鈴木大拙碑

Just at the bottom of the cherry-lined stone path down from Kodatsuno ridge is an unpretentious monument in a bamboo-lined corner. This marks the birthplace of the great Zen philosopher, Suzuki Daisetsu. Born in 1869 into the family of the Hondas' attending physicians, Suzuki went on to become the greatest interpreter of Japanese Zen Buddhism to the west, deeply influencing everyone from the Beat Generation and the hippies to the mainstream of America.

Suzuki left Kanazawa at age 21 for Tōkyō, where he attended Tōkyō University and studied Zen at Engakuji temple in Kamakura. Achieving satori in 1896, he began to produce a series of important essays on Zen in English, most of which are still widely read today. He later became a professor at the prestigious Ōtani University in Kyōto. Suzuki died in 1966.

Murō Saisei Monument　室生犀星文学碑

Beside the river which comforted him in youth and inspired much of his literary output, Kanazawa City erected a monument to Murō Saisei (1889–1962), the poet and novelist whose works helped lay the foundation of modern Japanese literature. The stone memorial was designed in 1964 by the architect Taniguchi Yoshirō in the shape of a *nagashibina* figurine. In the old days, such primitive dolls were sent floating down-river with prayers to protect family members from ill health. No one is sure exactly how *nagashibina* is related to Saisei, but the monument is suitably engraved with one of his lovliest poems, *Anzu Yo* (Impassioned Apricot):

Riverside monument to Murō Saisei. (H.Ikeuchi)

Burst into blossom, apricot:
Dear world, grow bright.

Blaze into blossom, apricot,
Come alive, come alight
That, in your shining passion for perfection,
All may come right.

Saisei's childhood was spent at Uhōin temple near the Saigawa Ōhashi bridge. Bitterness plagued him throughout. His schooling was uneven, and his early attempts at earning a living were unsatisfactory. Eventually Saisei set off for Tōkyō to pursue his budding career as a poet. But the economic difficulties which face most struggling artists reinforced Saisei's inherent instability--he continued to drift back and forth between Kanazawa and Tōkyō for several years. At last his literary reputation, based on the prose he produced to survive, became established. He returned to poetry once more and wrote prolifically until his death.

Daiwa Parking
Kanazawa Prince Hotel
Hideyoshi
Elle Bldg
Zeniya
Keizei
Hokkoku Shorin
Hananasa Florist
Gyahan
Akiyoshi
Iketen
Modern Literature Museum
German Bakery
Ichibinbo
Ishida
Kinjoki Bldg
Kokin
Shibazushi
Daiwa
Utsunomiya
Nissei Pal
Mr. Donut
Moroeya Pottery
Central Park
Nihon Rykoku
Shakei Pizza
Kinki Nihon Tourist
Daiichi Seimei
Bldg
Ito Shoyudo
Prefectural History Museum
Nisso Tourist
Kanazawa Gekijo
Robe
Fukui Bank
Boteju
Sunaba
Nakagoshi
Unashin
tsumoto Paper
Pilsen
Uchuken
Murataya
Saisei
Tokyo Store
Tableau
Blue Ribbons Bldg.
Hirosaka Catholic Church
Matsuiya YH
Londonya
Gion
United Church of Christ
Nosaku Lacquer
City Hall
Miyanaga Tabi
Miyabe
New Orient Express
Hideyoshi
Sato Cakes Mon
Seiyo Kojiki
Toichi Shokudo
Mokkiriya
Pied Piper House
Yamatoku
Lili Marlene
Saigawa Odori
Entora
Nakamura
Mon Ami
Daiichi Hotel
Goshuin Cakes
Imachu Lacquer
Police Station
Hirosaka Pension
Kanazawa U. Attached Primary School
to Kenrokuen
Ishiura Shrine
Tengu Meat
Sekitei
Kanko Kaikan
International Culture Center
Ofuji Chaya
Muro Saisei Monument
Shin Tatemachidori
Newspaper
Social Education Center
Youth Hostel Office
Nakamura Memorial Museum
M R O
Shofukaku
Dr. Iino
Mizuguruma
Honda Family Garden
Pottery Studio
Honda Museum
Goendama
Hondamachi
ura Ba shi
Uogashi
Suzuki Daisetsu Memorial
Former Bidai

TATEMACHI

To KOTATSUNO

to Hirota
to Satsuma Shrine

During his period of restless movement between Tōkyō and Kanazawa, Saisei wrote his best-known poem, *Furusato* (Hometown). It expresses a nostalgia which is at once universal in its appeal and widely associated with one specific hometown, Kanazawa.

Hometown

One's hometown is a place
　　　　　to be longed-for from a distance,
A yearning-lode, a magnet
　　　　　drawing, from sadness, song.

It's not a place to which,
　　　　　however dire one's failure,
A man might dare return
　　　　　beggared, the world gone wrong.

Now, lonely in this city,
　　　　　with, ah, what depth of feeling,
　　　　　what tears too sad for song,
I yearn for my heart's true capital,
　　　　　that town where I belong.

Sarumaru Shrine　　猿丸神社

Until the new Saigawa Road was built about 10 years ago, Sarumaru was a quiet shrine in the middle of the rice fields--a perfect spot for secret nocturnal visitors. Those who had some complaint about someone (usually a jealous wife with no other recourse) could find relief by visiting Sarumaru Shrine at the hour of the bull (around 2:00 a.m.). Wearing a white kimono and carrying a comb in her teeth, the sufferer would tack a straw doll, representing the object of her anguish, through the heart, to one of the great trees in the shrine grounds. These days, women have more direct ways of dealing with such problems, so the hollow clang of the hammer and nail is no longer heard in the neighborhood. The nails left from the Edo period have risen with the growing trees, way up above eye level, but they are still visible.

TERAMACHI 寺 町

When the Maedas took over Kaga, they were well aware of their position as foreign conquerors and the lasting threat of the Ikkō-shū sect and its native farmer-followers. In a brilliant stroke of city planning genius, Lord Toshitsune ordered in 1583 that various non-Ikkō-shū temples, including the scores that had moved here with the Maedas from Takefu and Nanao, should gather at two locations on the edge of town, the Saigawa riverside plateau and the Asano riverside mountain (Higashiyama). This unification move not only dispelled the fear of internal uprising, but it also made an external attack very difficult. Warriors from Echizen (Fukui) to the west or Etchū (Toyama) to the east would have to pass through a sacred temple district, cross a river, and then pick their way through the maze of narrow streets before having a chance to attack the castle.

What remains here is a unique ancient neighborhood on the edge of swinging Katamachi--majestic old temples and a geisha district, set off by a view so lovely that drivers are warned to be extra careful when crossing the bridge.

Before it became 'Temple Town,' when Izumi was still wild fields, there was an execution ground in this area. Thus memorial *jizō* statues are found here in abundance and provide the point of tourist interest in several of the temples. Few visitors will want to look at every temple--at some point, the proverbial 'if you've seen one, you've seen them all' satiation takes over--but the distinguishing features of several are included here for your choosing.

SHOPPING

Tsuda's Mizuhiki Shop (津田). Run by the son of Jukken-machi's Mrs. Tsuda, this 150-year-old shop preserves the three-story family hall of the original house, so look up when you go in. As you watch Mr. Tsuda fashion twisted-paper decorations for wedding gifts, he'll chat amiably about the future of his family craft. Although in rural Kanazawa he still gets orders, the *mizu-hiki*'s days are numbered, and he expects to branch off into other areas eventually. Stock up on ceremonial money envelopes or buy a small twisted-paper doll. 9:00–7:00, except Sun.

Tamondō (多聞堂) is a new shop making an old rice cracker, called Chiyo no Mon. Steamed, softened rice shaped around an almond is baked and flavored with cheese, soy sauce or salt, for a good sake snack. 9:00–7:30, except Sun.

Urata (浦　田) is famous for sweet bean-filled doll cakes, shaped like Kanazawa's local toy, Okiagari, and Maizuru, a triangular, ginger-spiced sweet. 9:00–8:30 except Thurs. Next door is a branch of the delicious **Fūgetsudō** (風月堂), a national Western cake chain. **Koide's** (小　出) best known cake is Shibafune, a ginger-frosted, oval cookie. But also try Senka, sugared walnuts sold in pretty cardboard boxes. 8:00–7:00 daily. Sun. until 4:00.

Moroeya (諸江屋) has specialized in making *rakugan,* dry molded cakes, for 150 years. Made of rice powder and sugar, and pressed into intricate, hand-carved molds, these cakes will keep (in a dark, dry place) for a year. The cakes boxed in *washi,* Japanese paper, are suitable for overseas mailing. If you ask (*Rakugan bunko o misete itadakemasenka?*), someone will show you the small museum two doors down, displaying old cake-making text books, wooden molds (the shop has about 300 of them) and even a perfect sugar replica of the ceramic bird in the Prefectural Art Museum. 8:30–7:00 daily.

Shineidō (真栄堂). Although there are several nice souvenir shops and tea houses clustered around Ninjadera, Shineidō is the most fun. For ¥250 and up, you can paint your own designs on a Kutani cup, sake holder or vase. Then you watch the old grandfather bake it in a small kiln while you sip a free cup of tea. Open daily, 8:00–6:00.

Yamada Geta (山　田). People don't wear *geta* (raised clogs) very often any more, and when they do, it's more likely a mass-produced, inexpensive pair. The population of craftsmen making *geta* by hand here is reduced to a single person, the younger Mr. Yamada, near Rokuto Plaza. He will custom-make a sturdy pair in a day, using fine-grained woods like paulownia (*kiri*), and your choice of colorful thongs. Or you can choose among the *geta* and

Painting Kutani at
Shineidō. (H.Ikeuchi)

zori slippers in the sales shop run by the elder Mr. Yamada. (He
got tired of cutting and sanding, and several years ago switched to
retailing only.)

Kabata (かばた). Surrounded by the flavorful aroma of *miso,*
customers happily choose among buckets of preserved fish and
showcases of various pickles– housewives for their family dinners
and tourists for 'famous product' souvenirs. The best sellers are
pickled *fugu* (blowfish) year-round, and *kabura-zushi* (a pickled
fish and turnip sandwich--but it's good!) between Nov. and March.
Try a sample. 9:00–7:00, except Sun.

Shankar (しゃんかある). All kinds of imports, jewelry, baskets,
pottery, sold by English-speaking Mr. Muroyama and his wife.
Kanazawa foreigners are especially grateful for his large-size Indian
shirts and dresses. Open 10:00–9:00 daily.

Hashimoto (橋 本) horse, dog and cattle equipment shop has
been run for the last 70 years by 87-year-old Mr. Hashimoto. Teramachi used to be lined with equestrian supply shops in the days
when Noda and Izumi were crowded with soldiers, but Mr. Hashimoto is the only one left. His son keeps hoping he'll retire and
relax, but he stubbornly sticks to his trade, cutting and stitching.
Look around at the chains, collars and saddles, and perhaps buy a
handsewn leather belt.

EATING

Terakiya (てら喜や) restaurant above and in back of the fishmonger's is cheaper than most, ¥1,400 at lunch and ¥3,000 and
up at dinner. The best part is that you can go downstairs and point
out the fish you'd like grilled or sliced into sashimi. Real down-
home food and atmosphere. 11:00–8:00 except Sun. and holidays.

Sankinrō (山錦楼). An old, elegant restaurant on Hamaguri Zaka, overlooking Saigawa. From both inside and out, Sankinrō looks like a Kyōto inn. The bright cobalt walls in the lobby and some upstairs rooms, as well as the general size of the place (it doesn't double as an inn) are remarkable. Perfect for a leisurely lunch or a long, boisterous evening. ¥5,000 and up. Phone ahead for faster service, and fix the price. Tel. 43–5577.

Tsubajin (つば甚). Nationally famous for creative Japanese cooking served on old, valuable dishes (this explains the high prices). For the non-connoisseur of Japanese antiques, try a sample of their Kaga cooking at **Jimbei** (甚 平) in Century Plaza. ¥2,000 at lunch and ¥5,000 up at dinner. 11:00–10:00 daily. The Hakusui hotel next door has a nice ceramics gallery off the lobby.

Maison de Rose (メゾン・ローゼ). Delicious food and an admirable wine list. Mr. Nakatani, the proprietor, is a Cornell Hotel School graduate. Homemade ice cream and sherbets. Visit the gallery downstairs. 11:00– 9:30. Closed 1st & 3rd Wed.

Suginoi (杉の井). Elegant, but reasonable. *Bentō* lunch for ¥1,500 at the counter, or in a lovely room for an extra ¥500. Evenings, ¥8,000 up. Open daily from 11:00.

Toyoshima (とよ島). The ¥500 tempura lunch, with a view of Saigawa and Murō Saisei's old house opposite, is a great bargain. Open daily from 11:00.

Inakaya (田舎家). Great atmosphere and a jovial master. Order by pointing at the glass fish-case, or at some delicious-looking dish being attacked by a fellow customer. Recommended is *zōsui,* a savory rice gruel, after some sashimi, but *teishoku* set dinners are the best bargain. 5:00–11:00, except Mon.

Kabuto (かぶと). Fresh white bread sells out daily. Cheesecake topped with real sour cream is a favorite. 10:00–10:00.

DRINKING

Sodegae (袖ガ江) on the main street, has antiques in the front half of the shop and a good coffee bar, presided over by friendly Mr. Harita, at the back. 9:00–6:00, except Tues.

Jigeimu (自芸夢) beside Ninjadera, displays and sells the pottery of locally famous Takamitsu Issei, and is run by his lovely wife. Mr. Takamitsu designed the ceramic decorations in Musashi's underground walkway. 9:30–5:00 daily.

Fancy (ファンシー) in the basement of Hirokōji Kaikan, is run by Hiro-chan, a unique lady who has spent her life dressing, speaking and acting like a man. You may find her bar closed—she sometimes locks up and goes out to have a drink or two at other places —but generally it's open 5:00 p.m.–7:00 a.m. except Sunday.

Roppongi (六本木) offers another great view of the river, especially at night when it turns into a bar. 9:30–11:00 daily.

Tyrol (チロル) has a small coffee counter, but is better known for excellent tarts and chocolates. 9:00–9:00 except Sun.

Donkey (ドンキー). Outdoorsy atmosphere. Casual resting place for walks along the river bank. No liquor. 10:00–10:00, except Tues.

Ichirinku (一菓区). Budding artists can exhibit paintings and ceramics here. Cakes displayed in the glass case tempt dieting customers. 8:30–10:00, except 2nd and 4th Tues.

VISITING

Uhōin 雨宝院

Smack on the river banks, a quiet oasis in a neighborhood dominated by bars and busy streets, Uhōin temple preserves the atmosphere enjoyed by poet and novelist Murō Saisei as a boy. A week after his birth in 1889, Saisei was adopted by this temple's priest, and he lived here until 1909, playing along the Saigawa and going through what was probably a distressing childhood. In 1922, the temple was washed away in a flood, and Saisei was among those who contributed to its reconstruction. The old grandmother living here now will show you, for ¥150, Saisei's letters and other memorabilia.

In the front yard is a stone erected in 1827, a period of famine, inviting people to bring abandoned or starving children to the temple, where they would be cared for: *Mayoi-go koko e mote ku beshi.*

Shinmeigū 神明宮

Shinmeigū shrine is famous for its enormous, 900-year-old *keyaki* tree. Before the land along Saigawa was reclaimed by an expanding city, this shrine was on the river bank itself, and the tree was used at the boat landing as a sturdy anchor. Iron fittings for the boat hooks can still be seen half-way up the trunk. They have been covered by foliage as the tree has grown. The shrine is also known for its special roasted rice cake, *aburi-mochi,* sold at the lively semi-annual festivals, in mid-May and October.

Hamaguri Zaka--Clam Slope 蛤 坂

To the left after crossing Saigawa Ōhashi bridge, a diagonally sloping road leads up to Teramachi plateau. In the beginning of Edo period, there was a foot path here, which eventually was overrun with houses and other buildings. Then a fire destroyed the area, and a passage was opened up again, like a clam which opens when cooked.

Jōgakuji 成学寺

The front yard is occupied by the 50-year-old *migawari jizō* who will gladly serve as your substitute, bearing for you any ills and troubles that you ask him to take on.

Neko Dera--Cat Temple (Ryūshōji) 猫寺（竜昌寺）

One night, about 200 years ago, the cat kept by a childless old couple appeared to them in a dream. It said, 'If I die, build me a grave at Ryūshōji, and I'll answer people's prayers.' Upon awakening, the old people were grieved to find that their dear cat was dead. They took it to the temple, where the astonished priest told them he had had the same dream. They buried the cat, who subsequently received the supplications of many worshippers. Since then the story has spread, and many pet owners have brought their dead animals to Ryūshōji for burial. Until about 10 years ago, such ashes and corpses were placed under the small altar behind the temple, but it became so crowded that the priest now refuses any more. He does still perform *kuyō* memorial prayers upon request. But he doesn't encourage tourists, and as a matter of fact, the story is more interesting than the small altar itself.

Western Pleasure Quarter 旧西廓

'Nishi,' the second largest tea house area of Kanazawa, is quieter these days than when the boisterous district was marked by solid gates to keep enslaved geisha from running away. In these days, even the prime evening hours are rather subdued, except one night in August, when the geisha perform their *obon* dance. However quiet the Nishi atmosphere, the geisha here are reputed to be the city's most beautiful (Higashi is better known for artistic talent).

Nishi also boasts the youngest geisha in town. Kyōno of Kazunoya is a 21-year-old who rejected a career of serving tea as an 'office lady' and chose instead to be a geisha like her mother and grandmother.

A little to the east of the tea house street, beyond the *yōsui* waterway, is a true red light district, packed with sleazy bars and crawling with sleazier customers. Night-time strollers be warned.

Kōsen Kutani Factory 九谷光仙窯元

Kōsen is a regular stop on the tourist track and the only Kutani factory within the city limits. Visitors may watch the potters in action, and the tour is free, but entry to the painters' area is forbidden. 8:00−12:00 and 1:00−5:00 daily.

Nensaiji 念西寺

Kaga's greatest haiku poet, Chiyo, lived in this nunnery for three or four years in the 1750's. Not much is known about Chiyo except that she was born in Mattō and lost her husband and child at a young age. She found in Nensaiji solace and peace from a difficult world. Her serene frame of mind is evident in her most famous poem, *Asagao ni tsurube torarete morai mizu* ('My well bucket taken over by the morning glory--I'll go elsewhere for today's water.'). Because the temple has been expanded, the original well is now found inside. Recently little water can be drawn from it, but it is still treasured by admirers of Chiyo. A beautifully tended monument to her is in the front garden, and the nuns hold an annual memorial service, attended by Kanazawa haiku poets, on October 10.

Lost children pillar at Uhōin.
(H.Ikeuchi)

Chiyo's famous well-bucket as carved by Mr.Ishizaki Shūhō.
(S.Ishizaki)

Senjuin 千手院

On the path leading to the small temple are rows of *jizō,* all colorfully bibbed and capped, peeking out from their secure huts. Strange offerings of vegetables--an eggplant, an onion--can be seen before them.

Rokuto Plaza 六斗の広見

Kanazawa is famous for its winding narrow streets and frequent dead ends, which in the old days served to confuse enemy attackers making their way to the castle. The modern-day stroller will also notice that back streets suddenly widen in places, creating small breathing spaces in crowded neighborhoods. Such *hiromi* were used for town gatherings and as a means (no doubt ineffective) of fire prevention. One plaza is found in the heart of the Teramachi temple district. The road leading out of the Rokuto Plaza, past Gesshōji, Kaizenji and Ryūenji, is the former highway to Tsurugi town. It's still crowded with old shops, houses and craftsmen, especially carpenters, and one of the most picturesque tatami makers in town, Mr. Hayashi, on the left.

Gesshōji 月照寺

Gesshōji's grounds are lined with unusual *jizō*, gathered long ago from Utatsuyama and Tsurugi when modernizing road construction threatened their peaceful existence. Here they are sheltered and draped with strips, which look suspiciously like kimono underskirt belts. Usually a *jizō* will have a rather benign expression and a simple shape, but these at Gesshōji are more similar to the elaborate Buddhist statuary which originated in India.

Kiōin 希翁院

In Kiōin's front yard is a small house protecting their *enmeijizō,* who provides supplicants with a long life. It's worth a try!

Ryūenji 竜渕寺

A spacious, 400-year-old Zen garden is found behind this temple, and the friendly old priest will be glad to show it to you. Actually, it's designed not for walking, but for viewing from the temple porch. Particularly in the rainy season, when low areas flood and the lanterns seem to be floating, or in the spring when outdoor tea ceremonies are held here, one wishes that other temples had been able to keep up their gardens as well. In the graveyard, you may be introduced to the various lords, samurai and illustrious persons, notably several Oda Nobunaga relatives, at rest.

Kaizenji 開禅寺

Although since the war, abortion has become a widely accepted form of birth control in Japan, many women feel the need to pray for the souls of their *mizuko,* the 'washed away babies.' New *jizō* statues, comforted with rattles and pinwheels and identified by name, have been erected at Kaizenji. In late July the city's gynecologists and OB-GYN nurses all gather here for a memorial service.

Sankōji 三光寺

Although the fourth largest city in Meiji Era Japan and thus a political force to be reckoned with, Kanazawa did not play much of a role nationally in the revolutionary changes of the Meiji Restoration. In fact, the change from feudal *han* to national *ken* was stormy here--for the first year of the prefectural system, the government tactfully moved off to Mikawa town to avoid confrontations with recalcitrant samurai. Unfortunately, on the national political level, Kanazawa's notable 'contribution' was nothing to be proud of, and even today, people rarely mention the Kioizaka Incident. In 1878, a Kanazawa boy named Shimada Ichirō assassinated the great Meiji leader, Count Ōkubo Toshimichi, known for his influence in Japan's technological and political modernization. Shimada's gang of right-wing fanatics had their headquarters in this now disgraced and neglected temple, earning them the name of the Sankōji Faction. Not much of a tourist attraction, except perhaps for fans of modern history.

★ **Ninjadera (Myōryūji)** 忍者寺（妙立寺）

Imagine an innocent-looking temple, so cleverly built around a central well that 29 staircases provide escape (or attack) routes to 22 of the 23 rooms. Then try to imagine the purpose of all the hidden chambers, secret tunnels and trick doors. The tour guides will explain that the lord used the temple as a discreet route to the western geisha district or for an emergency escape if the castle defenses should otherwise fail. The experts will somewhat indignantly state that simple lack of space dictated Myōryūji's odd construction, and that the head priest is exaggerating the story for profit. Whichever explanation sounds most reasonable, a well-timed visit is fascinating.

Don't go at noon or on Sundays or holidays--the temple has

become a major tourist attraction, and the hordes destroy its charm. A reservation is necessary (tel. 41−2877--at least one of the student part-time guides should speak some English), but try to make it at 3:00 or 4:00 p.m. Often two or three people without reservations can squeeze into each 20-minute tour. Myōryūji is closed on the first and 13th of the month and at New Years. ¥400. 9:00−4:30.

The major attractions are as follows;

1. The well, at the bottom of which is said to be a tunnel to Saigawa river and the castle.
2. Stairs lined with translucent rice paper, warning those inside of intruders.
3. Trick doors behind which guards may hide.
4. A hidden stairway.
5. A secret room with stairs concealed in the closet.
6. A tea room with a very low ceiling, because there are more stories inside than the external view would suggest.
7. The tea room's kitchen, where water could be lifted from the well.
8. The one room without an escape-worthy stairway--the *seppuku* ritual suicide chamber.
9. A *tokonoma* alcove with a hidden door behind it.
10. A 5½-mat tea room for the lord's exclusive use. The scroll in the alcove was written by the 13th Maeda lord, Nariyasu. The bridge helped the guests at tea parties imagine they were on the banks of the Saigawa river.
11. Another secret stairway, constructed so that exit, but no entry, is possible.

Another item, which is emphatically not part of the tour, is the nicely housed *jizō* figure in the temple grounds. His facial features have been almost completely rubbed away, in the days before penicillin, by syphilitics who hoped the *jizō* would cure their own diseased noses.

Gannenji 願念寺

On his long return trip from the Narrow Road to the North in 1689, poet Bashō was looking forward to meeting a Kanazawa disciple, Kosugi Isshō, for the first time. When he got here, Bashō visited Gannenji, only to discover that Isshō had recently died.

Shōgetsuji's Giant Cherry tree. (H.Ikeuchi)

Entrance to the Nishi Geisha District. (H.Ikeuchi)

Bashō then composed a haiku epitaph, *Tsuka mo ugoke waga naku koe wa aki no kaze,* which is now engraved on a marker outside the temple gate:

> Move, if you can hear,
> Silent mound of my friend,
> My wails and the answering
> Roar of autumn wind.

Isshō's most famous poem, *Kokoro kara yuki utsukushi ya nishi no kumo,* serves as the epitaph on his gravestone, standing to the left inside the temple gate:

> How beautiful it is,
> The snow on the ground,
> And the cloud in the west
> That brings more of it.

Notice also the three horizontal lines decorating the outside wall. They signify the high rank of the priest, a distant relative of the Imperial Family.

Kaga Crafts Museum 加賀民芸資料館

The building right beside the Great Cherry Tree of Shōgetsuji contains two floors of wonderful Edo and Meiji period treasures, antiques and junk. Many items are poorly displayed, explanatory notes are sketchy or in difficult characters, and some of the things seem to be there only on the strength of their old age. But there are many unusual household goods, much lovely craftsmanship and an enormous variety--a visit is well worth the ¥200 entrance fee. Your imagination as to their function and background is probably better than any explanation could be. There's a small coffee bar on the first floor. Open 8:30—5:00 (April-Sept.) and 8:30—4:00 (Oct.–March).

Shōgetsuji 松月寺

Shōgetsuji is a small temple boasting a giant, 15-meter-high cherry tree bursting through the earthen wall in the front grounds. The 300-year-old tree was given to the temple's second priest by Lord Toshitsune, from Komatsu Castle where he was living in retirement. Now the temple has little else to offer, except acupuncture and moxa treatments in the mornings.

Fushimidera 伏見寺

Fushimidera has an interesting background and is one of the few Teramachi temples open for public tour, but an actual visit rates only mixed reviews. Because of the head priest's uninspired explanatory spiel, there's something to be said for limiting one's visit to the front grounds only. Here we find, on the left, the grave of Imohori Tōgorō, the famous Nara-period potato digger of local legend. Fushimidera was built by Tōgorō in the Yamashina area and moved to Teramachi in the early Edo period.

If you do decide to suffer the tour, it will cost ¥150, but you will have a chance to glimpse the 1200-year-old National Treasure, a Buddha supposedly built by Tōgorō from the gold washed up in the well. Other items of interest: the rusty remains of some swords and tools found in Tōgorō's grave when it was moved here; two side-altars, one dedicated to merchants (there's supposed to be an erotic Indian statue behind those tiny gold doors) and one to traffic safety (the black wooden statue dating from the Heian era was originally the Buddhist deity who accompanied souls to heaven-- now he oversees transportation). Notice, too, Lord Toshiie's 12 Buddhist guardian figurines, each with an animal on his hat representing a year of the oriental zodiac. Open 8:00—6:00 daily.

Daienji 大円寺

Looking somewhat like a Swiss chalet, with its unusual white-washed walls, Daienji's main attraction is its four-meter-high *jizō* statue, made in 1700. The priest-sculptor took pity on people who never receive proper burial, and inserted some of their bones into the face, neck, chest, hands and feet of the statue. Thus, those unfortunates will receive the benefits of people's prayers to the *jizō*. This is the world's largest human bone statue. You can offer some coins and a prayer at the little house to the left as you enter the temple grounds. Then, remove your shoes and step up onto the platform for a close look through the wooden screen. The *jizō* is dressed in colorful, exotic robes and surrounded by hundreds of small gold statues.

Ryūzōji 立像寺

This temple has a new, eye-catching gate, built two years ago, at a cost of 20 million yen, by expert carpenters called all the way from Tochigi Prefecture. Ryūzōji has the largest area of any temple in Teramachi, and in its interior garden is a 'Christian lantern' with a cross-shaped neck and a figure of Jesus carved in the base. It is reputed to have been brought to Kanazawa by the Christian daimyō, Takayama Ukon, escaping Hideyoshi's anti-Christian wrath. Either ask at the door (Try *'Tōrō o misete itadakemasenka?'*) or go around back to the right by yourself.

In the front yard notice the rare two-storied belfry. The upper floor holds a wooden drum. The 17th-century bell on the lower floor is rung at 5:00 a.m. daily. Peek in the windows of the old storehouse, where sutras are kept in a revolving container.

W Slope W坂（ダブル坂）

Just up from Sakura Bridge is a W-shaped stone stairway, a favorite strolling path of poet Muro Saisei and Shikō (Fourth Higher School) students. But the boys were careful not to mount the stairs during exam time, since in Japanese pronunciation, 'W' is a homonym for 'double,' suggesting a retake of a failed test. Perhaps the students also felt premonitions of the ghost which appeared to several different people about six years ago. A thin, pale woman, with a long Edo-period hair style and a red sash across the front of her white kimono, floated around the bottom-most corner, always on the second of the month. The police investigated, but found no legends or documents relating any suitable tragic incident. Even a gangster living at the top of the slope declared that although he's afraid of no living person, this ghost has him nervous. The best time to catch a glimpse of her is 1:00 or 2:00 a.m. Good luck.

Keiganji 桂岩寺

Keiganji was destroyed by fire in 1961, but replaced with an unusual modern temple structure, a lesson to those who assume that interest in religion is on the wane. Only one of the unique

500 Statues of Rakan (Buddhist monks who have attained nirvana) was saved, but they are gradually being replaced, and now line, somewhat gaudily, the inside balcony. Walk in freely. You're also welcome to contribute a statue, for about ¥100,000.

Hōshūji 宝集寺

One of Kanazawa's Three Big Buddhas, this one looking like a smaller version of the Daibutsu in Kamakura, is found in Hōshūji's Rokkakudō (six-sided hall, which actually has eight sides). The massive copper head is from the original statue, dedicated to the health and safety of Minamoto Yoritomo (late 1100's). It was burned, but the body was rebuilt in wood by a Maeda relative in thanks for the birth of a long-awaited child (a son, of course). The hall is always open.

Kōshi Vengeance Monument 孝子碑

On the main street passing through Heiwa-machi to Daijōji, a stroller will come across a lot filled with monuments. They memorialize dutiful sons who avenged the senseless deaths of their father and grandfather. The family lived by a bamboo grove in this area on the edge of town. When a Kaga samurai named Yamada Gonzaemon was passing by one day, the lovely bamboo caught his eye. Drawing his sword, he boldly cut off a piece, and when the father and grandfather protested, he cut them down, too. The two elder sons immediately sought revenge, but were themselves killed. The youngest son, only 19 years old, patiently went into training and secretly plotted his strategy. At last his chance came when he heard that Gonzaemon was to pass through Jūichiya town again. The boy laid in wait, and struck down the arrogant samurai, much to the satisfaction of everyone concerned. Such legends of honorable behavior are rarely forgotten.

Daijōji 大乗寺

This temple is one of the most beautiful places in Kanazawa-- serene and cosy, with a sense of the past and a stunning view of the sea. Although it's an active Zen temple and a branch of the famous Eiheiji in Fukui, it hasn't yet been 'discovered' by tourists. Visitors in the morning (around 4:30) are welcome to join in Zen meditation, and those in the evening can sit on the cool stone steps and listen to the resonant peal of the temple bell. If you ring the inside gong three times, a monk will appear and show you the

Lord Maeda Toshiie rests
here (H.Ikeuchi)

Mysterious W Slope. (Oasis)

meditation room (*zazendō*) and the cavernous kitchen. (For this
service, an offering would be gratefully received.)

Daijōji was built in 1263 by Togashi, the local ruling family, in
their stronghold of Nonoichi. Although the Togashi were eventually overthrown by peasants incited by the Jōdo Shinshū sect, Daijōji
managed to survive under the protection of the Honda family and
other aristocratic supporters. They rebuilt the temple in its present
spot in 1697, and most of the original structures remain.

Of all the graves dotted around Daijōji, the most impressive are
those connected with the Hondas. The family's massive stone
graves lie behind a wooden gate at the end of the second path on
the left. Such magnificent slabs cost a fortune these days, so the
family has decided that future Hondas will join their ancestors
under the same markers. Just this side of the Honda graves, on the

left, lie the 12 identical headstones of the Honda family samurai who participated in a dramatic local Meiji Restoration incident. When their lord, Honda Masahira, a farsighted reformer, was killed by conservative fanatics, these 12 noble retainers dutifully killed his assassins. Then, to avoid trial by the new Meiji law, they solemnly disemboweled themselves.

Up to the left behind the Honda plot lie the 69 former head priests of Daijōji. Their graves are lined up in a U shape, with the founder in the center, and the stones getting progressively newer, and less mossy, towards the edge.

On a warm day, particularly in April, a hike up behind Daijōji is very pleasant. The hill is occupied by a strange mixture--a mammoth auditorium, a mental institution and a great statue of St. Rennyo set among the cherry trees.

A note for meditators: be prepared to join the cleaning and sweeping of the grounds after prayers. And don't be surprised when the monks, in deference to the politics of the present head priest, turn to the Rising Sun flag tacked onto the wall and break into a verse of 'Kimigayo,' the semi-official national anthem.

Nodayama Graveyard 野田山墓地

A visit to this hill on the edge of town combines a pleasant stroll with a history lesson. Among the shady trees and mossy rocks lie various Kanazawa luminaries, including novelist Murō Saisei and most of the Maeda family. Even poor, misguided Shimada Ichirō, the right-wing fanatic who assassinated Meiji statesman Ōkubo Toshimichi, is granted a spot here.

At the top of a stone stairway (250 steps, count 'em), find Lord Toshiie's gravestone, proclaiming him Ruler of Kaga, Noto and Etchū. He is surrounded by his descendants and their wives, all enclosed in high wooden fences and marked by *torii* gates. Then down the hill beneath him, arranged by rank and generation, lie Maeda retainers and officials, on down to the graves of the common people in the lowlands at Lord Toshiie's feet. On the way out, drop into Tōunji (桃雲寺) temple, which guards Lord Toshiie's grave (his posthumous name is Tōun).

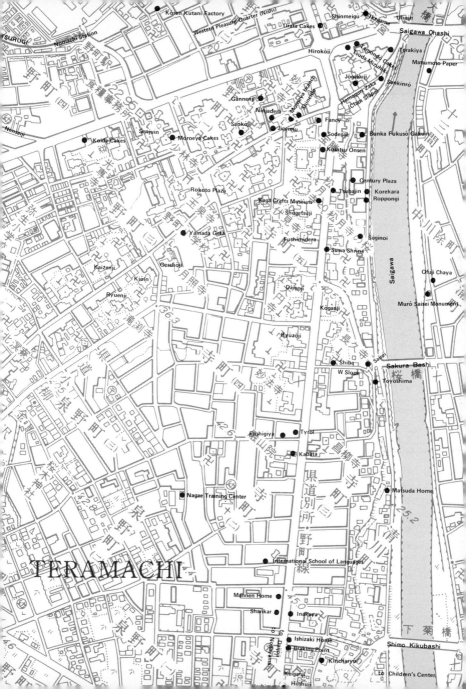

Kōzen Kutani Factory

Western Pleasure Quarter (Nishi)

Shinmeigū

Ikegame

Uhain

Nomachi Station

TSURUGI

Saigawa Ōhashi

Urata Cakes

Terakiya

Hirokōji

Amondō Cakes

Tsuda Mizuhiki

Matsumoto Paper

Jōgekuji

Sōkinrō

Hemuguri Zaka (Crash Slope)

Gannenji

Ninjadera

Moroeya branch

Shinatei

Sankoji

Fancy

Jigemu

Sodegae

Bunka Fukusō Gakuin

Senjuin

Koide Cakes

Moroeya Cakes

Kōatsu Onsen

Rokuto Plaza

Century Plaza

Kaga Crafts Museum

Tsubajin

Korekara

Shagetsuji

Roppongi

Nensaiji

Yamada Geta

Fushimidera

Suginoi

Suwa Shrine

Kaizenji

Gesshoji

Saigawa

Kioin

Ofuji Chaya

Ryuenji

Daienji

Murō Saisei Monument

Kōganji

Ryūzoji

Shiba

Saisei

Sakura Bashi

W Slope

Toyoshima

Fushigiya

Tyrol

Kabata

Matsuda Home

Nagae Training Center

International School of Languages

TERAMACHI

Mannen Home

Shankar

Inakaya

Matsuda Home

Ishizaki Home

Braking Point

Kincharyō

Keiganji

Hoshuji

Shimo Kikubashi

Children's Center

KANAZAWA SUBURBS （郊 外）

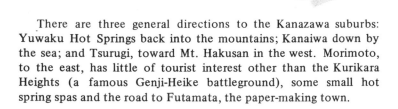

There are three general directions to the Kanazawa suburbs: Yuwaku Hot Springs back into the mountains; Kanaiwa down by the sea; and Tsurugi, toward Mt. Hakusan in the west. Morimoto, to the east, has little of tourist interest other than the Kurikara Heights (a famous Genji-Heike battleground), some small hot spring spas and the road to Futamata, the paper-making town.

YUWAKU HOT SPRINGS——EDO MURA 湯涌温泉

★ Edo Mura and Danpūen 江戸村と檀風苑

It may take half a day to visit Edo Village and its neighboring Yuwaku Hot Spring spa, but each minute has something interesting to offer. The bus (#12), loaded with mountain villagers, travels out Kodatsuno ridge, on a road so narrow that you can see the Saigawa and Asano rivers way down below on either side. Get off at the end of the line and head up the path for Edo Mura, a spacious, Williamsburg-like village settled with buildings from Hokuriku's feudal period. Each is representative of a different social class, in an era when architecture was strictly dictated by law.

The town is laid out in impressive order, beginning with an inn from along the Hokuriku North Road, where the Meiji Emperor actually spent the night. The road itself, passing in front of the inn, is surprisingly narrow (when a daimyō procession passed by, peasants were ordered off to the side to bow to the ground). Next comes a piece of the original *namako* wall from Kanazawa Castle, with a glass section offering a rare glimpse at its inner bamboo and wood construction. Around the corner are two peasant houses, a small one which vividly illustrates the grim life of feudal farmers, and a larger one from Noto, displaying the annual *aenokoto* ceremony when farmers invite the gods into their homes to eat, bathe and spend the night.

Another house along the path illustrates the life of peasants who moonlighted as paper makers. Next is a Shinshū sect temple, housing an unusual drum tower. Beside that are two samurai houses, one of the wealthy Maeda advisor family, Yokoyama, and the other of the low-ranking Takamine samurai family. (Biochemist Takamine Jōkichi became internationally famous for his synthesis of diastase, a digestive enzyme.) Across the courtyard, see two merchant's houses. The first, roofed with boards and stones, belonged to a seed dealer. The other is a former pawnshop, comfortable enough to demonstrate that although they were forbidden ostentation, Edo-period merchants did live well. Open 8:00−6:00 between April and Sep; 8:00−5:00 from Oct.−March. ¥800.

Every 20 minutes, a minibus makes the round trip between Edo Mura and Danpūen, its sister village. Danpūen concentrates on crafts, and although a ticket is included in the Edo Mura price, it is often neglected by tourists. Several old structures, including an unusually elaborate gate to a private home and a good museum, are scattered around the three hillside plateaus.

On the return trip from Edo Mura, drop into the outlandish Hakuunrō Hotel, which has hosted emperors and prime ministers, as well as the American Occupation Forces. If you call ahead (tel. 35−1111, Ms. Kato speaks English), you can arrange for luncheon, a rest, and the chance to use their fantastic variety of baths. It will cost about ¥10,000 a person. Or you may prefer to try the public bath in Yuwaku Hot Spring village, the waters of which are reputed to benefit burns, cuts and female troubles(?). Kanazawa people often take their own jugs and fill up with water to drink at home. Open 1:00−10:00 daily. Otherwise, Yuwaku Hot Spring is notable only for its quiet mountain atmosphere and one excellent country restaurant, Zenigame.

Zenigame 銭 瓶

Tokyoites may consider Kanazawa to be the sticks, but for

those who live here, it's a big town, with rush hour traffic, neon lights and sweltering summers. At every opportunity, Kanazawa people escape to the mountains for a stroll, a picnic or a Sunday drive. One of the best mountain hideaways, still relatively unknown, is Zenigame, a restaurant and inn run by an elderly farming couple. Every morning they gather mountain grasses, young vegetables from their garden, and *iwana* fish from the cold stream beside the house, to prepare fresh country meals at noon and evening. Delighted customers sit around the open hearth in the 150-year-old spacious farmhouse, enjoying especially the *kotsuzake,* hot sake poured over grilled fish, and the homemade pickles served on old family dishes. (As you drink the *kotsuzake,* notice the old gentleman in the picture on the inside of the bowl. He's drinking the same thing from the same saucer.) During the final rice course, old Mr. Takagi sits down to chat about the house (the chandelier was the first ever in Kanazawa, and the 120-year-old clock is still working) and his life (for years he'd been planning this restaurant for his retirement). After your meal, he'll show you the ornate family Buddhist altar, and you can browse (touching permitted) among the museum pieces, Taishō-era illustrated magazines, old pottery and household utensils. Take the bus for Yuwaku (#12), get off at Shibahara and walk 30 minutes. Or a taxi from downtown costs about ¥2,000. Call 35−1426 for reservations, specifying the price (¥3,500 and up per person). You can stay overnight with 2 meals (and no mosquitoes) for about ¥6,000.

KANAIWA 金 石

Yūzen Danchi 加賀友禅染色団地

After visiting Saihitsuan in Nagamachi to see Yūzen hand-painting techniques, dedicated Yūzen fans may want to make the trip out to the Yūzen Development, a section near Kanaiwa where most of the dyers have gathered. Each step involved in the Yūzen process is handled by a different artisan (mainly hand-painters, dyers and tailors), and bundled back and forth by middlemen. The dyers, however, were dependent on the cool, clear waters of the Asano and Saigawa rivers, where they washed the stiff paste out of the fabric. About 8 years ago, the problems of pollution and increasingly shallow river water forced them out. They organized an association, dug wells out near Kanaiwa, and built a series of workshops. These days we can only rarely see the colorful fabric floating in the rushing rivers--it's all done in tile troughs at the development. But it's still fascinating, particularly due to the enthusiastic explanation of Mr. Ichizuka, who speaks English and will gladly guide anyone who calls in advance (tel. 67–3291). There is also a video-taped English introduction to Yūzen available. Unfortunately, transportation is limited. There's one bus an hour to Utsugi (#52). Get off at Hama Senkōji. Taxis are about ¥1,000 one way from town. Closed Sun. and holidays.

Ōno Minato Shrine 大野湊神社

Get off the bus (#60 or 61) at Nishi Keisatsusho, the last stop before Kanaiwa. On the left is one of the most beautiful shrines in this area. There is a rare, sacred quality here, perhaps because the lonely buildings are sheltered by greenery and an ancient moat, or perhaps because Ōno Minato Shrine is so old. It was moved here in 1252 from a site farther out of town, now taken over by the advancing sea. The shrine is dominated by the outdoor noh theater, built here by Lord Maeda Toshinaga to celebrate the Tokugawa victory at Sekigahara. An annual performance has been held (on May 14 and 15) for the last 370 years—an impressive record, given Hokuriku's unpredictable weather.

Kanaiwa 金 石

If you think you've found real, provincial Japan in Kanazawa, take the bus out to Kanaiwa (#60 or 61) and walk around. In the narrow streets and salt air lingers the atmosphere of town life in the Edo period--housewives gossiping at the local *miso* shop, *geta*-shod children scampering noisily to the beach, and sleepy cats basking in the sun. One of the main occupations is still lumber--giant logs from Russia and Korea can be seen lying about everywhere. A few hours of strolling around Kanaiwa, and perhaps over to neighboring Ōno town, makes a pleasant afternoon.

In the late Edo period, Kanaiwa did enjoy a period of prosperity, thanks to the ingenuity of Zeniya Gohei (1773–1852). Zenigo, as he is also known, caught on early to the idea of sea trade. As his fleet grew, Kanaiwa became a boom town. Most of its historical interest--temples, shrines and one museum--centers around him.

Zeniya Gohei became phenomenally successful with his trading.

Zeniya Gohei at the height of his
wealth and influence. (G. Shimizu)

Wooden tramcars connect the city and suburbs.
(H.Ikeuchi)

Legally, it was limited to other coastal towns along the Japan Sea,
but there is some evidence that he dealt with foreign ships as well.
The Kaga government was experiencing an economic crisis at the
time, and such wealth was difficult to overlook. Shaky finances
were combined with jealousy, political jockeying, and pressure
from the shōgunate, to insure Zenigo's downfall. He was thrown
into jail on trumped-up charges, and he died soon after. Tragically,
this was the year before Perry's Black Ships arrived in Edo Bay to
open up Japan to free trade, and topple the feudal government.

Zenigo Museum 銭五遺品館

A proud little museum about Zenigo has been opened right
across the street from the Kanaiwa bus station. It is stocked with
documents, chests and other memorabilia likely to be found in a
sea-going merchant's home. Mr. Shimizu, who is the 11th generation Gohei and the museum director, will show you around. Some
years ago, an English magazine called *The East* carried a detailed
narrative of Zenigo's life. Ask to see Mr. Shimizu's copy. Open
9:00–5:00, except Tues. ¥250. (tel. 67–2333)

The rest of the Zenigo tour begins down the road and across the
street at **Honryūji** (本竜寺), the site of Zenigo's unmarked grave.
From there, continue to the intersection, where you will find
Zenigo's home. The house belongs to another family now, but
even from the outside, it's easy to tell how wealthy he must have
been. His tea house is now in the grounds of **Senchōji** (専長寺), a

little further down the street toward the beach. Go back to the main intersection and turn north toward Ōno town. Along the road, there's a dignified statue of Zenigo, set among the gnarled, wind-bent pines. It's relatively new; the original figure was melted down for munitions during the war.

Ōno　大　野

Ōno is another sleepy little town, known for *shōyu* production. Until 1970, when the individual family businesses organized a cooperative, the whole town reeked of soy sauce. Now the base is made at the factory on the edge of town and distributed to each of the families for seasoning and bottling. The smell in the factory is almost overpowering, but for people with strong stomachs, it is fascinating to visit. The head of the factory, Mr. Shintani, will be delighted to show you around. Call 68—1301.

IN THE DIRECTION OF TSURUGI　鶴来方面

Yamashina Fossil Beds　山 科

The mountain waters of Fushimi River have eaten away the riverbed, clearly exposing layers and layers of white, petrified shells imbedded in the dark rock. The fossilized marine life, also visible in basin-like whorls, dates from the Pleocene Age (that's 3 million years ago) when this area was still under the sea. There are several such sites of geological interest around Kanazawa, but Yamashina's sample is accessible, well-marked and protected with ropes and guard-rails. Secluded Yamashina Hot Spring, on the edge of the woods below the fossil beds, is inviting for a bath, dinner or overnight. (Tel. 41—0414) Take a #30 or 31 bus, get off at Kubo and walk from there.

Ace Kanazawa　エース金沢

Although some distance from the center of the city and geared to the tour-bus trade, Ace's thorough and interesting explanation of Kutani-making is worth the trip. Chatting about their life experiences, elderly potters amiably demonstrate at the wheel. Posters show the four stages of firing. Souvenirs are on sale, but after a look at the 'famous masters' exhibition, you may not be satisfied with an inexpensive tea bowl or an everyday vase. There's no pressure to buy. Visitors may inspect the kilns and even try their hands at making *rakuyaki* between 9:00 and 5:00. From

¥300 (for a dish) on up, it takes two or three days to fire, and if you don't have time to come back, they'll send your masterpieces anywhere in Japan. Take #44 bus and get off at Nishi Izumi Jūtaku. Open 9:00–7:00. Tel. 41–3147. Perhaps it's worth calling to avoid running into a busload of souvenir-seekers.

Kita Family House 喜多記念館

The Kita family of sake brewers moved out of their lovely old home in 1972 to open it to the public. Most striking is the spacious entry hall with a 3-story-high ceiling of narrow, but sturdy, beams over an open hearth. The ashes surrounding the silvery hanging kettle are combed into intricate designs every morning by the mistress of the house. The same pattern has been handed down for generations, taught to the incoming brides by the mother-in-law. Elsewhere in the house are a scroll mounted with a get-well letter from Lord Toshitsune, a narrow stairway with storage closets in its base, and a sliding trap door to prevent drafts. The various utensils, furniture and rooms are described in the excellent English pamphlet. The architecture is typical of a prosperous merchant's house. It's amazing to think that the whole thing was dismantled at its original site in Kanazawa and rebuilt in Nonoichi. Sake is still made in the back and on sale in old-fashioned jugs. Tea is included in the ¥300 entry fee. Open daily. Take #46 bus and get off at Nishi Nonoichi.

Rhein Halt (ラインハルト). Excellent German and French breads including rye and pumpernickel. German pastries. Mr. Shirakawa trained in Kobe and Germany. 7:00–7:00. Closed Sun.

La Mola (ラ・モーラ). Central American home cooking. Authentic dishes can be ordered in advance. Spanish music. Near the International Hotel. 11:00–10:00. Closed Tues.

Mattō City 松任市

There are two good reasons to visit Mattō. One is **Futsukaichiya** (二日市屋), a delicious *kappō*-style place run by Matsumoto Masashi, who spent a year at Berkeley. Make a reservation in advance (tel. 0762–75–0628) and he'll give you directions. Open daily from the late afternoon on, except Sundays. Take the bus to Mattō (#40), or a taxi (about ¥2,000).

The second attraction of Mattō is an excellent cake shop called **Saikadō** (彩霞堂), a ten-minute walk from the station. It does no advertising and has no branch sales outlets, but word has spread among tea-lovers. It is worth a trip only for their tiny walnut-filled confections, Chitose-kurumi. 8:00–8:30 Closed Sun.

Tsurugi   鶴来町

Tsurugi is the largest of the mountain towns surrounding Mt. Hakusan. It is also the most modern and accessible, but it still retains an air of uncomplicated rural life. To get there, take the electric train from Nomachi. Get off at either Tsurugi or Kaga Ichinomiya and cover the distance between them on foot. This guide begins at Ichinomiya and works back.

Tsurugi's famous products include *kikuzake,* a sake made from the clear waters of Hakusan; walnuts, found in several local cakes like *kurumi-mochi* (try Tsuruya, up the street from Manzairaku); and fine steel knives, particularly a small, well-shaped fruit knife. Also famous are the Gomadodaiko drums. On special occasions, young men wearing demon masks and loose kimono beat the giant drums in a stimulating rhythm. Performances are erratic, so call the Tourism Section of the Town Hall to find out if they are playing (or any other information you need). Tel. 07619–2–1111.

Shirayama Hime Shrine   白山比咩神社

Like trees, mountains are considered sacred in Japan, and the most magnificent of them are revered as gods. Hakusan is one of these. In 717, the Shinto priest, Taichō, became the first person to climb it. At the summit, he was greeted by the god of the mountain, riding a white horse, who granted him enlightenment. (Buddhism and Shintōism tend to get confused in such legends.) Taichō founded a central shrine, Kaga Ichinomiya, also called Shirayama, which is the Japanese reading of the Chinese characters for Hakusan. Shirayama serves as head to the 2716 Hakusan shrines scattered around the country. Its immaculate grounds surrounded by great cedars, Shirayama is one of the most beautiful spots in Kaga. It is also one of the busiest, with weddings and frequent purification services. New cars, houses, babies, or anything else that needs protection, can be blessed here. The busiest time is New Year's Eve, when the crowds sweep down from Kanazawa for their first prayers of the year.

Wataya   和田屋

This is a country restaurant specializing in fish, mountain

vegetables and strange mountain animals like badger, pheasant and bear. Fix the price (from ¥5,000) when you call for a reservation (tel. 07619—2—0570). 11:00—9:00, except the 2nd and 4th Tues.

Rindō りんどう

Rindō is a branch of Wataya, also specializing in mountain cooking. The menu is limited to various vegetables, bear sashimi, and grilled fish, but you can choose freely, and the prices are reasonable. Try *soba* noodles, *aburage* fried *tōfu,* or *ayu* (sweetfish, only between June and September). Attractive country atmosphere. 11:00—8:00, except Mon.

Funaokayama 舟岡山住居跡

In 1949, some neolithic, Jōmon hearthstones were discovered on this hill. Over them, the prefecture has constructed replicas of the houses of that period--curious, uncomfortable-looking straw and bamboo huts. Archeologists speculate from unearthed utensils and pottery that Tsurugi was a trading center between mountain and coastal dwellers.

Chida Lion Head Carving Shop 知田工房

Mr. Chida seems unusually young for a master carver, but the orders for lion heads keep pouring in, and he and his apprentices are kept very busy. Heads for actual dancing use are few, but people still want large ones for interior decoration. Mr. Chida also finds time every now and then for work on a pet project in the back--a lion head so big it will require a truck to take it away. Visitors are welcome. There are some tiny lion heads on sale if you ask.

Shishiku Heights 獅子吼高原

On one of the steep hills at the back of Tsurugi, there are a ski slope (advanced skiers should go farther into the mountains) and a 'ropeway' sightseeing gondola open all year. The view is magnificent. Near Shishiku Heights is Jumoku Kōen, a forestry experimental station planted with many unusual trees, and nice for family picnics.

Manzairaku Sake 万歳楽

Manzairaku, a *kikuzake* made from the waters of Hakusan, is produced between November and March. The family's eldest daughter, Kobori Masako, is willing to take visitors around the factory. Call her at 07619-2-0012 to set a time. She will feel more relaxed if you take along an interpreter. Other than the usual *isshōbin* (1.8 liters), Manzairaku is also sold in attractive Kutani containers. The Koboris will ship it anywhere in the world, but sometimes it loses its flavor in transit. It's best to try it while still in Kanazawa.

Ikkan-in 一閑院

When the priest Taichō passed through here 1300 years ago, he stopped to carve a giant *fudō* in the rock on the steep hillside. Over the years, the relief statue almost disappeared, so it was recarved in 1631 and covered with a protective temple. Since it's standing against the stone wall, the Ikkan-in building is very chilly and damp. But it's popular with the weak-sighted--the *fudō*, whose own wall-eyes look none too strong, is a patron of eye trouble. This is the largest *fudō* statue in Asia. Decorated with red flames and holding a mammoth sword, it's very impressive.

Chūgū Hot Springs 中宮温泉

A few old inns, famous for the wooden bathtubs, are clustered around this mountain mineral spring, far past Tsurugi. They open when the snows begin to melt in April and serve quiet-seeking customers until October. There are several attractions at Chūgū, the monkeys which gather around the Hakusan Nature Conservation Center, the bear-meat sashimi and the gorgeous foliage in the fall. Kokutetsu runs a few buses a day. Make reservations through JTB.

Hakusan Super Forest Road 白山スーパー林道

Recently opened, this beautiful mountain highway is very popular with Sunday drivers. The rest of us try to go on weekdays, or get an early start on Sunday and be just returning when the cars begin to pile up at the entrance's toll booth. The road is only open from May through November, the best time being autumn foliage season. Cars are most convenient (¥2,700 toll), but Hokutetsu does run bus tours regularly. No bikes or motorbikes allowed. The highway extends from Chūgū to Hatogaya in Gifu.

Hanibe Caves ハニべ巌窟院

Visitors to Hanibe don't know whether to tremble or laugh. In the side of a cliff, someone has installed plaster of Paris statues of demons inflicting ludicrous forms of torture on poor earthly sinners. The punishment fits the crime, according to these macabre scenes from Buddhist hell. Even more surprising is the recently installed Kama Sutra room of erotic Indian statuary. 9:00−5:00 daily. From Komatsu train station, take the Ugawa Yūsenji electric train to the end of the line. To continue on to Natadera temple, return to Komatsu and take the bus.

Makes you Lucky : FUKU-MASAMUNE

Please remember the characters of our name,
Fukumasamune : 福正宗
The 福 means luck and happiness. When you
visit restaurants displaying this sign, you'll really
be experiencing the Taste of Kanazawa.
The delicious companion to the gifts of the sea
and the mountains, that's Fukumasamune.
Please enjoy yourself!

EST.1625
HIGH QUALITY JAPANESE SAKE

福正宗

FUKUMITSUYA SAKE BREWING CO., LTD
KANAZAWA, ISHIKAWA, JAPAN

Glossary

bento--lunchbox: rice and accompanying side-dishes arranged in a lacquer box.

chome: numbered sections of a *machi* (town)

-dōri or *tōri*: road

Edo period--1600–1868: While the Tokugawa shōgunate ruled the nation from Edo (Tōkyō), the Maeda family controlled Kaga, the wealthiest fief in Japan.

gaijin: foreigner

Heian Period--794–1185: Japan's capital was at Heian (Kyōto), but the Hokuriku area was only loosely connected to the central government.

Hokuriku: The area midway along the Japan Seacoast side of Japan, consisting of Fukui, Ishikawa and Toyama prefectures.

Hyakumangoku--One million *koku*: five million bushels of rice, the wealth of the Kaga district under Maeda rule.

jizō: popular guardian god of children and travelers. Stone images of Jizō, often draped with bibs or hats, are found everywhere in Japan.

Jōdo Shin-shū--True Pure Land Sect: Buddhist sect founded by Shinran in the early 13th century transformed into the Ikkō (Single Minded) Sect in the 15th century. Shin-shū is still very influential in Kanazawa.

Kaga: the former province comprising the lower part of the present Ishikawa Prefecture.

Kamakura Bakufu: shōgunate established by Minamoto Yoritomo 1185, which ruled most of Japan until the mid-14th century.

Kannon: the Buddhist goddess of mercy.

kappō: counter-style restaurant serving seasonal Japanese dishes, mainly fish.

kinpaku--gold leaf: Most of Japan's gold leaf is produced in Kanazawa and used to decorate screens, fans, pottery and fabrics.

kiri--paulownia wood: a light, wide-grained wood used in vases, koto and *geta*.

koku: a measure of rice equal to about 5 bushels. The rank of samurai and daimyō was determined by the number of *koku* they received annually.

kotsuzake: hot sake poured over salt-grilled river fish in a wide shallow bowl. You pass the dish around drinking the scented sake and leaving the fish.

Meiji period--1868–1912: The feudal Edo period ended with the Restoration of the Meiji Emperor to political power. Japan was opened to modernization and foreign trade.

minshuku--people's lodge: cheaper than a *ryokan,* less strict than a youth hostel; most are run by families with big houses. Price usually includes dinner and breakfast.

mochi--rice cake: Steamed rice is pounded into a heavy, gluey paste. Often served roasted or sweetened with bean jam.

namako--sea cucumber: Kanazawa Castle and the wall around Seisonkaku Villa are decorated with the grey slate tiles lined with white adhesive which resemble slices of vinegared sea cucumber.

oden: chunks of various foods--eggs, fish paste, potatoes, meatballs, vegetables--simmered in a thin broth. Good in the winter.

rāmen: Chinese-style wheat noodles in soup.

ryokan--Japanese inn: sleeping on *futon* mats on the tatami--pure Japanese style. Dinner and breakfast included.

shabu-shabu: similar to fondue; you cook thin-sliced beef and vegetables in hot broth at your table and eat them with various sauces.

soba: buckwheat noodles served cold or hot with a soy sauce-flavored soup.

tabi--foot mittens: tight socks with a separate section for the big toe.

teishoku--set meal: usually served on a tray, including a main dish with rice, soup, pickles and tea.

tomuro: stones taken from Mt. Tomuro behind Kanazawa City. Both the red and blue variety are valued for their beauty and durability. Often found as gravestones of the aristocracy.

torii: the gate to a Shintō shrine, often red-painted wood, of two narrow beams resting on two posts.

udon: thick noodles made of wheat, usually served hot in a soy sauce-flavored soup.

yakitori: cubes of chicken or other meats grilled with a spicy sauce.

Acknowledgements

I am deeply grateful to everyone who has offered assistance and support in this project. In particular, I wish to mention 'my group,' the tireless band which made this book a reality: Mrs. Matsuda Sonoko, Mr. Tatsuno Tatsurō, Mr. Matsuhira Isamu, Mr. Nishimura Minoru, and especially Mr. Kaneko Kenju, whose editing skills have turned an amateurish scribble into an actual book. I only hope that the steady dose of chaos and inconvenience I caused 'my group' hasn't impeded too seriously the progress of international understanding. Their patient sympathy and tolerance will never be forgotten.

With the enthusiastic support of Mr. Shibuya Ryōji and Mr. Hatta Kōhei we have set up the 'Society to Introduce Kanazawa to the World,' which has helped in the financial end of this project. I hope this book will be only the first of many Society activities.

I am indebted to the imaginative Mrs. Izumi Akiko for the book's design and Mr. Hana Kiyoshi for the *sumi-e* drawings. My gratitude is further due to Mr. Motoya Kimio and the Canon Camera Club who contributed many of the photographs and to 'the Boss,' Ms. Murai Sachiko, who suggested the idea of a guidebook in the first place.

The translations of Bashō's haiku are taken from *The Narrow Road to the Deep North* (Penguin, 1966) with the kind permission of the author, Professor Yuasa Nobuyuki. Murō Saisei's poetry is from *Murō Saisei Zen Shishū* (Tōjusha, 1979) with the permission of the poet's daughter, Ms. Murō Asako. The translations were composed for this volume by Mr. Graeme Wilson. I am very grateful for his generosity. The *jibu* recipe appears thanks to the skilled cook Mrs. Matsumoto Akiko.

Several people gave their time to reading parts of the manuscript and offering suggestions and advice. I am grateful to them all: Ms. Nancy Broadbent, Mr. Imamura Michio, Ms. Inoue Yuki, Mr. Kashimoto Hidehiko, Professor Komatsu Ryōichi, Ms. Jean Pearce, Ms. Patty Ratcliffe, Mr. Tim Riedler, Mr. Shimazaki Susumu, Professor Tanaka Yoshio, Mr. Tani Kenji and Mr. Tom West. I have also benefited from the generous guidance and support of Mr. Ataka Natsuo, Mr. Furuse Toru, Mr. Honda Masakazu, Mr. Matsumoto

Satoru, Professor Nishitani Tatsuo, and Ms. Barbara Adachi.

The following books have been valuable sources of information:

Imamura Michio, *An Inquiry into Living Folkways: Ishikawa* (生きている民俗探訪), Daiichi Hōki, 1978.

Inoue Yuki, *Kanazawa Customs* (金沢の風習), Hokkoku Shuppansha, 1978.

Mori Eimatsu, *Kanazawa Castle* (金沢城), Hokkoku Shuppansha, 1970.

Shinkura Tadashi, *Four Seasons at Kenrokuen* (四季の兼六園), Aoyagi Shobō.

Sugi Yasuko, *Kanazawa Superstitions* (金沢の迷信), Hokkoku Shuppansha, 1978.

I wish there were space to mention everyone. Suffice it to say that making this book has been the joint effort of the people of Kanazawa.

A Note to the Revised Edition

This updated edition appears thanks to the help of a multitude of interested people. We'd first like to thank all those who bought the 13,500 copies in the first edition's astonishing eight printings. With these revenues, the Society to Introduce Kanazawa to the World was able to publish a bilingual newsletter, run a language teacher training program, and sponsor an ongoing summer Japanese language institute for foreigners.

We were encouraged by Governor Nakanishi and particularly by Mayor Egawa to do a revision of this book, and we gratefully acknowledge their support. I personally am indebted to the many 'updaters,' especially Anne Torige, who contributed so much time and effort to their roles as combination guinea pig and foreign correspondent. We at the Society are all relieved and thankful to the Kanazawa Tourist Association, which has agreed to handle the publication and distribution of this book henceforth.

Finally, special credit is due to Sonoko Matsuda, who created and sustained the Society to Introduce Kanazawa to the World. It is her vision that first shaped this book and her energy that made it possible for a revised edition five years later.

Restaurant Index

This index lists restaurants by category, so if you have your heart set on steak or sushi, find some ideas here and look up the details in the Areas section.

Maison de Roze 210
Lili Marlene 200
Maison de France 118
New Tanuki 173
Pilzen 201
Rhein Halt 230

Chinese
Hachi-ban Rāmen 174
Kinkōrō 201
Tenryū 200
Wan-san 186

Korean
Kazue 173
Midōen 188

Steak
Hiyoko 201
Rokkakudō 124,187
Ron 186
Tamae 200

Curry
Parvati 186

Central American
La Mola 230

Lunch Specials

Most restaurants offer a special price at lunch, so noon is the best time to sample some of the famous places without forfeiting a week's travel expenses. The following are especially known for cheap set lunches.

Jimbei 210
New Grand Hotel Chinese Buffet
Rokkakudō 124,187   31
Toyoshima 210

Rock Bottom Cheap
Dai Nana Gyōza 174
Irohanihoheto 186
Tamura 144
Toichi Shokudō 199

Index

Ruth Stevens was born in Massachusetts, U. S. A., in 1950. After earning a B.A. in political science at Kirkland College, and teaching secondary-school history for two years, she came to Kanazawa in 1974. Now in her sixth year of residence, it's looking increasingly likely that she'll join that group of foreigners who came to Japan for a year and ended up staying a lifetime.

Ruth Stevens lived in Kanazawa from 1974 to 1980. She now resides in New York.

金　沢 ——もう一面の日本

著　　者：ルース・スティブンス
　　　　　108 E.38th St., 1107, New York, N.Y. 10016 USA

編　　集：おあしす編集室
　　　　　表紙カバーデザイン：小川デザイン

監　　修：金沢を世界に開く市民の会

印　　刷：中川大正印刷（株）

発　　行：金沢市観光協会
　　　　　920 金沢市尾山町 9−13
　　　　　☎ (0762) 63−1151（代）

改訂版定価　1,600 円